NORTHERN IRELAND
THE INTERNATIONAL PERSPECTIVE

Northern Ireland: the International Perspective

ADRIAN GUELKE

GILL AND MACMILLAN
Dublin

ST. MARTIN'S PRESS
New York

Published in Ireland by
Gill and Macmillan Ltd
Goldenbridge
Dublin 8
with associated companies in
Auckland, Delhi, Gaborone, Hamburg, Harare,
Hong Kong, Johannesburg, Kuala Lumpur, Lagos, London,
Manzini, Melbourne, Mexico City, Nairobi,
New York, Singapore, Tokyo
© Adrian Guelke 1988
Print origination in Ireland by
Graphic Plan, Dublin
Printed in Great Britain by
The Camelot Press, Southampton

British Library Cataloguing in Publication Data

Guelke, Adrian
  Northern Ireland: the international perspective.
  1. Northern Ireland. Political events, 1968-1988. International
  aspects
  I. Title
  941.60824

  ISBN 0-7171-1455-4

Published in the USA by
St. Martin's Press, New York
© Adrian Guelke, 1988
All rights reserved. For information, write:
Scholarly and Reference Division,
St. Martin's Press, Inc., 175 Fifth Avenue, New York, NY 10010
First published in the United States of America in 1989

Library of Congress Cataloging-in-Publication Data

Guelke, Adrian.
  Northern Ireland.

  Bibliography: p.
  Includes index.
  1. Northern Ireland—Politics and government—1969—
2. Northern Ireland—Foreign public opinion.
3. Northern Ireland—Foreign relations.   I. Title.
DA990.U46G77 1988   941.60824   88-26461
ISBN 0-312-02515-X

For my parents

CONTENTS

PREFACE

The first week of October 1988 marks the twentieth anniversary of the Troubles, a doleful reminder of the durability of political instability in Northern Ireland. The third anniversary of the Anglo-Irish Agreement, the occasion under the Agreement for a review of its operation, is due a month later on 15 November 1988. The manuscript of this book, apart from the Preface, was completed by the first week of October 1987. This is the reason why, for example, the comparison between Israel and Northern Ireland contains no reference to the Palestinian *intifada*, which began in December 1987. In the narrower context of Northern Ireland, much has happened since October 1987, though little has changed. Acts of political violence, actions of the security forces, and the emotive reaction of the two communities to bloodshed have continued to dominate Northern Ireland's political agenda, though this has been mitigated to some extent by weariness with the conflict, which cuts across the province's sectarian divisions, and by nebulous but persistent speculation about the possibility of negotiations among the parties.

A number of events of recent months have underlined the significance of the conflict's international dimensions and this has been reflected in the attention that both the British and Irish Governments have given to international opinion. At the beginning of November 1987 the French navy intercepted a Panamanian-registered ship, the *Eksund*, with 150 tons of arms and ammunition, including twenty Soviet-made surface-to-air missiles, on board. From those arrested with the ship the French authorities quickly established that the massive arms shipment had been destined for the Provisional IRA and that the arms had been supplied by Libya. Both the British and Irish Governments gave credence to reports arising from the *Eksund* case which suggested that there had been earlier shipments of smaller size and that one of these had included a few surface-to-air missiles. However, no missiles had turned up in arms searches or been used by the Provisional IRA by May 1988. Gadafy's rhetoric suggests that antagonism towards Britain, dating back to the breach in diplomatic relations in 1984 and strongly reinforced by British involvement in the American air raid on Tripoli in 1986, provided the context of the revival of Libya's active involvement in the Northern Ireland conflict. It seems unlikely that Libya's feud with Britain will sustain a long-term commitment to aid the Provisional IRA.

A week after the interception of the *Eksund*, a Provisional IRA bomb killed eleven people and injured another sixty-three at a Remembrance Day ceremony in Enniskillen. This atrocity was one of the factors contributing to a sharp rise in the annual toll of fatalities in Northern Ireland as a result of the Troubles. (The total for 1987 was 93 compared to 61 in 1986.) The Provisional leadership acknowledged that reaction among Northern Catholics to the outrage had reduced the level of support for the IRA's political wing, Sinn Fein. The Enniskillen bombing also had a profound impact at the time on opinion in the Republic, influencing the debate on the contentious issue of extradition. New arrangements governing extradition were due to come into force on 1 December 1987 following the Republic's adherence to the European Convention on the Suppression of Terrorism in 1986. Implementation of the Convention had been delayed to this date in order to put pressure on the British Government to take steps to reform the administration of justice in Northern Ireland, particularly the system of single judge courts operating without a jury, which tried terrorist offences. This tactic had failed to produce a shift in the British position on the court system and consequently, strong opposition had grown to the implementation of the 1986 Extradition Act, despite the limited practical implications of the new legislation. Much of the opposition dissolved as a result of the Enniskillen bombing. Critics of extradition were further disarmed by the Government's introduction of an amendment to the 1986 Act which provided that the Irish Attorney General had to be satisfied that there was a clear intention to prosecute on the basis of sufficient evidence, before the extradition of any suspect could take place. The British Government strongly objected to this safeguard because of fears that as a result of this provision it might be forced to reveal the evidence it had against suspects, including the names of witnesses, in the Irish courts. The dispute between the two Governments over the issue was eventually resolved in May 1988 when they reached agreement on what in principle would constitute 'sufficient evidence' to satisfy the Irish Attorney General.

On 22 December 1987, John McMichael, a leading figure within the Loyalist paramilitary organisation, the UDA, was killed by a booby-trap bomb placed in his car by the Provisional IRA. His death led to recriminations within the UDA as a result of allegations that he had been betrayed from within the organisation and that his murder was linked to the internal inquiry he had launched into corruption, following a television exposé of the involvement of members of the UDA in protection rackets. The dissension sharpened divisions in the organisation and in March 1988, the Supreme Commander of the UDA, Andy Tyrie, was forced to resign after a vote of no confidence by the UDA's inner council. The changes at the top of the UDA were not accompanied by any outward change in the organisation's political stance and McMichael's ideas, in particular, have continued to be promoted in the UDA's publications. However, the new collective leadership of the UDA has declared that the organisation intends to step up attacks on Republican paramilitaries and the expectation is that the greater power which is now being wielded within the organisation by the regional commanders will entail a higher priority generally for violent activities.

During the first three months of 1988 a series of developments occurred that strained relations between the British and Irish Governments and led to widespread disillusionment with the functioning of the Anglo-Irish Agreement both in the South and among Catholics in Northern Ireland. On 25 January 1988, the British Attorney General announced that it had been decided on the grounds of national security not to prosecute police officers against whom evidence had been obtained by the inquiry into allegations of an RUC 'shoot to kill' policy in 1982 that they had sought to pervert the course of justice. Three days later the Court of Appeal in London rejected the appeal of six men against their convictions for the 1974 Birmingham pub bombings. The two decisions had a most damaging impact on confidence among nationalists in the administration of justice in Britain, the more especially because the Anglo-Irish Agreement had raised expectations that the British Government intended to address Irish grievances over the 1982 killings and over a number of apparent miscarriages of justice that had arisen from the Provisional IRA's bombing campaign in England in the mid-1970s. A survey of opinion in Northern Ireland in February, which was published in the April issue of *Fortnight*, provided evidence that the effect of the two decisions on Catholic attitudes towards Sinn Fein had outweighed the negative impact of the Enniskillen bombing on Catholic support for the party.

Two developments in February further compounded Catholic distrust of the British authorities. On 21 February, a civilian who had previously complained of harassment by the security forces was shot dead by a soldier at a Border checkpoint. Two days later, while controversy was still raging over the explanation that the shooting had been a freak accident, the news emerged that a soldier who had been convicted of the murder of a civilian in West Belfast in 1983 had been released after twenty-six months of a life sentence and had been permitted to rejoin his regiment. The next event to disturb Anglo-Irish relations was the shooting by the SAS of three members of the Provisional IRA on a bombing mission in Gibraltar on 6 March. The Irish Government's criticism of the killings, which was expressed in moderate terms, stemmed from eyewitness accounts which suggested that the three Provisionals, who were unarmed and had been under surveillance, had been shot out of hand with no attempt being made to arrest them. The attitude initially adopted by the British Government that the intentions of the would-be bombers from Belfast were sufficient justification in themselves for their deaths at the hands of the SAS served to stimulate controversy over the killings, since it failed to acknowledge the desirability of ending their mission without bloodshed. This attitude was one reason why the killings attracted the attention of Amnesty International, to the publicly expressed annoyance of the British Prime Minister. It was also a significant factor in arousing the emotions of Belfast's Catholics about the deaths. Tension in Belfast rose further after a Loyalist gunman attacked the funeral on 16 March of the Provisionals killed in Gibraltar. Three people died in the attack. Three days later two soldiers were killed by the Provisional IRA after they drove into the funeral procession of one of the victims of the Loyalist attack.

The violence in Belfast appeared to have a sobering effect on both the British and Irish Governments and a meeting of the Intergovernmental Conference in London passed off without recriminations. None the less, the events of the first three months of 1988 left their mark on the Irish Government. In a speech to Friends of Fianna Fáil in New York on 21 April, the Irish Prime Minister, Charles Haughey, listed the events of 1988 to justify his contention that the situation in Northern Ireland had become even worse than it had been in the past. While he acknowledged that the Irish government was committed to honour the Anglo-Irish Agreement as an international treaty, he expressed his belief that only a settlement that transcended the framework of Northern Ireland could achieve peace with justice and to this end he invited the leaders of Unionist opinion to enter into a constructive dialogue with the South. Haughey's apparent lack of enthusiasm for the Agreement and his revival of the theme of Northern Ireland as a failed political entity attracted sharp criticism from the Opposition parties in the Republic and an expression of regret from the British Government. Just as disturbing for the British Government as his strictures on the Agreement was Haughey's praise for a statement of policy on Ireland by Michael Dukakis, the leading contender for the Democratic Presidential nomination. The statement supported an active role by the United States on the issue of Northern Ireland and endorsed the objective of Irish unity. Haughey's comment raised the spectre of a renewal of Irish efforts to mobilise international opinion against British policy in Northern Ireland.

The British Government's sensitivity to international opinion on the issue of Northern Ireland was reflected in a speech made the day after Haughey's address by the British Foreign Secretary, Sir Geoffrey Howe. It was a conciliatory speech which recognised that recent events had antagonised Irish opinion, but argued forcefully that this had not been intentional or calculated on the British side. While declaring that the Government was willing 'to consider all creative proposals which can command widespread support and which recognise the international dimensions of the problem', Sir Geoffrey strongly reaffirmed the British Government's commitment to the Anglo-Irish Agreement. He also pointed out the progress that had been made in relation to discrimination in employment. (In March the Government had indicated its intention to make it compulsory for companies to monitor the religious composition of their staff and to report on their employment practices to a new Fair Employment Commission with the power to issue directives to firms on the steps they must take to promote equality of opportunity.) Sir Geoffrey's speech was well received in the Republic, not least because of its marked difference in tone from statements on events in Northern Ireland that were emanating from the British Prime Minister's Office. By contrast, the leader of the Democratic Unionist Party, Ian Paisley, described the speech as a 'studied insult' to Unionists.

The impact of the British Foreign Secretary's remarks on nationalists was partially weakened by his involvement in a row over television reporting of the Gibraltar killings. At the same time, emotions in Britain which had been stirred by the killing of the two soldiers on 19 March were aroused further by the murder of three off-duty servicemen by the Provisional IRA on 1 May in Holland. Internment and the legalisation of a 'shoot to kill' policy were two of the options canvassed in the British press following the killings in Holland. Such comment fuelled rumours in Northern Ireland that the Government was contemplating a major security initiative that would include internment on a selective basis, an option Unionists had long been pressing for. On 15 May three people died and ten were injured in a Loyalist attack on a Catholic-owned pub in the city centre of Belfast. Responsibility was claimed by the Protestant Action Force, a *nom de guerre* used by the Loyalist paramilitary organisation, the UVF. Violence and reaction to violence was once again dictating the political life of Northern Ireland. The inevitable consequence was the polarisation of the two communities. The situation had been made slightly worse than it might otherwise have been by the failure of the Government to scotch speculation on a change in security policy, allowing doubts to be nurtured about the strength of the Government's commitment to maintenance of the rule of law. In reality, due in part to external constraints, British security policy remains relatively liberal of necessity, though a rather different image of security policy often tends to be projected, especially by the Prime Minister, Margaret Thatcher, who is temperamentally unsuited to making a virtue of a liberal approach in this area of policy.

In spite of the continuing hostility of Protestants towards the Anglo-Irish Agreement and the disillusionment of many Catholics at the Agreement's failure to meet some of their grievances, there remains every reason to expect the Agreement to endure. In particular, the prospects of an accord among Northern Ireland's constitutional parties on a settlement replacing the Agreement are extremely remote. Further, in an international context the Agreement continues to play a significant role in securing support for British policy in Northern Ireland. This was underlined by the announcement by the European Commission on 24 May 1988 that it was contributing approximately £35 million to the International Fund which had been established under Article 10 of the Agreement to promote development in areas in both parts of Ireland which had suffered most severely from the effects of political instability in Northern Ireland. Why international opinion is of such importance to the conflict in Northern Ireland is the subject of this book.

In writing it, I have incurred many debts to many people, subject to the usual disclaimer that any faults or errors are mine. In particular, I would like to thank my colleagues in the Department of Political Science at Queen's University of Belfast and a former member of the Department, Professor John Whyte, for their encouragement. In this context, I must single out Frank Wright who read the first draft of the manuscript and helped me to reduce its length. Over the years, he and I have taught on many courses together. I owe much to his intellectual stimulation. Both postgraduates and undergraduate students have helped me to clarify my ideas and in this context I would especially like to thank past and present students taking the MSSc in Irish Political Studies. Their influence may partially be gauged from references in the notes to some of their dissertations. Thanks are also due to those political figures and others who granted me interviews in the course of my research. I hope they understand why I have decided they should remain anonymous. The publishers, Gill and Macmillan, in the persons of Fergal Tobin, Bridget Lunn, and Deirdre Rennison, have been of great assistance to me in completing the manuscript and I am particularly grateful to them for the tolerance they have shown at delays and other shortcomings on my part during various stages of the project. Finally, I would like to thank my wife, Brigid, and son, John, for their indulgence and support while the book was being written, as well as daughter, Kate, for being a good baby while I finished this Preface.

Belfast, May 1988   A.G.

Northern Ireland

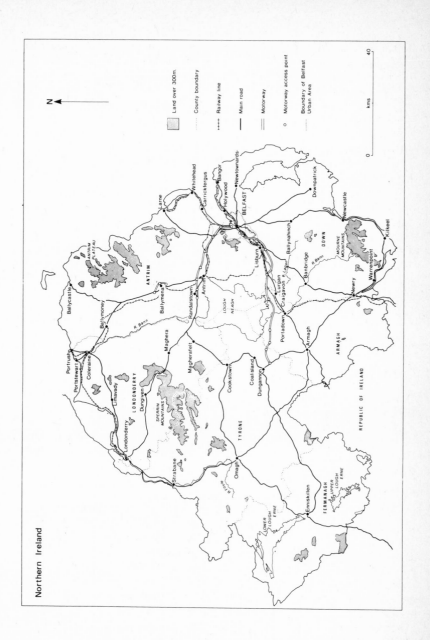

Land over 300m

County boundary

Railway line

Main road

Motorway

Motorway access point

Boundary of Belfast Urban Area

0   kms   40

N

1.

INTRODUCTION

BELFAST is as well known in most parts of the world as Beirut. Ian Paisley and Bobby Sands are names familiar to people in the farthest reaches of the Third World as the result of two decades of violent conflict in Northern Ireland. Yet the previous emergency in Northern Ireland, the Border campaign waged by the Irish Republican Army (IRA) between 1956 and 1962, caused scarcely a ripple in the outside world. While an Irish historian would see the present Troubles as the latest round in a conflict that stretches as far back as the seventeenth century, from an international perspective the onset of the present Troubles in 1968 and 1969 was the moment when most people in the world first became aware of Northern Ireland's existence as a political issue. There was another peak in international awareness of Northern Ireland during the 1981 hunger strike by Republican prisoners. By contrast, the Border campaign of the 1950s for the most part failed even to penetrate political consciousness in Britain itself. The change is too great to be explained by the difference between the scale of the Border campaign and that of the present Troubles, large though the difference now appears. In any event, international consciousness of the Northern Ireland problem was established in 1968 and 1969, prior to the major escalation of violence that followed the introduction of internment in August 1971.

The spread of modern communications appears to provide the most satisfactory explanation of the internationalisation of the Northern Ireland conflict in the late 1960s. Satellite television, which was instrumental in changing the course of the Vietnam conflict by bringing the war into American living rooms, also made people in New York as much as in London aware of the conflict in Northern Ireland at an early stage. When civil rights marchers were confronted by the police during 1969, they chanted: 'the whole world is watching', with good reason. This was before the main Republican and Loyalist paramilitary organisations, the Provisional IRA and the Ulster Defence Association (UDA), had even been formed. Consciousness of Northern Ireland as an issue was also stimulated by the dispatch of British troops to the province in August 1969. It made people in the outside world aware that Northern Ireland was a separate entity from Britain. This perception did not require any understanding of the precise constitutional niceties of Northern Ireland's position within the United Kingdom. However, it immediately raised questions as to the province's appropriate status in a post-colonial world, as the completion of the process of decolonisation in most parts of the world posed the obvious questions: what was left and where next? The outbreak of violence in Northern Ireland seemed to provide an answer on cue.

This book is about the implications and consequences of the internationalisation of the conflict. At least five distinct meanings of internationalisation or the international dimension can be identified. Firstly, it may be interpreted as referring to the territorial dispute between two states, the United Kingdom and the Republic of Ireland; secondly, as referring to the involvement of countries outside the British Isles in the conflict, both at a governmental and a non-governmental level; thirdly, as referring to the international affiliations of the parties to the conflict in Northern Ireland; fourthly, as referring to the impact of the conflict on the rest of the world; and fifthly, as referring to the influence of international opinion on the conflict. The most important of these different elements of the international dimension is the last, the influence of international opinion. This is the element with the most profound effect upon the conflict. In comparison with other well-known trouble spots such as Lebanon and Cyprus, the other four elements are of lesser significance. As to the first, the British and Irish Governments have avoided open territorial dispute, or, to be more precise, they have been less than enthusiastic in supporting 'their' sides in the internal conflict in Northern Ireland. As to the second, no other external governments — apart from Libya — have attempted to influence the course of the conflict except through pressure on the British and Irish Governments themselves. As to the third, with the important exception of Irish-American support for the Provisional IRA (see Chapter 7), the external affiliations of the internal groups are more a function of their own perceived needs than of the actual involvement of external affiliates. Fourth, the Northern Ireland conflict has so far been contained so as not to have much effect upon the outside world beyond the general awareness of its existence that dates back to the onset of the Troubles. By contrast, the international consensus about what would constitute the resolution of the conflict has had a powerful impact upon the expectations of internal groups in Northern Ireland and upon the stances of both British and Irish governments. This provides the context of the most significant external influences on the conflict, notably those emanating from the United States and the European Community.

At first sight, the consensus of world opinion in favour of a united Ireland might simply seem to be a judgment on the conflict as a territorial dispute, for at its most basic the conflict appears to be about whether the province will be incorporated into an all-Ireland Republic or remain part of the United Kingdom. In this context the high profile of the conflict might be attributed to the fact that the number of such disputes has been sharply reduced due to the trend within the international community towards the acceptance of existing boundaries. In particular, the Republic's continuing claim to jurisdiction over Northern Ireland stands out in Europe because it runs counter to the general acceptance by European states of the territorial consequences of the Second World War. In its most traditional form, the Irish nationalist viewpoint asserts that Britain is responsible for the continuing division of Ireland because of its deliberate encouragement of Unionist resistance to a united Ireland. In short, the Unionists are seen to be acting as proxies for the British state in its battle against a united Ireland. By contrast, from a Unionist perspective, Southern irredentism is viewed as the primary cause of the conflict, with nationalists in the North being seen as proxies for the Republic in the war being waged to achieve Irish unity.[1]

However, the equivocal attitudes of Britain and the Republic to their respective 'sides' in the conflict during two decades of the Troubles have done much to undermine this dimension of the conflict and the coherence of perspectives based on it. As a territorial dispute, the international dimension of the conflict has appeared to diminish as it has become evident that Britain and the Republic *share* the same objective of quarantining the conflict and preventing its intrusion into their domestic politics. In particular, the signing of the Anglo-Irish Agreement on Northern Ireland on 15 November 1985 makes it difficult to assert that there is still a conflict between the two states over this issue, even if they outwardly continue to differ in their ultimate objectives. In fact, even before the signing of the Agreement, the trend of academic interpretation was towards an internal model of the conflict that identified the antagonism between Protestants and Catholics within Northern Ireland as the root cause of the conflict, with external actors (including the British and Irish Governments) cast in a secondary role. John Whyte has argued that this has become the dominant interpretation among academic researchers into the conflict.[2] For this reason, the international influences upon the conflict will be explored in the *perceptions* of the internal actors in the conflict and only then in those of the two governments primarily involved. The starting point of the analysis has to be the nature of international norms.

Why does the overwhelming weight of world opinion favour a united Ireland? This is not simply a question of emotive support for Irish nationalism. Rather it is because Northern Ireland's *current* status as a conditional part of the United Kingdom·is seen as anomalous in an international context. The conditional nature of Northern Ireland's membership of the United Kingdom is reflected in the fact that British governments acknowledge Northern Ireland's right to secede from the United Kingdom.[3] This is simply the logical obverse of the constitutional guarantee that Northern Ireland shall not cease to be part of the United Kingdom without the consent of a majority of the people of the province. It makes Northern Ireland's position different from that of every other part of the United Kingdom, but comparable to that of Britain's remaining colonies. They too remain bound to Britain only by the consent of their inhabitants. In effect, the province enjoys a status somewhat above that of a colony but below that of, say, Scotland. Northern Ireland's position is unusual, even in a British context. It would be quite unthinkable in most other countries that part of the national territory should be regarded as, in principle, detachable. Thus, the Dutch political scientist, Arend Lijphart has described Northern Ireland as a plural society possessing the attribute of 'a colonial fragment',[4] while a report on the conflict for the European Parliament called Northern Ireland a 'constitutional oddity'.[5] Because Northern Ireland is not fully integrated into the United Kingdom either constitutionally or politically, it is seen internationally as a political entity in its own right and not simply as a subordinate part of the United Kingdom. What is more, as an entity in its own right, Northern Ireland lacks international legitimacy, to use a term developed by Martin Wight.

Wight defined international legitimacy as 'the collective judgment of international society about rightful membership of the family of nations; how sovereignty may be transferred; and how state succession is to be regulated, when large states break up into smaller, or several states combine into one'.[6] It should be emphasised that it is a political, not a legal, concept. International legitimacy is quite distinct from internal legitimacy—that is, the opinions of the inhabitants of a territory as to the rightfulness to rule of the state under which they live. Of course, internal legitimacy or its absence may be a factor in influencing the judgment of international society. The reverse may also be the case. International legitimacy or its absence may affect internal legitimacy. Interaction between these two levels of legitimacy is very evident in the case of Northern Ireland. However, there are also cases where the degree of interaction is minimal. There are many regimes with a low degree of internal legitimacy that nevertheless are treated as fully legitimate in international society. There are also a smaller number of cases of territories or regimes that enjoy a very high degree of internal legitimacy but lack international legitimacy. Gibraltar and the

Falkland Islands are the most obvious examples of the latter.[7]

As well as distinguishing between two levels of legitimacy, it is also useful to distinguish between two *types* of legitimacy: legitimacy in relation to territory or boundaries and legitimacy in relation to regimes or political systems. The difference is best illustrated by the example of South Africa, a byword as an international pariah. In South Africa's case it is clearly the regime and the system of apartheid that lack legitimacy rather than the territory itself or its boundaries. Indeed, the very legitimacy of the territory has proved an obstacle to the policy of apartheid. The Government's partitioning of the territory to create independent Bantustans has failed either to secure international recognition of the new entities or to alter international perceptions of the internal illegitimacy of the regime. South Africa has been no more successful in its attempts to incorporate territory. In contrast to South Africa, Northern Ireland's lack of international legitimacy concerns primarily the existence of the territory rather than the nature of the political system. An important difference between the two cases concerns the internal balance of forces in the two societies. In the long run it seems probable that the growth of Black power in South Africa will resolve the issue of the political system's illegitimacy. No such shift in the internal balance of forces seems likely in Northern Ireland. What South Africa and Northern Ireland have in common is that they both fall foul of the prevailing interpretation of the principle of self-determination. In South Africa's case this is because of White minority rule. In Northern Ireland's case, the conflict with the international norm is that its conditional status as a political entity appears anachronistic in a post-colonial world of permanent territorial units. To explain this point more fully, a brief analysis of the international norm of self-determination is necessary.

The prevailing interpretation of the principle of self-determination is that it is the right of the majority to establish an independent state within any area administered as a political entity by a colonial power. Under what one writer has disparagingly called 'the new UN law of self-determination',[8] the international community has opted to define the 'self' entitled to self-determination in terms of a territorial criterion rather than an ethnic or cultural one. This interpretation, which 'asserts the right of the majority within the frontiers prevailing at a given moment'[9] has dominated political practice since the end of the Second World War. It has been the basis of decolonisation in both Asia and Africa, with relatively few exceptions. In fact, it provides the basis of the international legitimacy of most states in the world. A significant feature of what can be called the majoritarian territorial interpretation of self-determination is that it makes no provision for the rights of minorities, an issue that figured prominently in the deliberations of the

League of Nations. By contrast, the Charter of the United Nations makes no mention of minorities.

The principal document setting out the position of the United Nations General Assembly on how the principle of self-determination ought to be interpreted is the 1970 *Declaration of Principles of International Law concerning Friendly Relations and Co-operation among States in accordance with the Charter of the United Nations* (superseding the 1960 *Declaration on the Granting of Independence to Colonial Countries and Peoples*).[10] The main points on self-determination are worth quoting at length:

> The establishment of a sovereign and independent State, the free association or integration with an independent State or the emergence into any other political status freely determined by a people constitute modes of implementing the right of self-determination by that people.
>
> Every State has the duty to refrain from any forcible action which deprives peoples referred to above in the elaboration of the present principle of their right to self-determination and freedom and independence. In their actions against, and resistance to, such forcible action in pursuit of the exercise of their right to self-determination, such peoples are entitled to seek and to receive support in accordance with the purposes and principles of the Charter.
>
> The territory of a colony or other Non-Self-Governing Territory has, under the Charter, a status separate and distinct from the territory of the State administering it; and such separate and distinct status under the Charter shall exist until the people of the colony or Non-Self-Governing Territory have exercised their right of self-determination in accordance with the Charter, and particularly its purposes and principles.
>
> Nothing in the foregoing paragraphs shall be construed as authorizing or encouraging any action which would dismember or impair, totally or in part, the territorial integrity or political unity of sovereign and independent States conducting themselves in compliance with the principle of equal rights and self-determination and thus possessed of a government representing the whole people belonging to the territory without distinction as to race, creed, or colour.
>
> Every State shall refrain from any action aimed at the partial or total disruption of the national unity and territorial integrity of any other State or country.[11]

Two points need to be strongly underlined. The first is the linking of adherence to the principle of self-determination to the legitimacy or otherwise of the use of force or violence. The second is the rejection of any right of secession from an independent state. Unlike the inhabitants of a colony whose right to self-determination remains an ongoing right which can be exercised in favour of independence at any time, the citizens of an independent state are bound to that state seemingly for all time. The right of self-determination has become *the right of self-determination once* at the point of independence. There is one major exception to this principle: the emergence of Bangladesh in 1971. The fact that Pakistan itself was the product of partition, the geographical separation between the two wings of the country, and the fact that the people of the East wing actually constituted a majority within the whole country were factors in legitimising this single and controversial example of contested secession.[12] However, the general hostility of the international community towards the principle of secession remains as strong as ever. Many secessionist movements have quite an impressive record in terms of attracting popular support and of establishing temporary control over territory but their lack of international legitimacy has been a major obstacle to their ultimate success. For example, recognition of an independent state for the Kurds would require a revolution in the interpretation of self-determination. On this ground alone the odds are heavily stacked against such an outcome, regardless of the local balance of forces.

The implications for Northern Ireland of the prevailing interpretation of the principle of self-determination are somewhat more ambiguous. Clearly, in political terms, Northern Ireland's current status does not comply with the model regarded as desirable in the 1970 *Declaration*. However, there is more than one answer to the question of what would be required to bring the situation into line with the purposes and principles of the Charter. In fact, a case could be made out for four different perspectives, even though one of these dominates international perceptions of the problem. Each is examined briefly below.

Firstly, there is the integrationist perspective. It takes as its starting point the fact that Northern Ireland is legally an integral part of the United Kingdom, which is itself an independent state and a fully legitimate member of the United Nations. From this perspective, the question of Northern Ireland's international legitimacy should not arise because it is simply a subordinate part of a state. Indeed, in terms of the Charter of the United Nations there is an obligation on other states and on the international community itself not to interfere in the situation. In particular, under Article 2, paragraph 7 of the Charter, the United Nations is precluded from intervening in 'matters which are essentially within the domestic jurisdiction of any state'. In fact, this was the basis on which Britain successfully opposed the efforts of the Irish Republic to include the situation in Northern Ireland on the agenda of the

Security Council when the major disturbances of August 1969 broke out.

The legal position has been of some value to Britain in preventing the formal internationalisation of the issue. But what would be required to make the integrationist perspective politically credible would be a declaration by the British Government that Northern Ireland was permanently part of the United Kingdom. Not only have successive British governments declined to make such a commitment to the permanence of the Union,[13] but with the signing of the Anglo-Irish Agreement in November 1985, Britain has committed itself in an international treaty to facilitate a change in the status of Northern Ireland, should its inhabitants so wish. Indeed, Professor John O'Connor, Dean of the Faculty of Law at University College Cork has argued that the Agreement has brought about a legal change in the province's status. He describes Northern Ireland's status under the Agreement as 'unique in international law' creating a situation in which the province 'for the first time has become subject to the legal right of two sovereign governments to determine how all matters which go to the heart of sovereignty in that area shall in future be determined'.[14] Integration was never a popular cause in Northern Ireland when the province had its own regional parliament. But since 1985 it has become much more popular as it is seen as a way of opposing the Anglo-Irish Agreement. However, there is little support for it in the UK mainland and it is unlikely that any British government would lightly accept the open-ended commitment to Northern Ireland that integration would demand, even if the abrogation of the Anglo-Irish Agreement permitted it to be made.

Secondly, there is the British Isles perspective. It acknowledges the illegitimacy of partition, but treats the territorial unit that has been partitioned as the British Isles as a whole. According to this view, partition occurred through the establishment of the Irish Free State in 1922. It was the first step in a process of secession, with the 1937 constitution, Irish neutrality during the Second World War, and the promulgation of the Republic of Ireland in 1949 representing further steps along that route. In this perspective the source of partition lies in illegitimate Irish secessionism. By implication, one way to end partition would be through a close association between Britain and Ireland that partially reverses the secessionist process. During the Second World War Winston Churchill saw the key to the achievement of Irish unity by consent as being 'de Valera [the Irish Prime Minister] showing some loyalty to Crown and Empire'.[15] Even in the 1950s, questioning 'Éire's' legitimacy figured prominently in the defence of the Unionist position.[16] However, in the world as it is today, any reversal of Irish secessionism would be bound to be very partial indeed since it is unimaginable that the Republic would cease to be a sovereign

independent state. The significance of this perspective has consequently declined although it still surfaces periodically in proposals for
a settlement of the conflict.

A persistent proponent of the British Isles perspective has been the
Conservative MP, Sir John Biggs-Davison. For example, when Irish
nationalists launched the New Ireland Forum in 1983, he put forward
the suggestion of a British Isles forum to work out 'a formula for the
reunification of these islands as a whole'.[17] It is a theme that has been
taken up by Unionists, also generally in reaction to nationalist political
initiatives.[18] Much more indirectly it can be seen in the proposal Harold
Wilson put forward in November 1971, as Leader of the Opposition, for
a united Ireland within the Commonwealth.[19] One can also see traces of
this perspective in some of the ideas floated in the early 1980s in the
context of the initial stage of the Anglo-Irish process, especially in the
widely canvassed suggestion that the Republic should join NATO as a
quid pro quo for unity.[20]

The strategic case for the British Isles perspective is that Ireland
constitutes an offshore island in relation to Great Britain, the control of
which by a hostile power could pose a threat to British security.
However, while Republicans and their sympathisers have asserted that
the strategic factor explains Britain's reluctance to withdraw from
Northern Ireland,[21] some Unionists such as Enoch Powell have alleged
that the goal of Irish entry into NATO provides the motivation for a
conspiracy between the Foreign Office and the American State
Department to bring about a united Ireland.[21] More reasonably, in
1986, Jonathan Alford, the Deputy Director of the International
Institute for Strategic Studies, argued that technology had greatly
reduced the strategic significance that Northern Ireland had once had
and that it was now largely a 'non-issue'.[23] This of course presupposes
that relationships between British and Irish governments remain much
as they have been. In 1983, the Secretary of State for Northern Ireland,
James Prior, warned a private meeting of Conservative MPs that Ireland
could become another Cuba if Sinn Fein came to power and linked the
warning with the need for progress to be made through the Anglo-Irish
process.[24] Only in this kind of context, can it credibly be argued that
Anglo-Irish relations have a strategic dimension, however far-fetched the
notion of Ireland as another Cuba might seem. But none of this makes a
reunified British Isles either attractive to the Republic or realistic
politics.

Thirdly, there is the independent Northern Ireland perspective. It
takes two rather different forms. At moments of particular tension
between Unionism and the British Government, the possibility of
independence has been canvassed by Loyalist politicians as a last ditch
resort to frustrate the British Government's plans. For example, the

threat of a Unilateral Declaration of Independence surfaced at the time of the imposition of direct rule by Britain and the suspension of Northern Ireland's regional parliament at Stormont in 1972. It has reappeared as a result of the Anglo-Irish Agreement, with Unionists warning that independence would have to be considered if the alternative was acceptance of the Agreement.[25] However, the idea of a negotiated independence has also been put forward as a positive solution to the problem of Northern Ireland's anomalous status. It has attracted a diverse range of supporters, including the Loyalist paramilitary organisation, the UDA, a former British Prime Minister, Sir James Callaghan, and the writer, Dervla Murphy. The case made out by the UDA for independence in *Beyond the Religious Divide*,[26] which was published in 1979, is examined in Chapter 4 on Loyalist perceptions. Callaghan argued in support of independence that British intervention had failed to produce a solution because it had 'undermined the sense of responsibility that the people of Northern Ireland should feel for their own destinies'.[27] His speech to the House of Commons in July 1981 was 'the first time since 1922 that a major British politician had seriously urged the secession of part of the United Kingdom'.[28] Dervla Murphy has put forward a similar line of argument, concluding that 'without a drastic *political* change, the Republican paramilitaries *cannot* be beaten'.[29]

The main weakness of this perspective is that independence has enjoyed negligible electoral support in the province, not least because of fears as to its likely economic consequences. Indeed, proponents of integration have exploited popular anxiety about the dangers of independence to argue against any form of devolved government for the province on the grounds that it could prove a stepping stone to independence.[30] However, in principle, were the majority (or simply a majority) to demand to exercise their right of self-determination within the boundaries established by the 'colonial' power, they would have a strong case in terms of the way that the principle of self-determination has been applied in other parts of the world. In fact, the present British Prime Minister has explicitly acknowledged the right of people in Northern Ireland to opt for independence;[31] and, if the British Government attempted to resist such a demand, it would find itself in a difficult position internationally. The international community has been disinclined to accept claims that Portugal and France have made at various times that their overseas territories constitute an integral part of their national territory. Admittedly, the physical proximity of Northern Ireland alters the case somewhat, but it is difficult to see on what basis a distinction could be drawn between the Republic of Ireland and Northern Ireland on geographical grounds.

Finally, there is the nationalist perspective. This is clearly the perspective that has by far the greatest influence on the views of the rest of the world. This is apparent from the coverage and comment that major events in Northern Ireland, such as the 1981 hunger strike, provoke.[32] The main tenets of the nationalist perspective are simple to state. In the first place, Northern Ireland was an artifically created entity. Its genesis was illegitimate not merely because it partitioned the island but because of the particular boundaries drawn.[33] Consequently, Northern Ireland's inclusion within the United Kingdom constitutes a denial of the right to self-determination of the majority within the island. In the second place, Britain's presence in Northern Ireland constitutes a form of colonial rule. Direct rule and the presence of British troops on the streets have enhanced the credibility of this proposition internationally, a point that the Provisional IRA was quick to appreciate and exploit.

One of the main strengths of the nationalist perspective is that the meaning of territorial integrity in relation to an island seems unambiguous, at least in a geographical sense. The geographical image has tended to influence the political (though admittedly not the legal) interpretation of the term, however much geographers may deplore the whole concept of natural frontiers. It is also a question of political practice. Divided sovereignties on islands are rare.[34] The fate of the island of Timor is instructive in this context. Up to 1975 the island was divided between Indonesia and Portugal. In that year, with the colonial power withdrawing, Indonesia forcibly and bloodily annexed East Timor against the clear wishes of a majority of the territory's inhabitants. Initially, there was a substantial majority in the United Nations General Assembly for a resolution condemning Indonesia's action as a violation of the right of the people of East Timor to self-determination within boundaries established by a colonial power. However, by 1982 this had dwindled to a majority of only four for a relatively weak resolution against Indonesia, effectively ending the international community's support for the division of the island. By contrast, Indonesia successfully asserted its claim to sovereignty over West Irian on the basis that this part of the island of New Guinea had been part of the Dutch East Indies. This issue also divided the General Assembly where there was considerable support for the view that the island's ethnic homogeneity and the issue of territorial integrity should override the principle of colonial boundaries.[35] In particular, the representative of the Republic of Ireland urged that self-determination should be offered to the people of New Guinea as a whole 'because New Guinea was a natural geographical unit'.[36]

Of the four perspectives examined, only the third, that of independence, actually treats Northern Ireland as a legitimate political entity in its own right, though under a changed status, but this option enjoys very little popular support in Northern Ireland. This and the dominant influence outside Northern Ireland of the fourth perspective provides a large part of the explanation for Northern Ireland's lack of international legitimacy. Even the support of much of the international community for the Anglo-Irish Agreement, while extremely important as an endorsement of the policies of the British and Irish Governments, does not represent support for the legitimacy of Northern Ireland as a political entity. On the contrary, it represents support for the approach the two governments have taken to cope with its illegitimacy, for the most part in the expectation that the Agreement constitutes a stepping stone to a united Ireland. While there is considerable appreciation in the outside world that the Protestant majority in Northern Ireland opposes a united Ireland, the political basis of Protestant opposition, because of its poor fit with existing norms, appears as anachronistic and illegitimate to much of world opinion as does White resistance to majority rule in South Africa.

What then are the most important consequences of Northern Ireland's lack of international legitimacy? What it does not entail should be stated first. It has not internationalised the conflict in the sense of drawing states outside the British Isles directly into the conflict. Very few states, if any, have a political interest of their own in the conflict that could possibly compensate for the impact that their direct involvement would have on their relations with both Britain and Ireland. The case of Libya, as yet exceptional, demonstrates the point. Libya is the only state that has ever publicly declared its readiness to supply arms to any of the protagonists in the conflict. Colonel Gadafy first declared his support for the IRA in June 1972.[37] The following March the Irish navy intercepted the freighter, *Claudia*, off the Irish coast and seized five tons of arms which had been loaded on to the freighter in Tripoli by soldiers of the Libyan army. However, the Ulster Workers Council strike in May 1974 appears to have modified Gadafy's view of the conflict and he even invited members of the UDA to Tripoli, although he apparently continued to give some aid to the IRA until 1977. But the value Libya placed on the establishment of diplomatic relations with the Republic and the growth of trade between the two countries appear to be the main reasons why Gadafy acceded to pressure from the Irish Government to stop the aid altogether at this time.[38]

The breach in diplomatic relations with Britain as a result of the killing of a policewoman by a member of the staff of the Libyan embassy in April 1984 re-awakened Gadafy's rhetorical interest in the problem of Northern Ireland. In an interview after the expulsion of Libyan diplomats from Britain, he declared, 'if the British call the honest Irish fighters terrorists ... we don't subscribe to that'.[39] In the same period he issued a public invitation to the IRA to set up an office in Tripoli.[40]

Following the American air raid on Libya using bases in Britain in April 1986, Gadafy chose the occasion of a visit to Libya by a group of West German MEPs in June that year to declare that he was planning to resume aid to the IRA.[41] The threat prompted a diplomatic protest from the Irish Government.[42] In an interview with *The Observer* in February 1987, Gadafy replied in the affirmative when asked if he had increased aid to the IRA after British participation in the American air raid, while in April 1987 on the anniversary of the American raid he once again promised, this time to a foreign audience that included two members of Sinn Fein, that Libya would open a centre for the IRA.[43] In effect, this was a repeat of the offer he had made to set up an office for the IRA in Libya three years earlier. However, for all his rhetoric, in practice Gadafy has not succeeded in making Libya a significant factor in the conflict in Northern Ireland. The most obvious constraint on Libyan intervention is the strong opposition of the Irish Government to its involvement in the conflict at any level.

Claire Sterling in a popular book on terrorism made much of the Libyan connection with the Provisional IRA. She grossly exaggerated both its significance and scale.[44] On the basis of even scantier evidence, allegations have been made from time to time of Soviet intervention in the conflict. For example, in 1983 the leader of the Ulster Unionist Party (UUP), James Molyneaux, alleged that Russian submarines had been landing arms on the West coast of Ireland for use by the Irish National Liberation Army (INLA).[45] No evidence for such landings emerged. However, it is possible that the allegation was prompted by the earlier claim of a defecting Soviet journalist that he had been present on a Russian trawler which had unloaded a crate of arms on to a boat close to the Irish coast.[46] Vaguer allegations of Soviet involvement have also been made by a number of writers in the field of international terrorism[47] and then recycled within Northern Ireland by local politicians. In fact, the scale of the conflict, particularly the character of the military equipment used by the paramilitaries, very clearly indicates the limited resources at their disposal, confirming the impression that emerges from court cases as well as from reputable studies of their finances that the paramilitaries are reliant for the most part on indigenous sources of funding. This is hardly surprising. The obvious reason why other states have not become actively involved in the conflict is, as Terrance Carroll has aptly put it, 'the lack of any discernible advantage to be gained from participation'.[48] So long as the Irish Republic and Britain are united in discouraging such involvement it is difficult to see what advantage could be gained by a third party. In particular, no states apart from Britain and the Republic of Ireland have any substantial economic interest in the outcome of the conflict.

Further, Ireland is remote from the strategic concerns of all states except the superpowers and Britain itself. Soviet strategic and political interests may be best served by the continuation of the conflict because of the damage it inflicts on Britain internationally and because of the diversion of military resources to the conflict. But the continuation of the conflict does not require Soviet assistance which—if it could be proven—could be counterproductive for the Provisional IRA, given the likely reaction of its American supporters. A settlement of the conflict is clearly in the best interests of the United States and has been reflected in American support for the Anglo-Irish process. No evidence has emerged that would justify placing a sinister interpretation on the failure of American governments to prevent the flow of funds and arms from the United States to Republican paramilitaries.

Much the same considerations apply to the external affiliates of parties to the internal conflict. The multitude of foreign contacts established by the paramilitaries are a reflection of their needs rather than of actual foreign involvement in the conflict. The foreign connections of the Loyalist paramilitaries are far less extensive than those of the Republican paramilitaries, reflecting the lack of sympathy for the Loyalist cause internationally. Sympathetic elements in the Orange Order in Canada and a variety of neo-fascist organisations in Europe have been their main contacts outside of the British Isles. The latter have been at best tenuous.[49] There have also been overblown reports of Loyalist contacts with right-wing groupings in South Africa.[50] The lack of international sympathy for their cause plays a larger part in the thinking of Loyalist paramilitaries than does any of the links they have been able to establish outside the British Isles, as will be evident from Chapter 4 on Loyalist perceptions of the conflict. The international connections of Republican paramilitaries have been much more significant. Most active in this field has been Sinn Fein, the political wing of the Provisional IRA. Sinn Fein's foreign contacts fall into three broad areas.

Firstly, there is the ethnic connection, Sinn Fein's links with supporters of the Republican cause in Irish communities in a number of countries, including Australia, New Zealand, and Canada, in addition to the United States, where Irish-American groups constitute far and away the most important external source of funds and arms for the Provisional IRA. Secondly, Sinn Fein has cultivated links with a number of separatist nationalist movements in Europe, including Basques, Bretons, and Corsicans. Thirdly, Sinn Fein has consistently supported the Palestinian cause and established links with a variety of Palestinian organisations. There have been several reports that members of the Provisional IRA have received training in the Middle East and particularly in Lebanon.[51] However, it is extremely unlikely that such training involved more than a handful of volunteers. In particular, Bowyer Bell's claim that 'who on the Falls Road had a suntan before cheap flights to Spain'[52] provided a clue to the existence of the training is a nice story but utterly incredible. The Middle East has also formed a secondary source of arms for the Provisional IRA after the United States.[53] However, while Sinn Fein has placed considerable stress on its support for the Palestine Liberation Organisation (PLO), the PLO has been embarrassed by reports linking it to the IRA. The issue was particularly important in the context of the PLO's diplomatic overtures to European governments in the late 1970s and the early 1980s. In January 1980 the chairman of the PLO, Yasser Arafat, denounced reports of links between the PLO and the IRA as 'a big lie' in a meeting with a parliamentary delegation from the Irish Republic in Beirut.[54] Sinn Fein has also strongly supported the South African movement, the African National Congress (ANC), but the links it has been able to establish with South African exiles have been even more tenuous than in the Palestinian case.

The reactions of the PLO and of the ANC to the IRA are mirrored by Sinn Fein's attitude towards violent organisations such as the Red Brigades in Italy or the Red Army Faction in West Germany. It is clearly recognised within the Provisional movement that any association with such groups would be politically damaging.[55] At the same time, the converse applies to such revolutionary terrorist organisations themselves and they have sought to identify their activities with those of the IRA, as in the reference to the IRA in the communiqué issued by the Red Brigades following the kidnapping of an American army officer, Brigadier General James Dozier.[56] It is evident that in terms of a pecking order of the world's violent movements, the IRA occupies a middle rank, but with much greater influence in the outside world than the Loyalist paramilitaries or other fringe Republican groups. With less to lose in terms of image or external influence, the INLA has forged links with a number of ideologically oriented, revolutionary terrorist organisations in Europe. The most important of these contacts, particularly as a conduit for arms, has been *Action Directe* in France.[57]

In fact, the main *practical* significance of the external contacts of the paramilitaries is as a source of arms or funds for arms. In their quest for arms, the paramilitaries have established very diverse contacts, some of which are essentially commercial and criminal rather than political. In particular, the attempt of the Provisional IRA to buy arms through an American intermediary from Omnipol, the sales organisation of the Czech arms industry, in 1971, almost certainly falls into this category, although Sterling inevitably seizes on the episode to support her contention of Soviet involvement in the conflict.[58] Moreover, contact with Eastern Europe was untypical. Both the Middle East and Western Europe have proved much safer areas for the purchase of arms by the paramilitaries. For example, in 1986 the Irish police, the Gardai, traced a consignment of arms they seized in raids in the Republic to Norway, where they had been stolen from an army base in 1984. A number of Norwegian nationals had been arrested in connection with the theft. There was no suggestion that their motivation had been political.[59] Stopping arms shipments from outside the British Isles would make a significant difference to the ability of Republican paramilitaries to sustain their campaign of violence, even at its present relatively reduced level compared to the early 1970s. However, it would make no difference to the currently much lower level of Loyalist violence. The variety and the scope of Ireland's links with the rest of the world, reflecting the impact on Ireland of growing international interdependence since the 1960s, has clearly made the task of stopping shipments more difficult and to that extent interdependence has played a part in aggravating the conflict in this context. The principal *political* significance for the paramilitaries of their external affiliations has been in reinforcing and legitimising their view of the conflict. This aspect is explored further in the chapters on Republican and Loyalist perceptions.

Finally, the Northern Ireland conflict can scarcely be said to have been internationalised in the sense that it is affecting the world beyond Northern Ireland. There has been some spill-over and potentially there might be much more. So far it has principally affected the UK mainland and the Republic. Close to a hundred people have died in Britain as a result of violence emanating from Northern Ireland, the vast majority in Provisional IRA bomb attacks. The most important episodes were the Birmingham pub bombs which killed 21 people in November 1974 and the attempt to assassinate the British Prime Minister in 1984. The Republic of Ireland has suffered a similar number of casualties. Almost a hundred people have died there as a result of Northern Ireland's Troubles, the victims of both Loyalist and Republican paramilitaries. The most serious episode occurred in May 1974 during the Ulster Workers Council strike when car-bombs killed 31 people in Dublin and Monaghan. There have also been a small number of violent incidents on the continent of Europe connected with the Troubles in Northern Ireland. In particular, the Provisional IRA has carried out a series of attacks on British military bases in West Germany. For example, a car bomb attack on the joint British army/Royal Air Force headquarters at Rheindahlen near Dusseldorf in March 1987 injured 31 people.[60] In 1979 the British Ambassador to the Netherlands, Sir Richard Sykes, was assassinated in The Hague. There were other attacks on British personnel in the same period, including the murder of a British army lieutenant at a base in West Germany, apparently carried out by the same Provisional IRA unit.

While the spill-over of violence from the conflict provides the most immediately concrete example of the Troubles' impact on the rest of the world, the potential impact of the conflict on the rest of the world is obviously of far greater significance. The possibility remains that the conflict in Northern Ireland will eventually destabilise the UK mainland or the Republic, or even both societies. Such an eventuality would clearly have the most far-reaching implications for Europe politically, particularly in the context of the EC, as well as having wide ramifications in the strategic field. If it was perceived as advancing the likelihood of a united Ireland, it might also provide a boost for other separatist nationalisms in Europe that have imitated the tactics of Republican paramilitaries in Northern Ireland. The Anglo-Irish Agreement of November 1985 has somewhat reduced the danger of the magnetisation of either Britain or the Republic by the conflict, though that possibility has not by any means been eliminated entirely. In particular, the combination of further damage to Britain's international reputation as a result of the conflict and the belief that externally dictated constraints on the security forces were disabling the fight against terrorism could eventually produce a backlash in Britain. In such circumstances, the demand for action to expunge the country's humiliation could prove irresistible, in spite of its implications for Britain's foreign relations. While such 'Falklandisation' of the conflict seems unlikely, it remains a hope cherished by Unionists in Northern Ireland. The present political impact of the conflict outside of Northern Ireland is difficult to measure with any precision. Perhaps the principal effect, contrary to the hopes of each side of the conflict in Northern Ireland, has been the alienation of the people of the UK mainland and the Republic from either side in Northern Ireland, a reaction that clearly reduces the likelihood of magnetisation.

Direct external involvement then in Northern Ireland is limited. Territorial conflict between Britain and the Republic is relatively low-key. But the international perception that the unification of Ireland is a proper solution to the conflict has a very considerable effect upon the course of events. In the first place, Northern Ireland's lack of international legitimacy plays a large part in shaping people's perceptions about the future of Northern Ireland. In a survey conducted by Edward Moxon-Browne in 1978 respondents in Northern Ireland were asked whether they thought the Border would disappear. The results are tabulated in Table 1.1 (Page 18).

Moxon-Browne also cites an NOP survey in 1967 before the Troubles began which found that 52 per cent of respondents believed the Border would go.[62] Given the weight and solidity of opinion within Northern Ireland opposed to a united Ireland, these are striking results that suggest that the expectations of people in Northern Ireland have been affected considerably by those prevailing in the outside world.[63]

These expectations reduce the scope for political compromise between the two communities because schemes for political accommodation tend to be viewed by both sides as transitional. A possible exception is the notion of an independent Northern Ireland, though even independence could be seen as a stage towards eventual reunification rather than an end in itself. All political initiatives of the British Government tend to be judged in a similar light. Despite the weight of government propaganda to the effect that the Anglo-Irish Agreement safeguarded the position of the majority opposed to a united Ireland, a considerable proportion of respondents in a poll of opinion in Northern Ireland on the Agreement concluded that it brought a united Ireland closer.[64] In particular, the very success of the Agreement internationally has contributed to Unionist suspicion of it, since Unionists recognise that world opinion favours a united Ireland. Consequently, Unionists tend to be hostile towards international organisations and sympathetic to those resisting the demands of the world community such as South Africa and Israel, while nationalists tend to identify strongly with world opinion on such issues. Both Unionists and nationalists are apt to draw conclusions about the direction of the British Government's policy towards Northern Ireland from its attitudes on these questions. Thus, the success with which the Conservative Government steered Zimbabwe to independence in accordance with international norms in 1980 both raised nationalist hopes and aroused Loyalist fears.[65]

Table 1.1

Question: Leaving your hopes to one side, do you think the Border will eventually disappear or not?[61]

	Protestants	Catholics	[All %]
Will disappear	50.6%	70.3%	[57%]
Will not disappear	49.4%	29.7%	[43%]

In the second place, Northern Ireland's lack of international legitimacy plays an important role in the legitimisation of political violence. It helps to promote a siege mentality among Protestants that provides a justification for the existence of Loyalist paramilitaries. At the same time, it gives external credibility to the Provisional IRA's claim that it is engaged in an anti-colonial struggle against British imperialism. These perceptions are analysed in depth in Chapters 3 and 4. In the third place, Northern Ireland's lack of international legitimacy places powerful constraints on the Government's response to the violence. If a conflict as serious as that in Northern Ireland were to break out within the legitimate boundaries of Great Britain, there is little likelihood that such constraints would be observed. The Government's sensitivity to international reaction to human rights violations in Northern Ireland stems in large part from a recognition that territories or regimes already seen as illegitimate by the international community attract a disproportionate degree of opprobrium for breaches of human rights.[66]

Fourthly, it gives credibility to the notion that the minority in Northern Ireland can defeat the majority. Allied to this is a belief that the international community would never permit the minority to lose and might just conceivably assist it to win. Thus the Provisional IRA is able to present a threat to the existence of Northern Ireland that has some measure of credibility despite the fact that the organisation's potential support is limited to the minority and that it has actually been supported only by a minority of the minority. The perceived durability of the threat is reflected in the wide assent given to the proposition that the IRA cannot be beaten. For example, it formed part of the argument that the former British Prime Minister, James Callaghan, put in favour of independence in 1981.

> At best, 'winning', in my judgment, would be merely—no, I withdraw the word 'merely'—would be a period, an uneasy period, of lower tension until the IRA had found another pretext to start the cycle again and plunge the people of Northern Ireland, once more back into disruption and death.[67]

The tendency to overestimate the strength of the forces on the nationalist side has another effect. It underpins the assumption that a united Ireland is bound to follow a British withdrawal.[68] The significance of this is that it enables the Provisionals to argue that they can be successful without winning the support of Protestants.[69] In fact, given the relationship between violence and sectarian divisions in Northern Ireland, it would be extremely difficult to sustain the credibility of a campaign of violence that depended for its success on support across the community divide. The assumption that Protestant opposition by itself cannot prevent the achievement of a united Ireland therefore forms a crucial element in Republican calculations.

Finally, Northern Ireland's lack of international legitimacy lies behind the persistent ambiguity in constitutional nationalism over the meaning of the commitment to seek unity by consent. On the one hand, there is a broad consensus among constitutional nationalists condemning the use of violence to achieve unity and some recognition that partition was the product of divisions and not just their cause. On the other hand, there is a reluctance to adopt any position that might be interpreted as according legitimacy to Northern Ireland as a political entity. The reluctance is understandable since the denial of legitimacy to Northern Ireland attracts international support for the nationalist case. At the same time, the ambiguous position of constitutional nationalists has fuelled Unionist suspicion of their intentions and has consequently been an obstacle to the achievement of political accommodation within Northern Ireland that constitutional nationalists desire. Unionist suspicion has not been allayed by the commitments entered into by the Republic of Ireland under the Anglo-Irish Agreement, because the assurances on the question of consent have been given in the context of a process that Unionists see as designed to achieve the result of a united Ireland. Attempts by British Ministers to reassure Unionists by suggesting that the Republic's commitments entail the permanent acceptance of the Border have simply made matters worse because they have prompted nationalist protests that this is not in fact the case.

From the perspective of the British Government, one of the main aims of the Agreement is to secure international support for the way that Northern Ireland is governed by associating the Republic with British policy in the province. It has so far achieved a considerable measure of success in this respect, mitigating the effect on world opinion of Northern Ireland's anomalous constitutional position. However, the support of world opinion is somewhat double-edged in so far as it is premised on the assumption that the Agreement constitutes a transitional step to a united Ireland. Further, while the Agreement has been a factor in checking the electoral rise of Sinn Fein, the political wing of the Provisional IRA, it has also been accompanied by an increase in the level of violence within Northern Ireland and an exacerbation of tensions between the two communities. What both the British and Irish Governments can fairly claim is that the Agreement has established a mechanism for limiting the internationalisation of the conflict. It is a measure of the intractability of the conflict that this represents political progress.

2.

VIOLENCE AND LEGITIMACY

THE overall impact of the internationalisation of the conflict has been to reinforce the fundamental role that the threat to Northern Ireland's existence as a political entity plays in entrenching the province's divisions. Because it is difficult to disentangle the external from the internal causes of the sectarian divisions in Northern Ireland, it remains open to argument just how much weight should be placed on the international dimension as a factor in the conflict. The thread connecting internal and external causes of the conflict is the question of legitimacy, particularly as it relates to the legitimisation of violence. Here this is examined from an internal perspective through the differences between the parties' attitudes towards violence. In his lucid book, *The Future of Violence*, the Christian pacifist, Gerald Priestland, argues that 'the essence of violence is that physical power is deliberately used with the ultimate sanction of physical pain and little choice but surrender or physical resistance'.[1] Two aspects of this attempt to identify the core meaning of the term need to be underlined. Firstly, the threat of violence or intimidation has justifiably been included by Priestland as part of the essence of the concept. In practice, such violence is often largely invisible to the external observer and unquantifiable as it encompasses all kinds of intimidation. Even more difficult than identifying actual incidences of intimidation is the problem of evaluating its indirect impact on communities through the spread of fear. Thus, comparisons between Northern Ireland and other places on the basis of homicide statistics are fundamentally misleading.[2]

In terms of the incidence of murder Belfast may be a less violent city than, say, Detroit in the United States, but this tells us little about the political impact of violence in the two cities. In a study of intimidation in housing, Darby and Morris estimated that in the period from August 1969 to February 1973, a total of between 30,000 and 60,000 people or between 6.6 per cent and 11.8 per cent of the population of the Belfast urban area were forced to leave their homes.[3] Violence on this scale is practically unknown in other Western industrialised societies except in the context of war. However, outside such periods of breakdown, the social constraints against violence in Northern Ireland are unusually strong, and this is reflected in the very low levels of ordinary crime during periods of tranquillity, much lower than those in more stable societies. There is awareness in both communities of the threat that violence poses to such tranquillity.

Secondly, the intentions of the perpetrator form part of Priestland's definition of violence. This excludes accidents as well as surgery and is more problematic. Most people think of a fatal car crash, for example, as a violent death. There is a small example of this usage in *Ireland: A Positive Proposal* by Kevin Boyle and Tom Hadden. To impress on readers the extent to which normal life is possible in Northern Ireland, they quote statistics showing that more people die each year in road accidents in the province than in the Troubles. They point out, further, that proportionately to population, more people die each year in road accidents in France than die in both road accidents and the Troubles in Northern Ireland.[4] By contrast, few people would find any relevance in a comparison of fatalities arising out of political violence with deaths caused by heart disease or by alcoholism. The weakness of the argument being put forward by Boyle and Hadden is that if violence encompasses events as ordinary as car accidents, then it becomes almost meaningless to treat the level of violence in a society as a yardstick of its normality. However, they are correct in questioning external perceptions of Northern Ireland as a society racked by extremely high levels of *overt* violence.

Priestland remains right to make intention a key element in his definition of violence. Indeed, common usage takes the issue of intention a step further than Priestland. Violence is not simply synonymous with kicking, punching, butting, or attacking an adversary with a weapon with a view to prevailing. There are a number of sports in which instances of such behaviour would be considered both unobjectionable and unremarkable. However, those engaged in any of these sports would disavow any intention to inflict lasting injury on an opponent and in most cases this disavowal meets with general public acceptance. The labelling of behaviour as violent typically entails a judgment that the perpetrator has malicious intent to harm another person or, alternatively, harms someone when not in full control of his or her actions due to drink or loss of temper. It is important to note that the use of the term almost invariably implies a negative value judgment. A strong element of censure is incorporated in the meaning of the term, violence. The point is well illustrated by a poll carried out for Ulster Television in November 1981[5] which asked respondents in Northern Ireland whether they approved or disapproved of the use of violence for political objectives. Not surprisingly, very few respondents said that they approved of the use of violence for this purpose, while 80 per cent strongly disapproved. However, the respondents' answers to other, more specific questions concerning the activities of paramilitary organisations showed that they understood the term violence implied disapproval. The 80 per cent were far from displaying pacifist attitudes towards violence. For most people, violence is only called by that name when it is disapproved of. Violence that is justified is usually called force.

In most societies the term, force, is applied to the actions of agencies enforcing the law such as the police. However, the use of the term is by no means confined to agents of the state. For example, private individuals are said to use force rather than violence when acting in self-defence, provided their reaction is not out of all proportion to the original provocation. As shown by the acquittal of Bernard Goetz, the subway vigilante who shot three men when approached for money in the New York Subway, what constitutes provocation and what self-defence may be given very wide parameters by a public that feels threatened by violent crime. What distinguishes force from violence therefore is less a question of the nature of the actions themselves than of their context and how they are perceived. Force tends to be associated with actions that are seen as legitimate and that can be justified as legal, regulated, reactive, and defensive. Violence, by contrast, suggests action that lacks legitimacy, is illegal, arbitrary, unpredictable, and aggressive. From a political perspective, action upholding the status quo tends to be seen as force while violence tends to be regarded as, by nature, anti-system. The conservative bias of the distinction has led radicals to challenge its validity,[6] but it is important to recognise the practical significance of the distinction. Politics in a society where there is a large measure of consensus over what constitutes violence or force has a stable frame of reference. This is absent in the case of deeply divided societies where the very definition of these terms is at issue. Misunderstanding is particularly likely to arise when the assumptions of a stable society are brought to bear on an unstable one. Analysis of the Northern Ireland conflict that treats political violence in the province as a problem of terrorism is especially prone to such error, basically because its point of departure in comparing Northern Ireland with other societies is the threat that terrorism poses to the existence and stability of liberal-democracy.[7] Since Northern Ireland is neither stable nor possessed of the consensus usually to be found in liberal-democracies, this approach tends to be unfruitful. It tends to underestimate the political influence of the paramilitaries and the hold that terrorism has over society.

It is no more fruitful to explain the durability of terrorism in Northern Ireland as a by-product of the intensity of sectarian hatred in the province, with emphasis being placed on the sharpness of political divisions on sectarian lines.[8] To sustain this picture, political differences within the province tend to be oversimplified through the equation of Protestant with Unionist and of Catholic with nationalist. In fact, as Unionists never tire of pointing out, there is not a simple correspondence between these categories as significant numbers of Catholics support the continuation of the Union.[9] Similarly, polls highlight considerable differences among Protestants as to their identity: British, Ulster, or Irish.[10] Further, pollsters' questions on possible solutions to the Northern Ireland problem from integration to independence also show that on many of the constitutional options opinion cuts right across the sectarian divide.[11] While polls of this kind may give a rather misleading impression of the extent of political fluidity across sectarian lines in the province, they do underline the weakness of explaining violence in Northern Ireland as the extreme by-product of more general sectarian political polarisation.

More relevant to an explanation of the Troubles than the intensity of political divisions is the fact that they centre on the issue of Northern Ireland's legitimacy and hence on what constitutes force and violence. Thus, it is often in respect of questions on force and violence that sectarian divisions emerge most clearly in polls of Northern Ireland opinion. A poll conducted for the *Belfast Telegraph* in January 1985 on the subject of law and order contained a number of questions that brought out the different perceptions of the two communities in this area quite starkly. The response to three of the questions is set out in Table 2.1.

Given the universalistic language in which the questions were posed, the degree of community polarisation is remarkable. In practice, it needs to be borne in mind that there would be less likelihood of Protestant approval of the death penalty for a Loyalist convicted of a 'terrorist murder', as was shown in the case of a member of the UDA who was sentenced to death in 1973 for the murder of a policeman prior to the formal abolition of the death penalty in Northern Ireland. Unionist politicians made numerous representations to the Government on his behalf prior to the sentence being commuted to life imprisonment, as had been expected from the outset. In 1985 the respondents would by and large have made the assumption that the question primarily referred to the Provisional IRA. Similarly, it would have been a realistic assumption at the time the poll was conducted that those likely to be injured by plastic bullets would be Catholics. In fact, there was a radical reversal in Unionist attitudes towards plastic bullets when a Loyalist was killed in protests over the Anglo-Irish Agreement in 1986. The third question shows unanimity in the Protestant view that the security forces were shackled by political restraints from tackling terrorism more forcefully. There would probably have been equal unanimity that they should not be restricted, had that question been asked. By contrast, it is likely that many of the Catholics who answered that the security forces were restricted in their duties would also have expressed the view that there should be political constraints on their operations. In short, the division of Catholic opinion on this question does not have the same significance as the unanimity on the Protestant side. The responses to these questions illustrate the existence of a division of opinion on sectarian lines in relation to issues of violence in Northern Ireland that is qualitatively different from the variations in opinion one would be likely to encounter in the UK mainland or in the Republic of Ireland.

Before exploring the attitudes of the two communities in greater

Table 2.1

Question 1: Do you approve or disapprove of the use of plastic bullets by the security forces as a weapon during riots?

	Roman Catholics	Protestants
Approve	9	86
Disapprove	87	8
Don't know	4	6

Question 2: Would you approve or disapprove of the re-introduction of the death penalty only for those convicted of terrorist murders in Northern Ireland?

	Roman Catholics	Protestants
Approve	21	74
Disapprove	71	18
Don't know	8	8

Question 3: Do you think the security forces are restricted by political policies in their security duties in Northern Ireland?

	Roman Catholics	Protestants
Are restricted	39	92
Are not restricted	40	4
Don't know	21	4

Source: *Belfast Telegraph*, 6 February 1985.

depth, the mainland British perspective on violence in Northern Ireland needs to be examined as it is the principal influence on the government's security policy, which is at the centre of political argument in Northern Ireland in both communities. In most essentials this perspective represents the extension to Northern Ireland of assumptions derived from the consensus on force and violence that prevails in Britain itself. In particular, through much of the Troubles a central assumption of British opinion has been that political violence is attributable to a tiny minority of the population. This view has a basis in reality. It is of course literally true that only an extremely small number of people has participated directly in shootings and bombings. The weakness of this perspective lies in the further assumption that it would be relatively easy to criminalise this minority of violent lawbreakers and to achieve their political isolation from their respective communities.

What this overlooked was the representative nature of political violence in Northern Ireland. That is to say, political violence is not seen as simply the actions of individuals, but is regarded as representative of the community from which it emanates, and that community is regarded as accountable for it.[12] Thus, it is usually very difficult for a Catholic in Northern Ireland to repudiate entirely and without qualification the actions of the Provisional IRA, because as a Catholic he or she will be held accountable for the IRA's violence by 'the other side'. At worst, this may mean being seen as a legitimate target by a Loyalist paramilitary organisation. At least, it means being conscious of being defined by leaders of Protestant opinion as part of 'the enemy'. At the same time, completely repudiating the IRA and its aims carries the risk of being seen as a traitor by one's 'own side'.

After the ending of internment, the British Government attempted to criminalise political violence through discontinuing the practice of according special category status to those convicted of crimes whose motivation was political. This policy was a spectacular failure. Far from isolating the paramilitaries, it served to highlight their political influence within their respective communities, reinforcing rather than weakening the community's identification with those engaged in political violence. One of the consequences of the battle over the policy was Sinn Fein's entry into electoral politics. The political wing of the Provisional IRA won just over 10 per cent of the vote in the Assembly elections of November 1982, outpolling in first preferences the moderate Alliance Party. Their success profoundly shocked opinion in the UK mainland since the result ran so completely counter to British assumptions as to the potential appeal of a terrorist organisation. The belief that it is abnormal, even in Northern Ireland, for terrorism to attract votes has also been a factor in the swiftness of British opinion's conversion to the alienation thesis advanced by the Irish Government and the SDLP to explain the Sinn Fein vote. This is the view that the electoral success of Sinn Fein reflects the special intensity of current Catholic dissatisfaction with government policies and can be reversed by tackling Catholic grievances.

A third feature of British opinion is the sharpness of the distinction drawn between political extremism and support for violence. Political extremism as a product of sectarian hatred is seen as encompassing a far wider section of the population than support for violence, especially among Protestants. The extent to which the 'constitutional' parties differ in their perceptions of what constitutes violence tends to be overlooked. Of Northern Ireland's main political parties only Sinn Fein is regarded by the British as committed to supporting violence. This perception periodically surfaces in policy pronouncements. In particular, at various times over the last few years the British Government has floated the idea that renunciation of violence might be made a condition of standing for election in Northern Ireland.[13] Nothing has come of this idea so far but clearly the assumption behind it is that it would be possible to define support for violence in such a way that it would provide a means of disqualifying Sinn Fein alone. This is partly a function of seeing Republican paramilitaries and the Provisional IRA, in particular, as primarily to blame for political violence in Northern Ireland. The fact that Republican paramilitaries have been responsible for the deaths of over half those killed in the Troubles is evidence that can be cited to support this judgment.[14] Occasionally, the popular press in Britain has gone further and attributed all the deaths in the Troubles to the IRA.[15] The notion that a duty should be placed on political parties to demonstrate their unreserved support for the constitution, the political institutions of the state, and law and order, ironically, forms part of the proposals put forward in 1987 by the Loyalist paramilitary organisation, the Ulster Defence Association (UDA).[16]

While British opinion draws a distinction between support for violence and extremism, it does see them as related. In the first place, political violence is seen itself as a by-product of extremism. Secondly and more importantly, political violence is perceived as a factor that polarises society and creates the climate for extremism. Conversely, it is assumed that a reduction in the overt level of violence will assist the growth of political moderation. A striking illustration of this assumption is to be found in Merlyn Rees's account[17] of his efforts to secure a ceasefire by the Provisional IRA so as to provide a fair wind for the Constitutional Convention taking place in 1975. Even with the benefit of hindsight, Rees appears blind to a significant by-product of this policy. This was to stimulate Unionist fears that there had been a deal between the British Government and the Provisionals. One reflection of these fears was a campaign of sectarian assassinations by

Loyalist paramilitaries. The result was that the policy was a failure in terms of securing a reduction in the level of violence. Rees's predecessor as Secretary of State for Northern Ireland, William Whitelaw, similarly sought a Provisional ceasefire in 1972 with comparable results in terms of accentuating Unionist distrust of the British Government and of triggering sectarian killings. In the event, the substantial fall in the numbers dying in political violence after 1976 was not accompanied by any lessening of political polarisation in the province.

Finally, the mainland British perspective on political violence in Northern Ireland is strongly influenced by their conception of their role in the province as that of an unbiased intermediary between bitterly contending political factions. The consequence has been a preference for grounding the difference between force and violence in Northern Ireland on the neutral concept of the rule of law rather than basing it on the assumption of Northern Ireland's legitimacy as a political entity. The latter could be construed as politically partisan, and even sectarian, given external perceptions of the conflict. The practical implications of emphasis on the rule of law are that Britain has had to be willing to defend its security policies on the basis of notions such as due process and minimum force. Deviations from these norms, in practice, have either had to be disavowed as an aberration or defended reluctantly as necessitated by the abnormal conditions prevailing in the province. Mainland opinion tends to make the assumption that the British army, the UDR, and the RUC conduct their operations as a matter of course according to the rule of law, and finds evidence to the contrary disturbing. This reaction smacks of hypocrisy to Republicans, while Unionists believe that such criticism of the security forces really does handicap them in the exercise of their duty, and suspect that it is motivated by a desire to appease nationalism rather than the depth of the mainland's commitment to the rule of law. An ambiguous statement attributed to a member of the SAS could be seen as supporting either of these suspicions: 'Letting the opposition shoot first is what we call "the Irish dimension".'[18] By contrast, a statement by Humphrey Atkins in 1980 that 'we do no service to Northern Ireland if we simply parallel the savagery of the gunman himself'[19] is a characteristic expression of the attitude expected of government by British opinion.

Within Northern Ireland, the attitudes of the Alliance Party, the small liberal party of the middle ground, come closest to those of mainland British opinion, though there are a few significant differences. Like mainland opinion, the Alliance Party emphasises 'universal respect for the rule of law'[20] as the foundation of its approach in this area. While the party acknowledges the need for emergency measures to deal with violence, it goes further than mainland opinion in advocating steps such as an enforceable Bill of Rights to ensure that the security forces adhere to the rule of law. The party strongly supported the policy of criminalisation even after the 1981 hunger strike by Republican prisoners.[21] The most significant difference with mainland opinion is the party's unequivocal support for the Union between Northern Ireland and Great Britain as presently constituted. Within this framework, the party advocates devolution in the context of accommodation between Catholics and Protestants within Northern Ireland. It has looked to Westminster to create the conditions for such accommodation through guaranteeing equality of rights within the province. Support for the party was at its strongest when it appeared that the British Government had both the capacity and the will to effect an internal settlement. It fell after the overthrow of the power-sharing Executive demonstrated the impotence of the British Government within Northern Ireland. The party attracts much greater support in the east of the province and in the areas that are furthest away from the Border with the Republic. For the most part, these are predominantly Protestant areas, though the Alliance Party itself attracts its political support in roughly equal numbers from Protestants and Catholics. The wealthier mixed suburbs within these areas are where Alliance tends to be most successful. Significantly, these are places where conditions for the operation of the rule of law are most favourable and where the resemblance to the situation prevailing in the UK mainland is closest. Residents co-operate with the police, and paramilitary organisations have little influence on their lives, except at moments of intense crisis.

However, it would be wrong to give the impression that hostility towards paramilitary organisations (of one's 'own side') was confined to affluent suburbs or to the middle classes. At various times during the Troubles the paramilitaries have encountered strong opposition to their activities within working-class areas. The most notable instance of such opposition was the mobilisation of opinion in Catholic West Belfast against the Provisional IRA in the summer of 1976. It sprang from an incident in August of that year in which three children were killed by a car carrying two Provisional IRA volunteers, which had gone out of control when the driver was shot by British soldiers in hot pursuit of the volunteers after a shooting incident. The dead children's aunt spoke out strongly against the Provisional IRA on television the day after the shooting, while a neighbour organised a petition for peace which rapidly attracted signatures. Large demonstrations and rallies followed in both Catholic and Protestant areas as the movement they had begun in Andersonstown gathered support across the whole of the province. In a matter of weeks the Peace People (as they were called) attracted the attention of the outside world, culminating in the award of the Nobel Peace Prize in 1977 to the two women who had started the movement. By the time of the award, support for the Peace People within Northern

Ireland had already declined. The award itself created resentment rather than pride in the province.

The credo of the Peace People was contained in a declaration that was read out at rallies in between prayers and hymn-singing. Reconciliation was the basic theme of the declaration alongside the rejection of 'the use of the bomb and the bullet and all the techniques of violence'.[22] The obvious difficulty from the outset was whether this rejection encompassed any of the activities of the security forces. What had impressed Protestant opinion to start with was that both Mairead Corrigan and Betty Williams had placed the blame for the children's deaths squarely and solely on the Provisionals. Such a position could be sustained as a judgment on a single incident. However, interpreted as a general statement of where responsibility lay for the violence in Northern Ireland, it had little prospect of securing the support of most Catholics, as the leaders of the Peace People themselves recognised. When a plastic bullet fired by the army killed a young boy in Turf Lodge in October 1976, the two founders of the Peace People strongly criticised the army's action. In response to hostile comment in the media, a further statement was issued by the Peace People placing their criticism of the army in the context of support for the rule of law. The clarification did little to prevent the further erosion of their support on both sides of the sectarian divide, and this was reflected in a decline in the numbers attending rallies and demonstrations. The problem was that the rejection of all violence, regardless of its source, identified the Peace People philosophically with pacifism, which was perceived as having little practical political relevance to the ending of the conflict.[23] In reality, pacifism was the only conceivable way in which the different perceptions that Protestant and Catholic working-class communities had of the conflict could be bridged. However, while the period in which the Peace People were able to attract mass support was relatively short-lived, it had a lasting influence in reducing the incidence of random sectarian murders in Northern Ireland, particularly through its effect on Loyalist perceptions of the conflict. (See Chapter 4.)

The perspective that most directly contradicts the mainland British view of the conflict is that of the Republican paramilitaries. It has been most clearly articulated by representatives of Sinn Fein, the political wing of the Provisional IRA. Their essential starting-point is that the British presence in Ireland is illegitimate. From this perspective, the genesis of the problem was partition, which constituted a denial of the Irish people's right to self-determination. According to Sinn Fein's interpretation of the international norm, the British and their local allies remain the aggressors in the conflict in Northern Ireland. The armed struggle waged by Republican paramilitaries constitutes resistance to occupation. It is notable how the language used by Sinn Fein inverts official British descriptions of the conflict. Thus, the security forces are portrayed as men of violence while Provisional IRA volunteers are cast in the role of the defenders of the nationalist ghettoes. Characteristic of Sinn Fein's response to criticism of the Provisional IRA as the main obstacle to peace is this statement by its President, Gerry Adams.

> We cannot have justice and peace in Ireland because we do not have a society capable of upholding them. Instead we have a system based on coercion, violence, sectarianism and exploitation. By its very nature British rule cannot be just or peaceful and, while this is so, revolutionary struggle will continue to strive to over-throw it in pursuit of true justice, peace, and happiness. Violence in Ireland has its roots in the conquest of Ireland by Britain.[24]

What gives added weight to this perspective is the extent to which it is shared by people in the Catholic community who have no connection with, and perhaps generally would not support, Republican paramili-taries. An open letter which seven priests sent to the Catholic bishops in 1982 in response to what they saw as one-sided criticism by the bishops of Republican paramilitaries illustrates the point clearly. They concluded their letter:

> If a political system has been created by force and maintained by force then leaders within the Christian community have a respon-sibility not only to speak against, but to actively resist such a system. Surely this is the primary violence in our society that must be confronted.[25]

It is worth pointing out that force here is being counterposed by impli-cation to consent and is being given a negative connotation similar to that of violence itself. The letter left vague what active resistance to the system or confronting the primary violence might entail. Despite .the ambiguity it was almost certainly not intended to be read as an endorse-ment of bombings or killings by Republican paramilitaries, though such an interpretation by Protestants would be perfectly understandable.

Of particular importance in the Provisionals' conception of the Northern Ireland conflict is the relationship between Britain and the forces of Loyalism. Their view of this relationship has undergone subtle changes as a result of the course of the Troubles and these are described in the next chapter. However, in this context, it is worth underlining what has been a more or less constant theme of Sinn Fein accounts of the relationship. This is the existence of active co-operation between the security forces under British control and Loyalist paramilitaries in attacks on the nationalist community. Sinn Féin has been able to point to a considerable number of court cases in which evidence of links between the security forces and Loyalist paramilitaries has surfaced. Almost all these have involved the Ulster Defence Regiment (UDR). In the most serious, there have been convictions of members of the UDR for murder. From a British perspective, these are cases of a very small number of rotten apples among the locally recruited forces least amenable to Westminster control. To Republicans they represent proof of the hollowness of British claims to be impartial or to maintain the rule of law. Beyond the element of propaganda in the arguments over such cases lies a very real difference of perception over how security policy operates in practice.

An indication of the wider significance of this difference is suggested by the judgment of a nationalist priest who fell foul of the Provisionals during the 1981 hunger strike. According to Father Faul, part of the explanation for continuing support among Catholics for the Provisionals is 'as the last insurance card against the madmen of extreme Protestantism, who have the guns, and even the co-operation of a few men in uniform to enable these attacks to take place'.[26] Similarly, an important factor in accounting for Sinn Fein's electoral success is that people's experience of the enforcement of the law in many nationalist areas tends to accord much more closely with Sinn Fein's description of the security forces as an oppressive presence than it does with British claims to uphold universal standards of justice. This is because their impression of the law is formed by daily encounters with soldiers in a situation in which they are heavily armed for their own protection, on the alert against snipers, and suspicious of the local population. Sinn Fein is not alone in attacking the nature of policing in nationalist areas. This is also one of the principal themes of the main constitutional nationalist party, the Social Democratic and Labour Party (SDLP).

The SDLP rejects the legitimacy of Northern Ireland as a political entity, at least as it is currently constituted. However, its rejection is by no means absolute. While the SDLP regards partition in much the same way as Sinn Fein, in short, as a violation of the right of the Irish people to self-determination, the party accepts the notion that the consent of people in Northern Ireland is necessary, even if only in a somewhat qualified form, to reverse the island's division. The clearest statement of the constitutional nationalist position on these points was put forward in the *New Ireland Forum Report* in May 1984. The Report describes 'the imposed division of Ireland which created an artificial majority in the North' as the origin of the Northern Ireland problem, while it accepts that 'the political arrangements for a new and sovereign Ireland would have to be freely negotiated and agreed to by the people of the North and by the people of the South'.[27] However, the Report was careful not to accord to a majority in Northern Ireland the right to reject the principle of a united Ireland.

Like the British the SDLP grounds the distinction between force and violence in Northern Ireland in the notion of the rule of law. However, there are two significant differences. The SDLP stresses that the reality of policing in the North falls very far short of that standard. Secondly, the party argues that meeting the minimum requirements of the rule of law is impossible outside of an overall political settlement of the Northern Ireland problem. The practical implication of this approach is that the party adopts attitudes towards violence in Northern Ireland somewhat akin to the pacifism of the Peace People. That is to say, the party condemns the violence of Republican paramilitaries, the violence of Loyalist paramilitaries, *and* that of the security forces. A statement by the chairman of the party following a shoot-out between the Provisional IRA and the security forces in February 1984 in which a soldier and two members of the Provisional IRA were killed illustrates the SDLP's outlook. Sean Farren commented: 'The tragic and needless loss of life in Dunloy underlines the futility of seeking a solution to Northern Ireland's political problems through violence.'[28] At the time the comment was directed as much to the British as to the Provisional IRA, though the emphasis within SDLP statements does vary somewhat with the fluctuations of British policy.

The point of departure of Unionists in their attitudes towards the maintenance of law and order is the legitimacy of Northern Ireland as a political entity entirely separated from the Republic of Ireland and underwritten by membership of the United Kingdom. Unionists see defeating the threat to Northern Ireland's existence as a political entity as the primary duty of the British Government and of the security forces. In fact, Unionist perceptions of what constitutes force and what violence largely hinge on the question of Northern Ireland's legitimacy. They regard the defeat of the threat to Northern Ireland's existence as naturally taking precedence over the rule of law and considerations such as due process and the doctrine of minimum force. It could be argued on behalf of Unionists that defeating Republicanism was a necessary pre-condition for the establishment of the rule of law, though such an argument would in practice be somewhat artificial since most Unionists have little expectation that the threat to their position will ever disappear.

Indeed, prior to the current Troubles, when a Unionist Government at Stormont was responsible for security policy, periods of tranquillity did not lead to the repeal of emergency legislation and reliance on the rule of law. This was because Unionists saw order as a function of the 'right' relationship between the two communities rather than as the counterpart to the existence of universal respect for the law. Put brutally, the 'right' relationship was one in which Catholics knew their place and were reminded of it on each anniversary of the Battle of the

Boyne by the parades of the Orange Order. To Unionists British insistence on restraints on the functioning of the security forces is a misguided attempt to appease international opinion and an indication that the British Government lacks the will and probably also the desire to defeat Republican terrorism. As the *Belfast Telegraph* poll in 1985 quoted at the beginning of this chapter showed, there is overwhelming support among Protestants for the view that the security forces are restricted politically from carrying out their duties.

If Unionists regard the British Government as unreliable defenders of Northern Ireland, their view of the SDLP is even more critical and contrasts extremely sharply with the view that has generally prevailed on the mainland of the SDLP as a moderate constitutional party. A particularly fierce clash of views between Unionists and the SDLP over security policy occurred at the beginning of 1983. This followed a number of 'shoot to kill' episodes at the end of 1982 in which unarmed members of Republican paramilitary organisations were killed by the security forces. To Unionists they represented a long overdue toughening of security policy. Harold McCusker, the Ulster Unionist MP for Armagh, responded bitterly to nationalist criticism of the security forces by issuing a statement that 'there are now two mutually exclusive and hostile communities in Northern Ireland and the sooner this fact is faced up to the better'.[29] He pursued the theme further in an article in *Fortnight* in which he launched a savage attack on the Deputy Leader of the SDLP, Seamus Mallon.

> And Seamus Mallon, who had witnessed the murder of two policemen at Markethill . . . has for the past month led a campaign of vilification against the RUC which will surely be used to justify the killing of more police, just as his anti-UDR campaign in the late seventies coincided with the virtual elimination of the part-time UDR in south Armagh.
>
> The inevitable conclusion that the Protestant community and its representatives are forced to is that, despite all the protestations to the contrary, Northern Ireland's Roman Catholics have decided, consciously or unconsciously, that they do not want the IRA defeated.
>
> This may well be the explanation for the oft-repeated assertion by the SDLP and Roman Catholic Church leaders that the IRA cannot be defeated. On top of this, they not only oppose new measures designed to curtail terrorism, but actually campaign to dismantle the existing ineffective legislation. A self-fulfilling prophecy?[30]

Another theme of Unionist criticism of constitutional nationalism is that in the pursuit of the same aim as that of the IRA, a united Ireland, they have wittingly or unwittingly legitimised the activities of the IRA. A variation on this theme is that IRA violence has been instrumental in furthering the aims of the SDLP and the Republic. According to Peter Smith, the author of *Why Unionists Say No*, 'everyone in Ireland knows that had there been no Republican terrorism there would have been no Anglo-Irish deal. The concessions made by Britain were won on the points of IRA rifles.'[31] In a somewhat similar vein the leader of the DUP, Ian Paisley, has frequently linked the Catholic Church and the SDLP to the IRA. Typical is this extract from Paisley's address to the Independent Orange Order in July 1987:

> The Church of Rome could stop the IRA tomorrow if she really wanted. How come when the two factions of INLA were locked in murderous conflict, the priests were able to call a halt to the killing of their own flocks? Yet they cannot call a halt to the IRA killing Protestants. The reality of the matter is this, that both the Church and the SDLP will use the IRA for their own ends. They will ride on the backs of the IRA to gain their own goals.[32]

A common response by the SDLP to Unionist attacks on the party's good faith on the issue of Republican terrorism has been to highlight the inflammatory rhetoric employed by Unionist leaders and to draw attention to the readiness of Unionist politicians to work alongside representatives of Loyalist paramilitaries in joint campaigns of one kind and another. The evidence is usually close to hand. Speeches by Unionists of every stripe abound in examples of inflammatory rhetoric with many aspirants to Paisley's reputation in this field. Characteristic of Paisley's style was the following climax from a speech he made in 1981: 'We have a choice to make. Shall we allow ourselves to be murdered by the IRA, or shall we go out and kill the killers?'[33] It does not require much imagination to understand that many Catholics, regardless of their political views, feel threatened by rhetoric of this sort. However, it is worth underlining that, in practice, Paisley has condemned instances of sectarian murder by Loyalist paramilitaries and has denied that his rhetoric is meant to encourage such activity. Understandably this has done little to assuage Catholic opinion, which has also been disturbed by the readiness of Unionist leaders to associate in public with Loyalist paramilitaries. A notable instance was the appearance of leading Unionist politicians at the paramilitary funeral in 1986 of John Bingham, who was murdered by the Provisional IRA and who had been the commander of the illegal Ulster Volunteer Force (UVF). While Unionists have justified their links with Loyalist paramilitaries, they have strongly condemned the British Government and the SDLP at various times for talking to the Provisional IRA. Their attitude is a reflection of the fact that they see Loyalist violence in quite a different light to Republican violence because of the different relationship it bears to the issue of the legitimacy of Northern Ireland as a political entity. None the less, Unionists have rarely been willing to approve specific actions carried out by Loyalist paramilitaries and have frequently condemned random assassinations of Catholics unconnected with Republican organisations.

Within the Loyalist paramilitaries themselves there is considerable dissatisfaction with the attitude of Unionist politicians and resentment at their repudiation of actions which, the paramilitaries argue, the politicians' rhetoric inspired. A leading figure in the UDA, John McMichael, encapsulated this disillusionment in an article published shortly before the Anglo-Irish Agreement. He wrote:

> I know of two prominent Unionists who believe that no country is worth fighting for and that there is no acceptable cause for violence. Yet those who believe this philosophy recognise the need to placate the masses with militant cliches and the promise of action which will never come. Their aim is to ride out each crisis and maintain order.... If some of the present Unionist leadership had been in power in 1912 Northern Ireland would never have come into existence.[34]

It is not fanciful to see McMichael's use of the term violence in this context as an acknowledgment that among Protestants breaking the law requires special justification. It has been a persistent theme of the publications of the Loyalist paramilitaries. The main line of argument presented in defence of their actions has been that of the necessity to take the law into their own hands due to the failure of the proper authorities to act against rebellion. As an early edition of *UDA* put it, 'it is simple logic that if there is no law being exercised, how can one be guilty of breaking the law?'[35] Distrust of the British Government's intentions plays an important part in the case made by the paramilitaries for Protestant self-reliance in the realm of security. It is a message to which Protestant urban working-class communities have been particularly receptive.[36] However, they have been less receptive to the UDA's advocacy of independence for Northern Ireland as the logical political counterpart of such self-reliance. This has not inhibited the leadership of the UDA from seeking to make a contribution to a political solution of the conflict. In direct contradiction of British assumptions about the connection between violence and extremism, moderation has been a hallmark of the UDA's occasional contributions to debate about a political settlement. These are explored further in Chapter 4.

In the course of this survey of attitudes towards force and violence in Northern Ireland five main perspectives have been identified: mainland British; Republican paramilitary; constitutional nationalist; Unionist;

and Loyalist paramilitary. In addition, the attitudes of the Alliance Party and the Peace People were referred to in the course of the consideration of the mainland British perspective. Of course, it would be relatively easy to subdivide these categories further, but that would obscure a point of major importance. The five main perspectives do not represent simply differences of emphasis or points on a spectrum. In their assumptions about Northern Ireland as a society and in their prescriptions for its ills, they are fundamentally at odds with each other. Indeed, it can reasonably be asserted that their coexistence within a single political entity is a basic cause of the conflict. That begs further questions about how such fundamentally different perspectives towards the maintenance of law and order have arisen in Northern Ireland. In particular, how have the paramilitaries been able to legitimise their activities? What accounts for the failure of political authority in Northern Ireland to establish a monopoly of legitimate violence? While these are by no means easy questions to answer, this approach has the advantage of treating violence itself as a central issue in the conflict and not as a symptom or by-product of division that has arisen for other reasons.

In their book, *Violence in Northern Ireland: Understanding Protestant Perspectives,* John F. Galliher and Jerry L.De Gregory argue that 'it is not so much that economic discrimination, religious, or political differences cause the conflict, but rather that violence is its own cause.'[37] From the interviews they conducted with representatives of a wide range of Protestant opinion they found that a dominant concern was that violence 'exists in, and even engenders an atmosphere which favors its endurance'.[38] Their treatment of violence as an input into the conflict rather than as an outcome is unusual. By contrast, violence is not included among the seven factors John Whyte examines in an article on the maintenance of the boundary between the two communities—that is to say, between Protestants and Catholics.[39] The factors he identifies from the literature as relevant are the Churches themselves, the Orange Order, social ranking, political differences, residential segregation, separate education, and endogamy. As Whyte himself points out, each has limitations as an explanation of the divide, though at least there seems to be no doubt that the dominant cleavage in the society is indeed that between Protestants and Catholics.[40] In particular, it is not that between Unionists and nationalists, as might be supposed from the importance of political differences as a source of conflict in the society. In other words, there appears to be a divergence between how the society divides and what it is divided over, for it is the perception of the constitutional issue, and certainly not any aspect of religious observance, that constitutes the main source of antagonism between the communities.

The answer to this conundrum is to be found in the factor Whyte leaves out, violence. The categories of Protestant and Catholic provide essential vehicles for taking the argument over the constitutional issue to the streets. It is immaterial that they do not correspond perfectly with political sentiment. The overlap is sufficient to ensure their utility as a means of political mobilisation. What is important is that individuals' identification with one or other of the categories is reinforced by consciousness of whose violence they are primarily threatened by and of whose violence they might be held accountable for. In fact, identification may be largely involuntary or even imposed. Hence one encounters the phenomenon in Northern Ireland of Catholic atheists and Protestant Jews, and vice versa. In the last resort, identity in Northern Ireland reflects how one would be treated at the outbreak of violent conflict between the communities. The fact that in Rose's 1968 survey 1,287 out of 1,291 of those interviewed accepted the label of Catholic or Protestant[41] provides an indication of how total the categorisation of the society in sectarian terms is.

Each of the factors that Whyte looks at is more explicable as a factor in the maintenance of the boundary between the communities when examined in relation to violence. This also explains why it is both correct to see religious identity as central to the conflict and wrong to see religiosity *per se* as a cause of conflict. Indeed, strong religious convictions provide an important social constraint on violence. In particular, it is quite common for the relatives of victims of sectarian assassination to appeal for no retaliation. Such appeals are almost invariably couched in religious rather than political terms. The movement of population in Belfast in the early years of the Troubles as a result of intimidation provides a graphic illustration of the role of violence in underpinning the very high level of residential segregation that exists in the province. Residential segregation for its part strongly facilitates the operation of separate education at school level. The parades of the Orange Order represent at the most basic level an assertion of the physical dominance of the Protestant community in the territory of Northern Ireland and although the aggression such parades display towards Catholics takes a ritualised and symbolic form, they do underline the importance that Protestants attach to the deterrence of Catholics as a community. At the same time, assumptions of Protestant superiority, where they exist, derive more from a belief in the majority's capacity and right to dominate the minority through the exercise of coercive power than they do from the recognition that Protestants tend to be generally better off than Catholics.[42] The threat that a united Ireland would pose to their position as a dominant community constitutes the main reason for Protestant hostility towards Irish nationalism. It is why they suspect Catholics as a community of desiring that end. Finally, endogamy reflects both the relative isolation of the two communities and the disincentives to intermarriage in a society where existing at the margin of either community is likely to mean greater exposure to risks of physical violence.

The obvious objection to this line of argument—and perhaps the reason why Whyte left out violence—is that the sectarian divide and all the factors he identifies as relevant to its maintenance have existed through periods of tranquillity in Northern Ireland. What this overlooks is the role that the threat of violence has played in shaping social relations in Northern Ireland even in periods of apparent peace. This is most clearly reflected in the failure of the rule of law to take root in such periods and in the fact that institutions espousing the need for community deterrence have continued to flourish. In short, peace has merely been a truce. The fact that society has not advanced beyond this point can perhaps best be explained by the insecurity of the dominant community's position which has arisen from the conditional character of Britain's commitment to the province and from the questioning of Northern Ireland's legitimacy as a political entity. While the periods of tranquillity in Northern Ireland have by and large coincided with times when Northern Ireland's position in the world has been relatively more secure, neither the degree of security nor the time it has lasted has ever been sufficient seriously to erode the sectarian divide.

That is not to say that the creation of the sectarian divide can simply be explained as the consequence of Northern Ireland's anomalous position within the United Kingdom or, alternatively, as the by-product of partition, since the divide preceded the creation of Northern Ireland as a political entity. Indeed, it can be traced back at least as far as disturbances in Belfast in the 1830s or earlier to the conflict in the countryside between the precursors of the Orange Order, the Peep O'Day Boys, and the Defenders in the 1780s. In particular, there has been a long history of population movement within the North of Ireland as a result of direct intimidation or the more generalised fear of being isolated from the protection of one's co-religionists. According to Darby, 'there is evidence that Catholics and Protestants have regarded their communities in such strategic terms since the 1835 riots, and have carefully monitored the shifting patterns of religious demography.'[43] However, while the genesis of sectarianism in the North of Ireland constitutes an important subject of historical research, the circumstances of its genesis are of limited relevance to explaining the sectarian polarisation of society in Northern Ireland in the late twentieth century. What matters now is what sustains the divide. Conflicting perceptions of the legitimacy of force and violence play a central role in the process, not as a legacy of the past but as reinforced by the conditions prevailing in today's society.

3.

REPUBLICAN PERCEPTIONS

IN Northern Ireland Republicanism usually refers to the strand of Irish nationalist opinion that is distinguished from constitutional nationalism by its advocacy of the use of physical force to end British rule. The leading role of the Provisional IRA in perpetuating the conflict is reflected in the fact that the organisation has been the agency directly responsible for well over a third of all the fatalities during the Troubles,[1] while Sinn Fein, its political wing, has been the only Republican political organisation to achieve a substantial level of electoral support in Northern Ireland since the onset of the Troubles. At particular junctures, other Republican organisations completely outside of the Provisional movement have exerted a significant influence on the course of the conflict. For example, in the early years of the conflict, the Official Republican movement was an important political and paramilitary actor in the province, but in the 1980s, as the Workers Party, it has moved away from policies and practices that fit the definition of Republicanism given above. Other organisations remaining within the ambit of Republicanism, such as the INLA, are best described as splinter groups. They illustrate the wide range of ideological positions encompassed by Republicanism.

Because of their central role, this chapter will be largely devoted to an examination of the perceptions of the Provisionals, principally employing the extensive publications of the movement's political wing. While the fundamental goal of the Provisional IRA has not changed, the movement has responded to the attention that the international community has paid to the Northern Ireland conflict. Thus, while the primary role of armed opposition to British rule has remained, it has become overlaid with other features which increase its legitimacy in the international arena. Paradoxically, the Provisionals were formed in 1970 as a reaction against an earlier effort by the leadership of the Republican movement to adapt itself to the perceived international realities of the 1960s. In the early 1970s the Provisionals were still steeped in much local particularism, which has gradually peeled away in the 1980s. An important consequence has been a change in attitude toward the place of Unionists in their strategy. Thus they no longer believe that Unionists will ever voluntarily accept a united Ireland or that Unionist antipathy towards Westminster can be harnessed to this end. Less realistically they believe they can win in spite of the opposition of the Protestant community. The change in attitude is reflected in the manner in which they have couched the demand for an end to British rule. In particular, the demand for British withdrawal has been extended to include disbandment of the UDR and the disarming of the RUC as the Provisionals have slowly come to recognise that ending British rule by itself might not lead automatically to a united Ireland because of the strength of Loyalist opposition to Irish nationalism.[2]

Likewise the justification of the goal of Irish unity remains essentially unchanged. The denial of the right of the people of Ireland as a whole to self-determination after Sinn Fein won a large majority of the votes in Ireland in the 1918 general election still constitutes an important element in (Provisional) Sinn Fein's justification of the use of force to end British rule in Northern Ireland.[3] But the grounding of the legitimacy of the Provisional IRA's campaign in a traditional Republican interpretation of Irish history is now much less emphasised than it was at the start of the campaign. This was a significant factor in the debate at the Sinn Fein *ard fheis* (convention) in 1986 which led to the abandonment of the historically hallowed principle of abstentionism.

From the outset the Provisionals saw themselves as an anti-colonial liberation movement against British imperialism. As a result of the internationalisation of the conflict, there is a greater awareness of the importance of securing external legitimacy for the campaign and this is reflected in the explicit appeal the Provisionals make to international norms as enshrining Ireland's right to self-determination as a single unit. For example, in 'A Scenario for Peace', a Sinn Fein discussion paper published in May 1987, there are references to a number of resolutions of the United Nations General Assembly relevant to the interpretation of the principle of self-determination, including the *International Covenant on Civil and Political Rights*, the *Declaration on the Granting of Independence to Colonial Countries and Peoples*, and the *Declaration of Principles of International Law Concerning Friendly Relations and Co-operation Among States in Accordance with the Charter of the United Nations*, a document quoted at length in Chapter 1. The discussion paper argues, in particular, that partition is in contravention of Article 6 of the *Declaration on the Granting of Independence to Colonial Countries and Peoples*, which describes any attempt at the partial or total disruption of the national unity and territorial integrity of a country as incompatible with the purposes and principles of the Charter.[4] This article may be less helpful to their case than the Provisionals imagine since their own campaign could be described as an attack on the territorial integrity of a legally fully legitimate member of the United Nations, the United Kingdom of Great Britain and Northern Ireland. But this attempt to root the legitimacy of the 'armed struggle' in international norms is a step beyond simply calling the Northern Ireland conflict 'Britain's Vietnam'[5] and several steps beyond preoccupation with the historical legitimacy of the Second Dáil and the result of the 1918 general election.

At the time of the onset of the Troubles in 1968, physical force Republicanism was at the nadir of its fortunes. In the 1960s there had been a revolution in attitudes in both Sinn Fein and the IRA itself as a result of the complete failure of the Border campaign initiated by the IRA in 1956 and formally called off in 1962. This was long after it was apparent that its impact on the stability of Northern Ireland had been negligible. The movement came under the influence of left-wing intellectuals in the Republic who rejected what they saw as traditional Republicanism's élitist militarism. They argued in the style of the New Left of the 1960s that the Republican movement's failures were due to its political isolation from the concerns of ordinary people and advocated the movement's involvement in community politics as the way to re-establish its relevance to the Irish people. In the South this brought about the movement's participation in campaigns over housing, jobs, land questions, and fishing rights. However, the implications of the new strategy for the North proved rather more problematic. There, sectarian divisions were clearly an obstacle to establishing Republicanism as a mass movement involved in economic and social issues. Furthermore, Sinn Fein was an illegal organisation in Northern Ireland.

Consequently, the new strategy was adapted to fit the circumstances of Northern Ireland with a degree of difficulty. What emerged was a studiously moderate and reformist set of policies with the long-term aim of overcoming the sectarian divisions in the North. Unifying the Protestant and Catholic working-class was seen as the key to more radical possibilities at some time in the future. Republicans were urged to participate in the civil rights movement that was developing in the North. They were strongly represented at the formation of the Northern Ireland Civil Rights Association (NICRA) in February 1967, though only four of those elected to the 14-member steering committee had Republican affiliations. Their reluctance to play a prominent leadership role in the civil rights movement reflected their awareness that such a role might jeopardise the broad appeal of the movement. None the less, the strength of their presence behind the scenes was sufficient to arouse Loyalist fears that the civil rights movement in its various manifestations was simply a Republican conspiracy against Northern Ireland in a new guise. The radicalisation of the civil rights movement in 1968 and 1969, which resulted from the violence the demonstrators encountered, further fuelled Unionist suspicion that civil rights had all along been a deliberate tactic to destabilise the province. In fact, the violent turn of events in the North came as a considerable shock to the Southern leaders of the Republican movement. It was an eventuality for which they were manifestly unprepared. Indeed, the upsurge in sectarianism that accompanied the violence ran directly counter to their aim of unifying the Protestant and Catholic working class as the first stage in a long-term strategy for achieving a united socialist Ireland.

In retrospect, the hopes placed on the development of class politics appear naïve. However, at the time, it seemed much more in tune with the general trend of politics in the North and the rest of the world than did traditional Republicanism. The civil rights movement with its emphasis on reform within the context of Northern Ireland was itself in part a product of social and economic changes that were eroding sectarian divisions. This was particularly apparent in the trade union movement. The decline of traditional industries and the opening of new factories as a result of foreign investment were reducing the influence of sectarian labour practices. Residential segregation was also breaking down, particularly as the result of the movement of Catholics into previously Protestant suburbs of Belfast. Their improved position in occupational terms, as much as O'Neill's reformist attitudes, resulted in a number of Catholics actually joining the Unionist Party. Numbers of others were attracted by the prospect that class politics would displace the sectarian basis of political divisions and supported the Northern Ireland Labour Party, a party committed to maintaining the link with Britain.

However, the violent confrontations arising out of the civil rights campaign in 1968 and 1969 polarised Northern Ireland once again on sectarian lines, though with the difference that there was no longer any prospect that Catholics would ever again passively accept being a subordinate minority within Northern Ireland. Their resolve was strengthened by the prospect of Westminster intervention if the Unionist Government proved incapable of containing the violence. When prolonged rioting followed the Apprentice Boys' parade in Londonderry in August 1969, the leaders of the action in Londonderry appealed for diversionary protests elsewhere in the province to stretch the resources of the local security forces. These tactics and the threat to intervene by the Irish Prime Minister infuriated Loyalists, who launched their own ferocious attacks on Catholic neighbourhoods in Belfast. By the time that British troops arrived on the streets of Belfast, they were welcome not merely as a symbol of Westminster's political involvement but also as a defence against Loyalist mobs. The readiness of Belfast Catholics to welcome the British army in this role was a measure of the failure of the traditional exponents of physical force in the Catholic community, the IRA.

The incapacity of the IRA to defend Catholic areas against Loyalist attacks reflected the organisation's weakness in the city. Its lack of military preparedness was a consequence of the Republican movement's new political direction. In Catholic ghettoes derisive slogans appeared that IRA stood for 'I Ran Away'.[6] Traditional Republicans regarded these events as a vindication of their criticism of the leadership. In Belfast itself the bitter reaction to the humiliation of the IRA was a virtual coup within the organisation in September 1969. The Belfast IRA turned its back on the leadership by agreeing that there would be no communications with Dublin for a period of three months.[7] Matters came to a head at a meeting of the IRA's Army Convention in December 1969, which Belfast boycotted. The split came over the principle of abstentionism. The IRA's refusal to accept the legitimacy of the parliaments at Westminster, Stormont in Northern Ireland, and Leinster House in the Republic, was embodied in an electoral commitment by Republican candidates not to take their seats if elected to any of these bodies. The leadership was committed to abandoning the principle and a majority of the Convention supported this logical extension of the movement's new political strategy, reportedly by 39 votes to 12.[8] The outvoted minority withdrew in a pre-arranged move to form the Provisional Army Council, providing the leadership of what consequently became known as the Provisional IRA or the Provos in popular parlance. By a similar process the body supporting the existing leadership became known as the Official IRA.

The same division appeared in Sinn Fein at the *ard fheis* in Dublin in January 1970. Shortly after a resolution in favour of abandoning the principle of abstentionism was passed, the dissenters staged a walkout and reconvened in a hall hired for the purpose where they elected the Caretaker Executive of (Provisional) Sinn Fein with a mandate to support the Provisional Army Council. The first issue of a periodical supporting the Provisionals, called *An Phoblacht* (The Republic), was published in February. It contained a wide-ranging statement by the Caretaker Executive making it clear that the disagreement with the Dublin leadership went far beyond the question of abstentionism. It accused the Official leadership of having as its ultimate objective 'nothing but a totalitarian dictatorship of the Left' and rejected its 'extreme socialism'.[9] The new movement described its own commitment to socialism as follows:

Our socialism envisages the nationalization of the monetary system, commercial banks and insurance companies, key industries, mines, building land and fishing rights. Ours is a socialism based on the native Irish tradition of *Comhar na g-Comharsan* (neighbours' co-operation) which is founded on the right of worker-ownership and on our Irish and Christian values.[10]

Part of the inspiration of this notion of socialism came from Catholic social philosophy, especially distributism, a theory that was first developed by the English Catholic writers, Hillaire Belloc and G. K. Chesterton.[11]

Another major area of disagreement was the stance the leadership had taken over the issue of the retention of a parliament in Northern Ireland, following the arrival of British troops in the province.

We find absolutely incomprehensible from any Republican stand-point the campaigning in favour of retaining the Stormont parliament in August, September, and October last when it was in danger of being abolished altogether by the British Government. In any future struggle it would surely be preferable to have a direct confrontation with the British Government on Irish soil without the Stormont junta being interposed.[12]

The attitude of the (Official) leadership reflected a continuing attachment to the idea of building working-class unity within the context of Northern Ireland's existing institutions, although that looked increasingly unrealistic as sectarian conflict intensified. The Provisionals also largely contrived to ignore this reality, viewing the conflict simply as a war between Britain and the Irish people. They still remained attached to the arcane theory that the only rightful source of legitimacy in Ireland was the Second Dáil, elected in 1921 as the parliament of the Republic proclaimed in 1916 and, according to Republicans, betrayed by the members who signed the Anglo-Irish Treaty establishing the Irish Free State or who subsequently accepted its authority. In this view the IRA derived its legitimacy from the decision of the surviving Republican members of the Second Dáil to transfer authority for the government of Ireland to the Army Council. Just before the split the Provisionals themselves had sought and received the endorsement of Tom Maguire, by this time the sole surviving Republican member of the Second Dáil.

The March 1970 issue of *An Phoblacht* described the aims of the Provisionals as being:

to end foreign rule in Ireland, to establish a 32-county Democratic Socialist Republic, based on the proclamation of 1916, to restore the Irish language and culture to a position of strength, and to promote a social order based on justice and Christian principles which will give everyone a just share of the nation's wealth.[13]

In practice, the overriding concern of most of the new recruits joining the Provisional IRA in Northern Ireland was to secure the means to defend the areas in which they lived against the attacks of Loyalist mobs. Ideological considerations boiled down to a demand for guns rather than books and pamphlets. At this time, there was considerable sympathy to be tapped in the Republic both among the general public and at an official level for the plight of Northern Catholics. Indeed, in the early stages of the conflict Government Ministers became involved in efforts to supply Northern Catholics with weaponry for their self-defence as well as in encouraging the split within the Republican movement. Although the logic of Provisional ideology pointed towards confrontation with the British army to rid Ireland of foreign rule, the assumption was that the role filled by the Provisional IRA would, in practice, be confined to that of defending Catholic ghettoes.

Legitimacy even in this role depended on the alienation of the Catholic population from the British army and loss of confidence in the army as a defence against Loyalist violence. It took place in stages. Perhaps predictably, an Orange parade, the aggressive meaning of which tended to be lost on outsiders, was instrumental in the process. Against the advice and appeals of local Catholic politicians, Orangemen were permitted by the authorities to march through a Catholic area of Belfast in April 1970. The inevitably violent reaction of the local population to this display of Loyalist triumphalism brought Catholics directly into conflict with the British army. An even more important turning point in the relations between the Catholic community and the army was the Falls Road Curfew in July 1970 during which the army carried out house-to-house arms searches of the area, a poor working-class Catholic neighbourhood, in an exceptionally brutal manner. The operation followed shortly after a change of government in Britain which brought the Conservatives into power. This was at a time when the Conservative relationship to the Unionist Party still had some meaning and it may also have reflected the army's frustration over constant Unionist criticism that it was reacting passively to violations of the law in Catholic areas. Provisional propaganda quickly exploited the new mood of Catholic hostility towards the troops.[14]

The transformation of the image of the troops meant that the Provisional IRA could now be presented as defenders of the community against the British forces of occupation, as they were dubbed, a role much more consonant with the basic ideology of the movement. The change had far-reaching implications for Provisional IRA operations, for, in terms of this role, offensive action against the British presence could be justified in a wide area, on the grounds that forcing the British to disperse their military resources took pressure off the ghettoes.[15] At the beginning of 1971 the Army Council approved offensive operations against the British army and in February 1971, a British soldier was killed in a gun battle with a unit of the Provisional IRA in Belfast, the first army victim of the Troubles. By the end of the year forty-three members of the British army and five members of the UDR had died. Bombings of commercial targets also occurred with increasing frequency, justified as increasing the cost to Britain of its occupation of the North since the British Government footed the bill for compensation.[16] The bombs also spread terror, as civilian deaths were a common consequence of inadequate or bungled warnings.

In its publications, Sinn Fein continued to deride the notion that political accommodation within Northern Ireland offered any prospect of a solution to the conflict. *Republican News* declared that Stormont had 'no autonomy—not a shred of self-determination'.[17] It saw these advantages in direct rule from Westminster:

> British forces of occupation could then be clearly seen as forces of invasion on Irish soil. The lines of demarcation could be fairly and squarely drawn between those whose wish would be to sell their birthright and nationality and those who would strive to maintain it and defend it.[18]

However, the basis of the Provisionals' opposition to Stormont became obscured when they became part of a much wider Catholic movement demanding that Stormont be abolished, after the Unionist Government of Brian Faulkner introduced internment in August 1971. Far from reducing the violence, internment united 'a large section of the Catholic population behind the IRA Provisionals and recruitment to the IRA became easier than ever before'.[19] Bloody Sunday, when paratroopers shot dead thirteen demonstrators in Londonderry, at the end of January 1972, alienated Catholic opinion further. It also forced a change in the British Government's policy towards Northern Ireland.

When the British Government suspended the Stormont parliament and imposed direct rule in March 1972, the SDLP issued a statement appealing to 'those engaged in the campaign of violence to cease immediately'[20] so as to allow internment to be ended and a positive response to be made to proposals for the constitutional future of the province. Both the Provisional IRA and the Official IRA came under considerable pressure within the Catholic community to suspend their campaign in order to give British mediation a chance. It was pressure the Official IRA ultimately acceded to, when it announced an indefinite ceasefire at the end of May. But while the fall of Stormont was welcome to the Provisionals as a first step, they wanted negotiations to start about a British withdrawal before any ceasefire. Their first political initiative had been the announcement in August 1971 of proposals for the establishment of four provincial parliaments within a united Ireland.[21] One of these would be a parliament for the province of Ulster, consisting of nine counties, as it had done prior to partition. The proposal was designed to allay Protestant fears of being swamped within a united Ireland, as they would still constitute a small majority within a nine-county province of Ulster. The holding of free elections to a nine-county parliament of Ulster was one of the points in a peace plan issued by the Provisionals on the eve of a meeting between the British and Irish Prime Ministers in September.[22]

In June 1972, in what *Republican News* had dubbed 'the year of victory',[23] the proposals for a federal Ireland, including a *Dáil Uladh* (Ulster Assembly) were reissued and incorporated in Sinn Fein's existing social and economic programme for a new Ireland, *Éire Nua*.[24] The context was the announcement of a truce by the Provisional IRA, starting on 27 June. The initiative had begun with an offer by the Provisionals to enter into negotiations with the British Government earlier in the month at a press conference in Londonderry. It was a measure of their political influence at that time that the British Government agreed to the demands made by the Provisionals as preconditions for a truce and negotiations between the two sides. The most important of the British concessions was the introduction of special category status for prisoners convicted of politically motivated offences, although a hunger strike by a leading Belfast Republican was probably the decisive factor in exacting this particular concession. Another demand acceded to by the Government was the release from internment of Gerry Adams so that he could attend the talks. These were held in London on 7 July. They made little headway. The Provisionals presented their demand for a declaration of intent from the British Government to withdraw from Northern Ireland, while, according to Provisional sources, the British side responded that withdrawal would lead to a bloodbath.[25] Two days later the truce broke down as a result of a clash between the army and the Provisional IRA at a sectarian interface in Belfast, a clash precipitated by the Loyalist UDA. In 1987 Martin McGuinness, who had been a member of the Provisional delegation to London, recalled the reasoning behind the Provisional initiative as follows:

> In a war situation the Republican movement was attempting to show the world that it was reasonable and prepared to talk. Furthermore, if the two sides were involved in a ceasefire the Brits

were actually recognising the legitimacy of the IRA and the Republican forces, and this in itself was a major international victory.[26]

The breakdown of the truce did not spell an end to the hopes that leading figures within the Provisional movement, particularly Daithi O'Connaill and Ruairi O'Bradaigh, placed in the federal proposals. The hostility of Loyalists to the imposition of direct rule fuelled their hopes that Britain might yet be driven out of Northern Ireland by an alliance of extremes. O'Connaill even welcomed the Ulster Workers Council strike that brought down the power-sharing Executive in May 1974 as being in the 'Wolfe Tone tradition'.[27] It was an outlook that many Provisionals in the North found incomprehensible. In fact, the moment at which the prospect for an alliance of extremes appeared most credible was before the strike when the imperative of undermining the Sunningdale Agreement created a tactical basis for co-operation. In January 1974 Desmond Boal, a lawyer and politician with close links with the Loyalist paramilitaries, put forward proposals for a federal Ireland under which the old Stormont system would be restored in Ulster. *An Phoblacht* reported the Boal plan as the breakthrough that the Provisionals had always been seeking under the headline: 'Loyalists and Republicans on way to peace'.[28] However, Loyalist interest in the Boal plan evaporated after the success of the UWC strike, though the indirect contacts that had been established between the Provisionals and the Loyalist paramilitaries were maintained after the strike.[29]

The next avenue pursued by the Provisionals was talks with Protestant clergymen from Northern Ireland. These took place in December 1974 against the background of bombs in Birmingham the previous month which had killed 21 people, the culmination of the Provisionals' decision at the beginning of 1973 to extend the campaign of violence to the UK mainland to put added pressure on Britain to withdraw. Once again the Provisionals put forward a package linking a ceasefire with a British declaration of intent to withdraw and reiterating the constitutional proposals in *Éire Nua*. To underline the significance of the initiative, the Army Council announced a unilateral ceasefire over the Christmas and New Year period. The Secretary of State for Northern Ireland, Merlyn Rees, responded to the ceasefire by authorising officials to establish contact with the Provisionals, releasing a number of detainees, and reducing the number of army patrols. The prospect of an end to internment and the withdrawal of the army to barracks that Rees presented, persuaded the Provisionals to announce an indefinite suspension of hostilities against Crown forces in February 1975. They were still hopeful that these moves were a prelude to withdrawal. However, the ceasefire did not lead to any reduction in the level of political violence in Northern Ireland. Suspicion that there had been a deal on withdrawal between the Provisionals and the British fuelled a Loyalist campaign of random sectarian assassinations during 1975 and 1976, reflected in a substantial increase in the level of civilian fatalities. The terror created in Catholic areas by the Loyalist campaign damaged the Provisionals' claim to be effective defenders of the Catholic community and drew units of the Provisionals into action of a similarly crude sectarian character. The Provisionals' reputation was further damaged by internecine feuding with other Republican para-militaries.

In retrospect, these years in the mid 1970s came to be seen by the Provisionals as ones in which they came close to defeat. As Bishop and Mallie have put it:

> The current leadership of the movement regard this period with superstitious dread, an age of decadence in which republicanism lost its way and was led to the edge of the precipice by the cunning of the British.[30]

The failure of the ceasefire to produce any political dividends for the Provisionals prompted a revolt against the Southern leadership of the movement, reflected in the establishment of a Northern Command of the Provisional IRA towards the end of 1976. The existence of new political thinking within the movement was signalled by the address of a former Vice President of Sinn Fein, Jimmy Drumm, at the annual Wolfe Tone commemoration ceremony at Bodenstown in June 1977. It warned of the dangers of the political isolation of the armed struggle. Perhaps even more significantly, it explicitly rejected what had been a central tenet of Provisional thinking in previous years, the view that a British withdrawal from Northern Ireland was imminent. This expectation had been sustained by a number of factors including opinion polls showing that a majority of people in the UK mainland favoured withdrawal, disinvestment from the province by some British firms, and the resistance of Loyalists to British authority that had so impressed O'Connaill. It was the basis of predictions of victory and had led to the gearing of the campaign of violence to a short-term perspective. The change in thinking went further than speeches. It provided the justification for a radical reorganisation of the Provisional IRA. An internal Provisional IRA Staff Report explained the change as follows: 'We must gear ourselves to Long-Term Armed Struggle based on putting unknown men and new recruits into a cell structure.'[31]

Northerners from Belfast increasingly came to dominate the movement and this was reflected in three trends within the movement: of secularisation, radicalisation, and politicisation. In particular, emphasis on the secular nature of the movement became a consistent feature of interviews given by Sinn Fein representatives from the late 1970s. The old dictum that the Provos went to Mass every week where the Stickies (a popular term for members of the Official IRA) went only once a year lost the credence it had once enjoyed. At the 1983 Sinn Fein *ard fheis*, the references in the party's constitution to 'Christian principles' were replaced by the words, 'Irish Republican Socialist principles in accordance with the Easter Proclamation of 1916 and the democratic programme of the First Dáil in 1919'.[32] By this time, there was no question of treating Catholic social theory as an important influence on the movement's ideology. However, while the influence of religion on the movement has diminished, it has by no means disappeared. For example, the use of religious symbolism played an important role in the mobilisation of Catholic opinion behind the hunger strike by Republican prisoners during 1981. Clashes between the Provisional leadership with the Catholic Church hierarchy over the issue of violence have centred on the question of how far the Church's authority should extend into the realm of politics and on the consistency of the Church's pronouncements. The Church's authority within its own realm has not been challenged. While not emphasised, religious piety is still a common personal characteristic of leading figures within the movement.

Radicalisation was reflected in a much greater emphasis being given to the socialist aims of the movement and even in an openness to the influence of Marxist ideas. In particular, by the late 1970s the anti-Communism that had been a feature of the Provisionals' hostility towards the Officials at the time of the split had largely faded and Castro was no longer portrayed as a totalitarian dictator in the pages of *Republican News*.[33] However, the shift to the left had limits. Suggestions made by Government Ministers in Northern Ireland of a conversion of the movement to Marxism elicited strong denials from Sinn Fein.[34] In policy terms, one of the most important consequences of the process of radicalisation was the ditching of the federal proposals in *Éire Nua*. The Northern radicals regarded the proposals as a sop to the Loyalists and as an obstacle to the pursuit of socialist policies by the central government. They met fierce resistance from the old Southern leadership and their task was made more difficult by the fact that the policy had been entrenched in the constitution. The 1981 *ard fheis* voted by a simple majority to throw out the federal proposals. In 1982 the rejection of federalism received the two-thirds majority required to secure its removal from the constitution.

Part of the impetus behind the process of radicalisation was the influx into Sinn Fein of former internees and those who had served prison sentences of one kind or another. They were particularly keen to see an enlargement of Sinn Fein's role from merely being a support group for the Provisional IRA. The politicisation and expansion of Sinn Fein created opportunities for other interests to influence the direction of policy. One of these was feminism. Following a decision of the 1979 *ard fheis*, a Commission of Women's Affairs was established at a meeting in Belfast in November 1979. The Commission presented a policy document, 'Women in a New Ireland', to the 1980 *ard fheis*. It called for equal opportunities for women in work and in education and advocated support for legalisation of divorce and availability of contraception. Most of the impetus for the development of Sinn Fein's policy on the issue of women's rights came from a grass roots movement among women in Belfast. It has enjoyed qualified support from the Northern leadership of the movement. As Claire Hackett's study of feminism in Sinn Fein puts it, 'while the conservative forces in Sinn Fein are in conflict with feminism, the radical forces are not always in collaboration with it'.[35] In particular, a resolution in favour of a woman's right to choose to have an abortion was narrowly passed at the 1985 *ard fheis* against the advice of the party leadership.[36] At the 1986 *ard fheis*, the policy was reversed to one of opposing abortion as a means of birth control but accepting it in cases where the woman's life was in danger.[37]

Politicisation has been the most important of the trends within Sinn Fein since the mid-1970s. While former prisoners provided much of the drive behind it, fundamentally it stemmed from the recognition that the movement's commitment to a long-term protracted struggle meant that a single-minded concentration on the 'military' campaign was no longer appropriate. In particular, there was a subtle change in the importance attached to popular support for the actions of the Provisional IRA. In the early years of the Troubles it was seen as important because alienation of the local population made it difficult to sustain the campaign of violence and increased the vulnerability of volunteers to the security forces. However, the reorganisation from a locally based pyramid structure to a cell system, in part itself a response to a loss of support, made the operational reasons for ensuring that there was local tolerance of the actions of the Provisional IRA less pressing. It increasingly came to be recognised that support was needed in a wider political context to give meaning to the campaign of violence, so that it could be sustained on a long-term basis. The change in perspective was reflected in assertions that 'armed struggle' on its own could not bring victory to the Republican cause and in criticism of the 'militaristic' tendency of the movement's early years.[38] At the same time, the movement remained wedded to the notion that the goal of a united Ireland could not be achieved without the use of force, a crucial point distinguishing the politicisation of the Provisionals in the 1970s and 1980s from the changes that took place in the Republican movement in the 1960s.[39]

The most significant consequence of the politicisation of the Pro-visionals was Sinn Fein's participation in elections. With the minor exception of local councils in the Republic, it had been the policy of Sinn Fein to boycott elections. By the late 1970s there were elements in the party demanding a change in policy and there was a debate inside Sinn Fein over whether the party should contest the direct elections to the European Parliament in 1979. However, those advocating partici-pation were in a minority. The later shift in opinion was the result of the situation in the prisons and its consequences. The decision of the British Government to end special category status for those convicted of poli-tically motivated offences after 1 March 1976 had led to protests in the prisons. The protests had gradually escalated to the point of a hunger strike by Republican prisoners. It had ended in confusion in December 1980. At the beginning of March 1981 a second hunger strike began, led by the Officer Commanding the Provisional prisoners, Bobby Sands. The impetus for the confrontation had come from the prisoners them-selves, spurred on by the physical manner in which the prison authori-ties attempted to break their resistance. The hunger strike had been embarked upon against the wishes of the Provisional leadership outside the prison, which feared that mobilising support for the prison protest would require winding down the campaign of violence. The leadership warned the prisoners that there could be no holding back on operations by the Provisional IRA during a second hunger strike.[40]

In a column in the *Irish Times* in January 1981, David McKittrick had concluded that 'prospects look bleak for the Provisionals' and reported that 'some of the top security people now see the Provos as a defeated organisation and view the next couple of years as essentially a mopping-up operation'.[41] In the event, the second hunger strike proved to be a watershed in the history of Northern Ireland. The transformation brought about by Sands's death was vividly reflected in David McKittrick's column in the *Irish Times*. In May 1981 he argued that 'this has been one of the best times the Provisional IRA has ever had', explaining why as follows:

> At this moment the Northern Ireland problem is seen worldwide as the Provisionals have always wanted it to be: the hammer and the anvil, the Brits versus the Provos, nothing in between and nobody else relevant.[42]

This impression had been reinforced by a fortuitous by-election. Shortly after Sands began his hunger strike, the Westminster MP for Fermanagh and South Tyrone died, creating a vacancy in a constituency with a narrow Catholic majority. Sands stood as a political prisoner and won the by-election. His election agent, Owen Carron, won the by-election that followed Sands's own death. Two prisoners were also elected in the Republic's general election in June 1981. In the local council elections in Northern Ireland in May, fringe Republican groups had done well in the absence of Sinn Fein's participation. For example, in Belfast, two candidates standing for the Irish Republican Socialist Party, the political wing of the Irish National Liberation Army (INLA) were elected. The enormous impact of the hunger strike on Catholic opinion in Northern Ireland flooded the Provisionals with recruits which the movement had difficulty absorbing. Participation in elections provided an obvious means of utilising the energies of new supporters and was endorsed by a majority of delegates at the Sinn Fein *ard fheis* that convened at the end of October 1981 in the aftermath of the hunger strike. One of the leading Northern radicals, Danny Morrison, used a striking metaphor to answer critics who feared that involvement in elections was a step towards the abandonment of the Provisional IRA's 'military' campaign. He declared in words that would be frequently quoted:

> Who here really believes that we can win the war through the ballot box? But will anyone here object if, with a ballot paper in this hand, and an Armalite in this hand, we take power in Ireland?[43]

A general election in the Republic in February 1982 provided the first test of the new strategy. However, Sinn Fein's candidates fared poorly in comparison with the vote that H-block candidates had received in June 1981. But in the Northern Ireland Assembly elections in October 1982, Sinn Fein secured 10.1 per cent of first preference votes and five of its 12 candidates were elected.

The result came as a profound shock to mainland British opinion, which had been nurtured on the stereotype of the Provisionals as terrorists without any popular support for their actions. This view had been shaken by the vote for Sands, but it had been possible to separate endorsement of the prisoners' demands from support for the methods of the Provisional IRA. The vote for Sinn Fein in October 1982 appeared to indicate that there was a substantial level of support in Northern Ireland for the Provisional IRA's campaign itself. Sinn Fein's quarterly, *Iris,* aptly described the impact of the party's electoral success as 'the ballot bomb'.[44] Sinn Fein encouraged its supporters in the view that voting constituted the continuation of the campaign of violence by other means, declaring before the election that 'while not everyone can plant a bomb, everyone can plant a vote'.[45] Further vindication of the electoral strategy came in the United Kingdom general election of June 1983. Gerry Adams was elected as the MP for West Belfast and across the province the party won over 100,000 votes and 13.4 per cent of the total votes cast. The gap between Sinn Fein and the SDLP had narrowed to less than 5 per cent of the vote.

The possibility that at some time in the future Sinn Fein might overtake the SDLP electorally and destroy the claim of constitutional nationalism to represent the aspirations of the minority alarmed both the British and Irish Governments[46] and gave a powerful impetus to the Anglo-Irish process. The second direct election to the European Parliament in June 1984 provided the next major electoral test for Sinn Fein. In the event, the Sinn Fein candidate, Danny Morrison, polled 10,000 fewer votes than the party's total in the general election the previous year, but almost the same share of the vote, 13.3 per cent. However, the SDLP candidate and one of the province's three MEPs John Hume, polled over 22 per cent of first preference votes. The result was seen as a major setback for Sinn Fein and prompted some criticism, within the Provisional movement, of the electoral strategy. This largely centred on the share of the movement's financial resources being devoted to elections. The strain on resources was evident from the risks being taken to raise funds. In particular, the Provisional IRA had resorted to kidnapping wealthy businessmen in the Republic for ransom. In December 1983 this had led to a shoot-out between a Provisional IRA unit and the Republic's security forces. A garda cadet and a soldier had been killed, severely damaging the credibility of the Provisionals' claim to pose no threat to the political stability of the Republic. None the less, on the same day as Hume convincingly defeated Morrison in the North, Sinn Fein won 4.9 per cent of the vote in the European elections in the South, considerably above its anticipated level of support.

After the European elections, Sinn Fein representatives spoke very cautiously about the party's electoral prospects. For example, Adams forecast that the party would win between 30 and 35 seats in the elections in May 1985 to Northern Ireland's 26 local councils,[47] implying a considerable drop in the party's vote. The profile of military operations went up. The most spectacular of these was an attempt to assassinate the British Prime Minister during the Conservative Party Conference at Brighton in October 1984 through a bomb placed in the Grand Hotel. The bomb killed five people, including a Conservative MP. In Northern Ireland, a mortar bomb attack on a barracks in Newry in February 1985 killed nine police officers. The change in emphasis did not end controversy over the electoral strategy, and argument over the amount of money being spent on the local council elections resulted in the expulsion of a senior figure from the movement. In the elections, Sinn Fein won 11.8 per cent of first preference votes and fifty-nine seats. Although a slight fall in the party's performance in comparison with both 1983 and 1984, the result caused consternation to the Government as its implications became apparent. The presence of members of the political wing of the Provisional IRA in the council chambers incensed Unionists who responded by disrupting the business of councils by way of protest. In a few councils Sinn Fein was in a strong enough position to secure the election of officers. For example, it was the largest party on Omagh District Council and a Sinn Fein Councillor was elected Chairman of the Council. A Sinn Fein Councillor was also elected the Chairman of Fermanagh District Council. The depth of the sectarian divide in Northern Ireland meant that, in practice, there was co-operation between the SDLP and Sinn Fein on the councils, further estranging Unionists from the party of constitutional nationalism.

On 15 November 1985, the British and Irish Prime Ministers signed the Anglo-Irish Agreement under which the right of the Irish Government to be consulted on policies in Northern Ireland was institutionalised. It immediately became the main focus of Unionist anger, subsuming the issue of Sinn Fein's presence on local councils. In its reaction to the Agreement, Sinn Fein was torn between wanting to claim credit for any substantive benefits for nationalists that might emerge from the deal and denouncing the pact as primarily concerned with security co-operation and suppressing Republicanism. While the Provisional IRA stepped up the tempo of its operations, the movement strongly disavowed suggestions that this represented an attempt to bring down the Agreement. The Provisionals' equivocation over the Agreement was attributable to their recognition of its likely impact on Catholic opinion in Northern Ireland rather than to any doubts as to the threat it posed to their movement. Adams described the objectives of the Agreement as follows.

> It is an attempt to isolate and draw popular support away from the republican struggle while putting a diplomatic veneer on British rule, injecting a credibility into establishment 'nationalism' so that British rule and the interests it represents can be stabilised in the long term, and insulating the British from international criticism of their involvement in Irish affairs.[48]

The threat to the Provisionals' position was evident in four different contexts. The first of these was in Northern Ireland itself. By-elections in January 1986, which followed Unionist resignations from Westminster as part of their protest against the Anglo-Irish Agreement, provided an early test of Catholic opinion on the Agreement in four constituencies contested by both the SDLP and Sinn Fein. The result was a substantial shift of opinion to the SDLP, only partly attributable to tactical voting. The Agreement also had a substantial impact on political opinion in Britain itself. In particular, support for the Agreement provided the basis of a new consensus among the British parties on the issue of Northern Ireland. Left-wingers favouring withdrawal were effectively marginalised. This represented a major setback for the Provisionals who had placed considerable hopes on the close links they had forged with elements on the Left of the Labour Party since the leader of the Greater London Council, Ken Livingstone, had supported the prisoners' demands during the 1981 hunger strike. The development of political contacts in Britain had initially been facilitated by Sinn Fein's move to the left in the late 1970s. The taboo in the Labour Party against association with the Provisionals had broken down further as a result of Sinn Fein's electoral successes in 1982 and 1983. The Agreement did not put an end to Sinn Fein's contacts with elements in the Labour Party, but it greatly reduced the value of such contacts, as most of the Labour Party rallied around the party leadership's support for the Agreement. Indeed, defeating the Loyalist challenge to the Agreement became a priority with sections of the party previously sympathetic to withdrawal. The difficulty Republicans experienced in explaining their opposition to the Agreement to British audiences comes out clearly in the journal of the Troops Out Movement.[49] The third context in which the Provisionals' influence was reduced as a result of the Agreement was the Republic, where public support for the Agreement was helping to establish new parameters to the debate on the North, effectively isolating the Provisionals. Finally, in a wider international context, the Agreement was interpreted as a step towards a united Ireland and helped to underscore the legitimacy of constitutional nationalism, making the Provisionals' campaign appear at best a destructive irrelevance.

The difficulties the Provisionals faced as a result of the Anglo-Irish Agreement were reflected in the crisis in the movement over abstentionism. Many of the Northern radicals had long believed that a key to increasing the impact of the Provisional IRA's campaign in the North was greater political support for Sinn Fein in the South. They regarded abstentionism, particularly in relation to the Republic's parliament at Leinster House, as an obstacle to the party's development in the South. The issue was a very sensitive one as abstentionism had been the basis of the split that had led to the creation of the Provisionals in 1969 and 1970. At Sinn Fein's *ard fheis* at the beginning of November 1985, a motion to change policy on abstentionism from the status of a principle to that of a tactic had been narrowly defeated.[50] However, after the Anglo-Irish Agreement, the cautious approach which the leadership had taken towards changing the policy was abandoned. Forcing through a change in time for the Republic's next general election was treated as a matter of urgency. For the first time in sixteen years a General Army Convention of the Provisional IRA was held to consider the question of abstentionism among other matters. In October 1986, the outcome of the meeting was announced, including the amendment of the

Provisional IRA's constitution to permit support for candidates ready to take their seats in Leinster House, if elected.[51]

The General Army Convention set the scene for the debate at Sinn Fein's *ard fheis* which met on 31 October and 1 and 2 November. It was clear in advance of the meeting that the conference was likely to pass the proposal that absentionism in relation to Leinster House be dropped and that some of the more traditional Republicans from the South would leave Sinn Fein as a result. What the debate revealed was how deep the sense of crisis within the movement was. A common theme of speeches in favour of change was that it was an urgent necessity for the movement to break out of its political isolation in the South.[52] After the motion altering the constitution to permit participation in Leinster House was passed by the necessary two-thirds majority, some of those who opposed the change walked out, including Ruairi O'Bradaigh and Daithi O'Connaill. As in 1970, the dissidents reconvened at a hotel booked for the purpose where they launched a new party, Republican Sinn Fein. The difference from 1970 was that Republican Sinn Fein had no armed wing, leaving the new body little option but to support the Provisional IRA from the sidelines.

Adams had cautiously played down the prospects of an early electoral breakthrough if Sinn Fein dropped absentionism and his caution proved amply justified. In the Republic's general election in February 1987, Sinn Fein fielded twenty-nine candidates, but won only 1.9 per cent of the first preference votes, a disastrous performance in the first test of the new policy. Ironically, in the same election, the Workers Party, descended from the Republican movement of the 1960s, won four seats in the Dáil. However, in the United Kingdom general election in June 1987, Sinn Fein could derive some comfort from the re-election of Adams in West Belfast with an increased share of the vote. Prior to the election there had been clashes in Belfast between the police and crowds attending the funerals of Provisional IRA volunteers and this may have contributed to the success of Adams. Over the province as a whole, Sinn Fein's vote fell to 11.4 per cent of the votes cast, a relatively modest decline in its fortunes compared to its performance in local council elections in May 1985.

The explanation for the continuing electoral appeal of Sinn Fein in Northern Ireland, despite the Provisionals' difficulties in a wider context, is to be found in the sectarian divide and in continuing uncertainty over Northern Ireland's political future. In particular, the Anglo-Irish Agreement has not reduced the threat of inter-community violence within Northern Ireland. Indeed, on the contrary, the Agreement has worsened relations between the two communities. The rise in sectarian tensions has been reflected in an increased level of fatalities as the result of political violence since the Agreement and the widespread incidence of intimidation, prompting movement of population from some mixed residential areas. The Provisionals have capitalised on Loyalist reaction to the Agreement by presenting themselves as the Catholic community's most reliable defence against the possibility of Loyalist violence.[53] At times, the Provisionals even appear to have come under pressure in the Catholic community to take offensive action following sectarian assassinations by Loyalist paramilitaries.[54]

One of the consequences of the Northern takeover of the Provisional movement has been a ready acceptance by the leadership of the sectarian underpinning of the conflict. It is reflected, on the one hand, in their confidence that the Provisional IRA cannot be defeated.[55] On the other, it constitutes one of the reasons why they are resigned to a long-term campaign. They fit Protestant hostility towards a united Ireland into their anti-colonial model of the conflict by treating it as a product of British manipulation and of the strength of Britain's commitment to the Union. (By contrast, the unreliability of Britain's commitment to the Union constitutes a fundamental tenet of Loyalism.) Sectarianism, itself underpinned by the violence, not only does much to underwrite the position of the Provisionals in their role as defenders of the Catholic community, but also helps to legitimise the Provisionals' larger ambitions. Given that the Provisionals are representative politically only of a minority of the Catholic minority in Northern Ireland, it might seem that the balance of forces would appear so decisively tilted against them as to make it impossible for hopes of ultimate victory to be sustained.

However, that is not how the Provisionals see the position. On the contrary, they base their expectations of the inevitability of a united Ireland on the support that the goal of Irish unity enjoys not just in Northern Ireland but in the Republic. In this broadly sectarian context the position of Unionists looks much more precarious. In *The Politics of Irish Freedom*, Gerry Adams reproduces an electoral map of Ireland, based on the 1985 local elections in Northern Ireland, which shows Unionists still able to command majority support only in a very small area of the whole island.[56] While the Provisionals cast public doubt on the commitment of the SDLP and the Republic to the achievement of a united Ireland, in their political calculations they count on their support for the nationalist cause. Where the Provisionals most clearly differ from constitutional nationalists is in their insistence that a united Ireland cannot be achieved without the use of physical force and in their belief in the impossibility of an accommodation with Protestants as a community outside the context of a united Ireland. The strength of the Provisionals' position is that in the context of Northern Ireland's Troubles, these propositions accord both with the widespread expectation that Loyalists will resist Irish unity by force and with the common-sense assumption that Protestant distrust of the nationalist aspirations of Catholics will prevent an accommodation between the communities within Northern Ireland.

A sectarian head count is not the only basis for their confidence in ultimate victory. The Provisionals also look outside Ireland for external legitimisation of their ambitions. They derive a considerable measure of encouragement from the fact that much of world opinion tends to see Northern Ireland as an anachronism. In recent years they have sought to identify similarities between their struggle and that of the African National Congress (ANC) in South Africa and the Palestine Liberation Organisation (PLO) in relation to Israel. In West Belfast the Provisionals' solidarity with the PLO and ANC is proclaimed on wall murals. The analogies serve to emphasise an ethnic dimension to the division between the communities in Northern Ireland by casting Protestants in the role of settlers in relation to a native population. They also carry the implication that the aspiration to a united Ireland is similarly grounded in universal norms with the potential to attract international support that might one day prove decisive, and imply that the alternative to violent resistance is humiliating subordination. However, neither the PLO nor the ANC encourage such identification. By contrast, the Provisionals' links with the Basque organisation, ETA, and its political wing, Herri Batasuna, are mutually reinforcing and have been strengthened by the two movements' common interest in cultural aspects of nationalism such as language.

The Provisionals' emphasis on the wider international context of the struggle for a united Ireland has been most apparent since the hunger strike in 1981 when the Provisional leadership began to realise the potential significance of external perceptions of the conflict and how crucial to the impact of the Provisional IRA's campaign had been the discrediting of the stereotype of the organisation abroad as terrorists without support. While it has not always secured universal support from Republicans, external legitimisation has provided the means for the organisation to free itself from some of the doctrines of traditional Irish Republicanism, such as insistence on the legitimacy of the Second Dáil, that have been an obstacle to the movement's political development. It has also facilitated the Provisionals in sustaining an image of themselves as engaged in a great and historic enterprise and has tended to obscure the actual day-to-day character of the Provisional IRA's campaign. This has changed rather less than have Provisional perceptions of the political course of the conflict. Its essential characteristic has been a very elastic notion of a legitimate target, wide enough to be used to justify attacks on off-duty and even retired members of the security forces, on Unionist politicians as well as British Ministers, on prison officers, on judges, and even on commercial contractors supplying services of one kind or another to the security forces, all in the name of a 'war' against British imperialism. It is a measure of the uncertainty that surrounds Northern Ireland's existence as a political entity, even after the Anglo-Irish Agreement, that it remains quite impossible to predict the duration or even the outcome of the Provisionals' campaign.

4.

LOYALIST PERCEPTIONS

THE division among nationalists between constitutional nationalism and Republicanism is mirrored by a division among Unionists between Ulster Loyalists and Ulster British.[1] However, the distinction is less clear cut and the term Ulster British is rarely used in Northern Ireland. Paradoxically, given its overtones of unqualified obligation, the term, Loyalist, is generally used to apply to those Unionists whose primary loyalty is to the Protestant community in Northern Ireland and who are only conditionally loyal to the British connection.[2] Politically, it constitutes the dominant tradition among Unionists, not merely numerically, but also organisationally, as it encompasses the Orange Order, the Democratic Unionist Party (DUP), and sections of the Ulster Unionist Party (UUP). Among Loyalists, paramilitary organisations represent only a minority tendency.[3] However, they provide the closest equivalent to the Provisional movement analysed in the last chapter and, consequently, this chapter will focus on the specific perceptions of the paramilitaries rather than attempting to provide a general overview of Loyalist attitudes towards the conflict. To avoid unnecessary complication and in line with the method adopted in the previous chapter, the analysis will concentrate on the principal Loyalist paramilitary organisation, the Ulster Defence Association (UDA).

Unlike the Provisional IRA, the UDA is a legal organisation. It has escaped the frequent calls that have been made for its proscription through the expedient of not claiming responsibility for the violent activities undertaken by its members. When made, claims of responsibility have been issued using a variety of *noms de guerre*, principally that of the Ulster Freedom Fighters (UFF). The other main Loyalist paramilitary is the Ulster Volunteer Force (UVF),[4] which is illegal and was first proscribed in 1966 after a number of sectarian murders in that year. None the less, it has also generally preferred to use *noms de guerre* when claiming responsibility for acts of violence, most notably, that of the Protestant Action Force (PAF). A variety of other paramilitaries have appeared on the scene. The DUP leader, Ian Paisley, has frequently been associated with such ventures, including the Third Force and Ulster Resistance. The staging of demonstrations and the mounting of the occasional patrol have formed the limit of their activities. Defensive patrolling of a more sustained and serious character was the main activity undertaken by a number of rural paramilitary organisations, such as Down Orange Welfare and the Orange Volunteers, which were active during the early 1970s. They disappeared with the Ulsterisation of the security forces from 1976.[5]

The UDA, unlike the Provisionals, has been unable to secure mass electoral backing. Because of their alignment with Britain, Unionists look to the security forces in the first instance for support for their position and at a political level the attitude of Protestants toward 'their' paramilitaries remains somewhat equivocal, notwithstanding Unionist doubts about the strength of Britain's commitment to their cause and hence the reliance that can be placed on British security policies. The effect of international opinion on Loyalists generally has been to make them acutely aware of the extent of their isolation in the world. At its foundation, the UDA exemplified this consciousness of the unpopularity of the Unionist cause. However, the UDA, partly because it is less constrained by electoral pressures, has gone further than the Unionist political parties in thinking out aloud about the problem of Northern Ireland's place in the world. In particular, since the late 1970s the UDA has published political proposals which demonstrate an awareness of the potentially important role that might be played by the international community in stabilising or, alternatively, undermining any settlement.

Like the Provisional movement, the UDA came into existence after the onset of the Troubles and after the dispatch of British troops to the province in aid of the civil power. Just as the violent disturbances of 1968 and 1969 had exposed the vulnerability of the many Catholic areas, paving the way for the rise of the Provisional IRA, so in exposed Protestant neighbourhoods in and around Belfast, vigilantes appeared on the streets to patrol the areas after dark as a precaution against attacks by Republicans. They were organised in locally based associations named after their particular neighbourhood. The most active and aggressive of these vigilante organisations appeared in Protestant working-class districts adjoining similar Catholic areas. Two of these, the Shankill Defence Association and the Woodvale Defence Association, convened a meeting to co-ordinate the activities of the different local associations in September 1971, at a time of high tension between the communities and a sharp escalation in the level of political violence following the introduction of internment. The meeting elected a steering committee with the task of integrating the different associations into a single organisation, which was named the Ulster Defence Association. To aid recruitment, a newsletter was published. In

the first issue of *UDA*, the organisation's aim was simply stated as being
'the defence of Ulster against all who would destroy her'.[6]

The newsletter also set out the rules of the organisation. They
included the following: 'because of the present situation in Northern
Ireland, in which a STATE OF WAR exists, no Roman Catholic can
become a member'.[7] That no Catholic could be trusted was a persistent
theme of early issues of *UDA*. Typical is the newsletter's explanation of
why the Government banned remembrance parades as part of a general
ban on processions.

> They were banned because the number of Roman Catholics who
> would have participated would have been less than .001% of
> the Roman Catholic population. They were banned because the
> Roman Catholic population do not regard themselves as part of
> Ulster. They regard themselves as part of the Republic of Ireland.
> They are on the side of murder, terrorism, intimidation, and the
> total destruction of all loyalists. The exceptions are so very, very
> few that we simply cannot trust any of them, despite Mr Brian
> Faulkner.[8]

Such distrust constituted an important element in the general
perception Protestants had of themselves as a beleaguered and
threatened population. Many of the discriminatory practices seen in
Westminster as the cause of the Troubles were viewed by Loyalists in
this defensive context. Consequently, many of the reforms introduced
by the British Government intensified Protestant fears as to their
political future. Reform of the security apparatus evoked a hostile
reaction because of the fear that Protestants were deliberately being
deprived of the means to defend themselves. Thus, the announcement
of the decision to disband the Ulster Special Constabulary, the B-
Specials, in October 1969 provoked riots in Protestant areas of Belfast,
during which a policeman was shot dead. He was the first RUC fatality
of the present Troubles.

The view that Ulster Protestants constitute a community under
siege, surrounded by enemies, was (and remains) central to the UDA's
interpretation of the conflict and to its justification of Loyalist violence.
It was powerfully expressed in a statement issued by the UDA in June
1973:

> We are betrayed, maligned and our families live in constant fear
> and misery. We are a nuisance to our so-called allies and have no
> friends anywhere. Once more in the history of our people, we have
> our backs to the wall, facing extinction by one way or another. This
> is the moment to beware, for Ulstermen in this position fight
> mercilessly till they or their enemies are dead.

A UFF press statement the following month took a similarly apocalyptic view of the situation, while drawing comfort from a foreign analogy, similarly characterised by the siege mentality of the dominant community.

> Our backs are to the wall. We have more in common with the State of Israel, the Star of David on our flag. Those brave people fought and won their battle for survival. We intend to win ours. And like the Jewish people, each time an act of aggression is committed against our people, we shall retaliate in a way that only the animals in the IRA can understand.[10]

Another common theme of early UDA publications was the failure of the authorities to enforce the law. Whereas Catholics in the inner city ghettoes complained bitterly of harassment by the army, Loyalist hostility towards the army stemmed from the Government's toleration of Catholic no-go areas. The perception that Loyalist paramilitaries only existed because lawlessness was permitted by the Government was reflected in the motto adopted by the UDA and unveiled in the second issue of its newsletter. The motto was *Cedenta Arma Togae*, literally, the gown before arms, but translated as Law before Violence.[11] It was an extraordinary slogan for an organisation whose members were about to embark on a campaign of random sectarian assassinations.

A Protestant backlash had arisen even before the mobilisation of Catholics through the civil rights movement. The Unionist Government under Terence O'Neill had discarded the traditional Loyalist belief that peace could only be maintained through ensuring that Catholics were kept in a subordinate position. The belief that the position of Protestants was being threatened by reform stimulated opposition to O'Neill's policies both within and outside the Unionist Party. In addition, some of the social and economic trends of the 1960s, particularly the erosion of residential segregation in parts of Belfast, were accentuating the fears of working-class Protestant communities most affected by the process of change. Their perception that they faced both a local and a general threat to their position found a violent expression. It involved only a handful of people. At the time, its political significance appeared slight. It first manifested itself in March 1966 in a series of petrol bomb attacks on Catholic-owned business premises. In May, a press statement was issued by an organisation describing itself as the Belfast UVF. It announced that it was declaring war on the IRA and that 'known IRA men will be executed mercilessly'.[12] In the weeks after this statement, two Catholics were murdered and others injured. None of the victims had any connection with the IRA. The police quickly identified and arrested the perpetrators, while the Government proscribed the UVF.

There were no further sectarian assassinations by Loyalist para-militaries until the second half of 1971. By that time, the men convicted of the murders in 1966 had come to be regarded by some Belfast Loyalists as heroes and as prophets of what needed to be done. The resumption of the attacks was prompted, in the first instance, by the escalation of violence by Republican paramilitaries that followed the introduction of internment in August 1971. By far the most serious episode was a bomb attack on a Catholic pub in North Belfast in December 1971 in which fifteen people died. The Loyalist campaign received further impetus from two events in 1972. The first of these was the imposition of direct rule by Westminster in March 1972. The second was the Provisional IRA's short truce of two weeks at the end of June and the beginning of July. It was a measure of just how great Loyalist suspicions of the British Government's intentions were during this period that these events were seen as steps towards the forced incor-poration of Northern Ireland into the Republic. The reaction to the truce was particularly savage. During the fortnight it lasted, 18 people died, most of them civilians wholly innocent of involvement in para-military activities, the victims of random sectarian assassinations. The same pattern was to be repeated during the Provisionals' ceasefire in 1975. The 1972 truce ended over an episode in a housing estate in West Belfast in which the UDA was involved in preventing Catholics from moving into property which they had been assigned after it had been vacated by Protestants. The unwillingness of the British army to take on the UDA to get the Catholic families housed prompted the Provisionals to end the truce.

The campaign of sectarian assassinations had important territorial dimensions, encapsulated in two phrases that have been used to explain the geographical spread of 'doorstep' murders in Belfast: 'clearing the decks', meaning the expulsion of Catholics from residential areas of overwhelming Protestant predominance, and 'holding the line', meaning preventing encroachments from a neighbouring Catholic area, so as to maintain the balance between the communities.[13] The political threat posed to Protestants by public housing policies and by movement of population has remained a persistent theme of UDA publications and clearly reflects the influence of such strategic thinking.[14] However, it is important to emphasise that only a very small proportion of the members of the UDA resorted to murder in pursuit of these or other objectives. At its peak in 1972 the UDA had 'about 25,000 dues-paying members'.[15] For most of these, membership of the UDA meant partici-pation in the military parades the organisation staged on the streets of Belfast as a demonstration of the force at its disposal or attendance suitably attired in combat jacket at the mass rallies that were held to promote William Craig as the leader who would save Ulster. Craig's violent rhetoric, especially his calls for the liquidation of Ulster's enemies, formed the main basis of his political appeal to the UDA in this period.[16]

Like almost all Loyalists, the UDA regarded the Sunningdale Agreement of December 1973, establishing a Council of Ireland to promote co-operation between the two parts of Ireland, as a plot to bring about a united Ireland. At the time, Loyalist politicians opposed to the establishment of the power-sharing Executive were organised in a coalition called the United Ulster Unionist Council (UUUC). Together, the UUUC, the UDA, and a number of smaller Loyalist para-militaries formed the Ulster Army Council. It co-ordinated the efforts of Loyalists to bring down the Executive and with it the Sunningdale Agreement. Plans for a general strike were made by yet another co-ordinating body, the Ulster Workers Council (UWC), which included Loyalist trade unionists in key industries. After the demand for fresh elections to the Assembly went unheeded and after the defeat of a Loyalist motion in the Assembly condemning the Council of Ireland, the UWC called a general strike in May 1974. Backed by the muscle of the UDA which set up road blocks and otherwise physically discouraged people from going to work, the strike rapidly paralysed the province. After 14 days the Unionist head of the Executive, Brian Faulkner, resigned, bringing to an end both the experiment in power-sharing and the Sunningdale Agreement. It was the UDA's greatest triumph.

However, in the aftermath of the strike, the UDA found itself no longer courted by the Loyalist politicians who had sought its support in their hour of need. Disillusionment with the politicians prompted new thinking within the UDA. Because of the variety and disparate nature of opinions that emerged within the organisation following the strike, it was some time before this was reflected in an independent political stance. In June the UDA declared a ceasefire on behalf of the UFF. In August 1974 talks were held with the SDLP, although nothing concrete came out of them. An even more startling development was the appearance of a UDA delegation in Libya in November 1974 to explore the possibility of Libyan aid for an independent Ulster.[17] Before this trip the UDA's external contacts had almost entirely been confined to sympathisers in the Orange Order in Scotland and Canada. The UDA organised and had members in Scotland. In December 1974 two men were convicted of smuggling arms to the UDA from Canada.[18] The Libyan episode caused considerable embarrassment to the UDA because of the presence in Tripoli at the same time of a delegation from Sinn Fein, although both denied that there had been any negotiations between them. These political murmurings proved short-lived. In 1975 political dialogue with other bodies was eclipsed by the campaign of sectarian assassinations that followed the Provisionals' announcement of an indefinite ceasefire. Once again, the Loyalist paramilitaries suspected a British betrayal of Ulster and vented their anger by killing Catholic civilians. Three broad perceptions formed the basis on which the UDA justified the Loyalist campaign of violence: firstly, that Catholics in general supported the Provisional IRA; secondly, that the security forces were incapable of, or being prevented from, upholding the law; and thirdly, that it was the settled intention of the British Government to sell out the Protestant community.

In 1976 the first of these perceptions began to change. In August 1976 when the Peace People came into being demanding an end to the Provisionals campaign, the large demonstrations in Catholic areas of the city made a considerable impression on the UDA. Although the Peace People were to stress their non-sectarian character and also held demonstrations in Protestant parts of the city, it was the fact that the movement had emerged from a working-class Catholic community that accounted for its impact on the UDA. The UDA's journal, *Ulster*, carried an editorial in September 1976 entitled 'Peace Perfect Peace',[18] which was notably sympathetic to the aims of the Peace People, if slightly sceptical as to its prospects for success. It readily conceded that the Provisionals' violence provided the only justification for the UDA's existence, declaring 'if there is no such thing as the IRA then that would equally apply to the Loyalist paramilitaries'.[20]

The same issue of *Ulster* contained a letter from a Catholic reader hostile to the Provisional IRA. This represented quite a substantial change from the attitudes prevalent a few years earlier when the constant refrain of UDA publications had been 'you can trust none of them' and when its supporters had been urged to harden themselves to put aside any friendships with Catholics as 'an obstacle to us in the protection and preservation of our community'.[21] A partial change was evident even before the formation of the Peace People. It was reflected in the terms in which the campaign of sectarian assassinations was justified. For example, the July 1976 issue of *Ulster* complained that what the media portrayed as random sectarian assassinations were in fact selective attacks on 'known Republicans',[22] notwithstanding the insistence of the police that the victims had no links with Republican paramilitaries. In 1977 the Loyalist campaign of sectarian assassinations stopped altogether. This ceasefire lasted through 1978 and the first half of 1979. Tim Pat Coogan suggests that it was the result of a specific agreement through intermediaries between the Provisionals and the UDA.[23] It is difficult to assess the significance of such contacts. However, the fact that the UDA never again attempted to justify random sectarian assassinations, while justifying attacks on Republicans, suggests that a change in perceptions was the more important factor in moderating the UDA's outlook and behaviour.

The UDA was also affected by a change in perceptions outside its own ranks. The Government's adoption of direct rule as a long-term policy[24] transformed Protestant attitudes with profound consequences for all the Loyalist paramilitaries. Protestant and even Loyalist fears that Britain intended to force them into a united Ireland diminished sharply. The worst of the crisis appeared over and Loyalist paramilitaries were no longer seen as necessary to protect Ulster from the machinations of the British Government. The process of Ulsterisation of the security forces added to the confidence of the Protestant community. Furthermore, the actions of the Loyalist paramilitaries during the early and mid-1970s now appeared in a much less legitimate light to most Protestants. The racketeering associated with paramilitary fund-raising also loomed larger in the negative attitudes towards organisations such as the UDA. The change in mood was reflected in the success the police achieved in tracking down the perpetrators of sectarian assassinations of earlier years and in a decline in the membership and influence of the paramilitaries. Loyalist politicians who had made inflammatory speeches, which the paramilitaries had seen as a green light for their actions, distanced themselves from any association with the men of violence. There was particular bitterness within the paramilitaries at the lack of interest of the politicians in the plight of Loyalist prisoners.

The year 1977 saw a further change in the UDA's outlook. In May the UDA gave its backing to an indefinite strike called by the Reverend Ian Paisley to demand a change in the Government's security policy. The revival of the UWC appeared to provide a lifeline to the UDA to regain lost influence. The role of the UDA was to provide muscle on the streets as it had done during the 1974 strike. However, despite widespread intimidation by the Loyalist paramilitaries, the 1977 strike was a failure. Key groups such as the workers at power stations refused to support the strike and it was opposed by much of the Unionist establishment. The police saw the strike as a welcome opportunity to enhance their position in the Catholic community by demonstrating their impartiality and took active steps to clear barricades and to stop intimidation. This was in marked contrast to the passivity of the security forces in the face of similar tactics in 1974. As a result of the strike, the UDA's confidence in Loyalist politicians was further undermined by what the UDA saw as the politicians' failure to judge the mood of Protestant public opinion correctly. Distrust of politicians has always been close to the surface within the UDA, but hitherto it had been ready to support Loyalist politicians who emphasised distrust of the British Government and the need for Protestants to defend themselves. These were after all the principal reasons why Loyalists joined paramilitary organisations like the UDA. After the failure of the 1977 strike, the leadership of the UDA resolved that the organisation should develop its own distinctive position on a long-term solution to the Northern Ireland conflict.

In January 1978 the New Ulster Political Research Group (NUPRG) was set up to carry out the task. It was clear from an early stage that the NUPRG would come out in favour of an independent Northern Ireland. It was by no means a new idea. At moments of crisis in relations with Westminster in the early 1970s, William Craig had threatened that Loyalists would declare a unilateral declaration of independence from Britain on the lines of Rhodesia's UDI and had been backed up by the UDA. However, the NUPRG's thinking was moving away from the notion of independence as a last resort to prevent betrayal by Britain and towards the idea of independence as a positive way forward that would permit accommodation between the two communities in Northern Ireland. This had first been put forward in a detailed exposition by Glen Barr at a conference in Amherst, Massachusetts, in September 1975.[25] Barr was a Loyalist politician who had come to prominence in Northern Ireland as a result of his leading role in the UWC during the 1974 strike. He had worked closely with the UDA and had been a member of the UDA's mission to Libya in November 1974. However, at the Amherst conference, he was speaking in a personal capacity and not as an associate of the UDA. His opportunity to get the formal backing of the UDA for his ideas came when he became a member of the NUPRG.

The NUPRG's proposals were published in March 1979 in a discussion document entitled, *Beyond the Religious Divide*.[26] It recommended negotiated independence for Northern Ireland as:

> the only proposal which does not have a victor and a loser. It will encourage the development of a common identity between all of our people, regardless of religion. We offer through our proposal, first class Ulster-citizenship to all of our people, because like it or not the Protestant of N.I. is looked upon as a second class British Citizen in Britain and the Roman Catholic of N.I. as a second class Irish Citizen in the South.[27]

Independence was to be on the basis of a new constitution along the lines of the American constitution with a Bill of Rights and to be supported by guarantees from Britain and the Irish Republic which would withdraw all their claims of sovereignty over Northern Ireland. These guarantees were designed to ensure that negotiated independence did not become either a stepping stone to a united Ireland or the basis for a Protestant dominated state.

Underlying these proposals was 'the concept of political unity in Northern Ireland between Protestants and Roman Catholics with the same ideology' which would allow people 'to decide their elected

Representatives on a political basis rather than religious bigotry and sectarian hatred'.[28] It warned:

> Without the evolution of proper politics, the people of Northern Ireland will continually be manipulated by sectarian politicians who make no contribution to the social and economic well-being of the people of the country, but only continue to fan the flames of religious bigotry for self gain and preservation.[29]

The notion of 'proper politics' was not defined explicitly in the document but it was evident that what the authors had in mind was the development of class-based politics that would permit the emergence of a broadly based Labour party in Northern Ireland. The Ulster Heritage Agency was set up to promote research into the early history of Ulster as a focus of people's loyalties prior to religious conflict in the seventeenth century.[30]

Despite the emphasis on accommodation between the communities in *Beyond the Religious Divide*, the reception for the document was relatively muted. Partly, this was because the idea of independence was anathema to Unionists of the Ulster British tradition who generally were more liberal in their attitudes towards Catholics than Loyalists. Partly, it was because lingering suspicion remained that the appeal of independence to at least some members of the UDA was that it would provide an opportunity for retribution against Republican para-militaries and their supporters. There was evidence in the UDA's own publications to support this suspicion. An article in *Ulster* in October 1978 on 'Why independence is feared by the IRA' argued that 'it is no secret that if Ulster were to "go it alone", the IRA would have their backs to the wall' making possible the destruction of 'the hiding places, the rat-holes, the sewers from which they emanate'.[31] However, another issue of *Ulster* quoted approvingly an altogether more sophisticated reason why independence could be expected to undermine the position of the Provisionals. This was the argument that the Provisionals 'could not claim with any conviction that an indigenous government of Ulster politicians would be "colonial" or "imperialist"'.[32] In the end, the failure of the NUPRG proposals to make greater headway was due to limited support for independence even among the rank and file of the UDA, and still less in the wider Protestant community.

This became clearly apparent when the UDA took its political development a stage further by forming the Ulster Loyalist Democratic Party (ULDP) in June 1981. In the previous month, three candidates had stood in the local council elections under the banner of the NUPRG, and the UDA derived encouragement from the fact that one of the candidates succeeded in getting elected to Belfast City Council.

The first election to be fought by the ULDP was a council by-election in East Belfast in August 1981. Its candidate received 8.4 per cent of the vote, an unexciting if respectable performance. However, the first major electoral test for the ULDP was a Westminster by-election in South Belfast in March 1982 that followed the murder of the constituency's MP by the Provisional IRA. The ULDP's candidate was its chairman, John McMichael, one of the leading figures within the UDA. He fought the election squarely on the issue of negotiated independence and fared extremely poorly, receiving a miserable 1 per cent of the total votes cast, indicating that not even all members of the UDA had voted for him. Two ULDP candidates stood in the Assembly elections of October 1982 and also received a derisory level of support, a striking contrast to the success of Sinn Fein in the same elections. ULDP candidates fared little better in the local council elections of 1985. After that, the ULDP disappeared from view and the NUPRG was revived, though this time simply as the Ulster Political Research Group (UPRG). The failure of the ULDP was partly due to concern about the economic implications of independence. In addition, the hunger strike crisis had made the ULDP's hopes of accommodation with nationalists appear unrealistic to most people, and the more so because of the resumption of Loyalist political violence.

In fact, the political climate had begun to change only a few months after the publication of *Beyond the Religious Divide* in March 1979. A change of government as a result of the Conservative victory in the May 1979 general elections led to the appointment of a new and inexperienced Secretary of State for Northern Ireland, Humphrey Atkins. In his first months in office he managed to create uncertainty as to the future direction of government policy. The rising tension was reflected in the UDA's reaction to a Provisional IRA publicity stunt at the beginning of August. After gunmen appeared on the streets of West Belfast openly displaying their weapons, the UDA issued a warning that it might be forced to resume its operations. Later that same month, *The Guardian* published a report that a new Loyalist assassination squad had been established to attack selective targets and that it comprised members of the UDA, the Red Hand Commando, and the UVF.[33] On the same day 27 August 1979, a bomb placed on a boat in the Republic by the Provisional IRA killed Lord Mountbatten and three others, while in a separate incident eighteen soldiers were killed at Warrenpoint in Northern Ireland in an IRA ambush. These events were followed by a resumption of sectarian assassinations of Catholics and by a statement from the UFF that it was embarking on a campaign against known Republicans.[34]

The role of the UDA leadership during this period remains unclear. At first, the leadership emphatically distanced itself from the resumption of Loyalist violence and especially from instances of random sectarian assassinations. However, as tensions rose in the province as a result of the hunger strikes by Republican prisoners against criminal-isation in 1980 and 1981, UDA spokesmen showed a greater willingness to acknowledge that the UFF was associated with the organisation. In an interview published in December 1981, the Supreme Commander of the UDA, Andy Tyrie, explained the relationship between the UDA and the UFF as follows:

> The UFF consist of a group of people who are members or associated members of the Ulster Defence Association and they decided that the only solution to the problem is a purely military one. And their attitude is, well to remove active Republicans and active nationalists who are trying to overthrow what exists here in the form of a government. People who are assassinating or bombing Ulster people. The UFF feel they are justified in taking military action against them. Now, if that's the type of action they do stay strictly to, and do bomb and shoot only active Republicans, no way would the UDA disapprove of it. We would have no objection to it whatsoever.[35]

In the pages of *Ulster*, the trial of the men who tried to assassinate Bernadette McAliskey in January 1981 was reported with pride.[36] McAliskey was a leading figure on the National H-block/Armagh Committee, the main support group for the Republican prisoners' demands, but she was not a member of Sinn Fein or any other party associated with a Republican paramilitary organisation. The attack on her and other episodes involving the UFF, such as the murder in 1980 of John Turnley, a Protestant member of the constitutional, if strongly nationalist Irish Independence Party, showed how elastic was the notion of 'active Republicans and active nationalists who are trying to over-throw what exists here in the form of a government'.

None the less, by the standards of the early and mid-1970s when Loyalist paramilitaries caused hundreds of fatalities, Loyalist violence in this period was by and large selective and limited in its scope. For example, according to the RUC, Loyalist paramilitaries were responsible for the death of twelve of the 101 victims of political violence during 1981,[37] the traumatic year of the second Republican hunger strike, when much of the Catholic community was mobilised behind the prisoners' demands. This seems at least partly attributable to the restraint exercised by Andy Tyrie, the dominant figure in the UDA since about 1974. Tyrie remained committed to the view that winning the support of Catholics for a united Northern Ireland was the key to defeating Republicanism. While the election of Bobby Sands in the Fermanagh and South Tyrone by-election during the course of the 1981 hunger strike was seen by the UDA leadership as a blow to hopes that the Catholic community would repudiate the Provisionals, the UDA's comments on the political developments within the Catholic community remained restrained. Unlike the DUP, the UDA did not suggest that the election of Sands proved that Catholics in general supported the IRA.[38] Sinn Fein's success in the Assembly elections in October 1982 was not open to the same interpretation and represented a more unambiguous blow to the political accommodation between the communities sought by the leadership of the UDA. At the same time, the organisation itself was prospering as sectarian polarisation was bringing fresh recruits into the ranks of the UDA. One of the obvious reasons for the gulf between the leadership's political ideas and those of the rank and file was that what impelled Loyalists to join the UDA had little or nothing to do with the organisation's political stance. It was in the expectation of active participation in the defence of Ulster, not to engage in debate about Northern Ireland's future, that they turned to paramilitaries.

How to meet this expectation constituted a considerable problem for the leadership. Its stake in the ideas produced by the NUPRG was only one reason for restraint on paramilitary operations. Another compelling reason for the pursuit of a selective and limited campaign was the fear that history would repeat itself and that when the immediate crisis created by the rise of Sinn Fein was over, Protestant opinion would once again turn against the paramilitaries and that their members would end up in jail for crimes commited during the crisis, as had happened in the 1970s. The leadership was determined that this should not occur again. Despite the rise of Sinn Fein as an electoral force in 1982 and 1983 and despite the Anglo-Irish Agreement in 1985, the number of killings attributed to Loyalist paramilitaries continued to remain relatively low, with thirteen murders in 1982, seven in 1983, seven in 1984, five in 1985, and fourteen in 1986. For the same period, the RUC put the number of murders by Republican paramilitaries at 248.[39] One answer the UDA found to the problem of inactivity was to put its most energetic members through a rigorous programme of training to prepare them militarily for the possibility of a final showdown with Republicanism.

The establishment within the UDA of a small professional army, trained to a high level of military proficiency in tasks such as tracking, map-reading, and target-shooting, was an expensive programme and represented a considerable financial commitment by the UDA. The new body, variously described as an 'officer corps' and an 'elite commando-style nucleus of paramilitary supermen',[40] was called the Ulster Defence Force (UDF). Members who qualified through the training programme were awarded a badge of golden wings and enrolled in the UDF. The force's motto was *'sans peur'*. It was described by *Ulster* in the following terms in 1986:

The Ulster Defence Force was formed in 1982 as part of the UDA's reorganisation programme. Comprised largely of young men, led by senior members with ex-army qualifications, this comparatively-new group is a well-trained force which many believe is being held in readiness for a potential 'Doomsday' situation in Ulster.[41]

It was the UDA's policy that the UDF should be kept in reserve and that the existing campaign against Republicans should be carried out by the UFF.[42] By this time there was little attempt to disguise the close relationship between the UDA and the UFF. The UFF was even accorded its own symbol of a Red fist and represented on one of the four quarters of the Ulster flag, along with the UDA, the UDF, and Loyalist Prisoners Aid (LPA) on a new coat of arms adorning the cover of *Ulster*.[43] The same coat of arms was reproduced as a wall mural outside the UDA's headquarters in East Belfast.

The notion of a doomsday situation became a significant element in the UDA leadership's thinking in response to the rise of Sinn Fein. In July 1983 following Sinn Fein's success in the Westminster general election the previous month, John McMichael called on the Provisional IRA to declare a ceasefire and issued the following warning:

> If the representatives of the Ulster Catholic community continue to pursue its united Ireland or nothing attitude, then Ulster Protestants are forced to conclude that a political solution is beyond reach. Should this indeed be the case, they are left with no alternative other than to single-mindedly prepare ourselves (*sic*), both psychologically and physically, for the final and seemingly inevitable conflict.[44]

At the time, McMichael complained that the press played up the threat of civil war and ignored his pleas for reconciliation between Protestant and Catholic in Northern Ireland.[45] Two years later in April 1985, McMichael reiterated his warning in a pessimistic article in *Ulster* which argued that there was a general perception that Northern Ireland was heading for open conflict within ten years and that it might be preferable to precipitate the conflict sooner rather than later. The same piece insisted that there were 'great numbers of Catholics in Ulster who play a constructive role in our society and must not be confused with our enemies'.[46]

A continuing commitment to political accommodation was the most important survival of the thinking that had produced *Beyond the Religious Divide* in 1979. Much else did not survive the rise of Sinn Fein. The move to the left within the UDA that accompanied the politicisation of the late 1970s went into reverse. *Ulster* became stridently right-wing in reaction to the links being forged between Sinn Fein and the Left of the Labour Party in Britain, and much more traditionally Loyalist in its approach, emphasising that Ulster was British in seeming contradiction of the leadership's support for independence on the basis of a common Ulster identity. The links of the IRA with international communism became a regular theme of *Ulster*, although it also reproduced what purported to be an IRA oath to engage in a religious war on behalf of the Pope to exterminate Protestants.[47] The right-wing character of *Ulster* was also reflected in its occasional coverage of foreign affairs. For example, the March 1985 issue of *Ulster* carried a laudatory article on 'The South African Defence Force in Anti-Terrorist Operations'.[48] (Shortly after the existence of the UDF was first revealed towards the end of 1983, a UDA spokesman in Londonderry claimed that the force had been trained in Israel, South Africa, and Lebanon. A member of the UDA's leadership, Sam Duddy, would confirm only that there had been contacts as regards training with the three countries.)[49]

The UDA's political isolation, together with its reputation for racketeering, had created difficulties for the organisation in the late 1970s and a renewed working relationship between the UDA and the politicians was clearly in evidence during the 1983 campaign of Loyalist prisoners for segregation. During the summer of 1985, the UDA joined forces with other Loyalist organisations to set up the United Ulster Loyalist Front (UULF) to oppose the re-routing of Orange parades. Shortly before the British and Irish Governments entered into the Anglo-Irish Agreement, the UULF took the further initiative of setting up Ulster Clubs, comprising members of Unionist political parties as well as members of the paramilitaries.[50] After the signing of the Agreement, the UDA made it clear that it would follow the lead set by the politicians in the campaign to bring it down. The UDA's thinking on the 'doomsday situation' was that it was up to the politicians as the representatives of Ulster Protestants to take the responsibility for declaring unequivocally when the moment for civil war had arrived. The UDA was determined to avoid the position where its members took violent action in response to violent rhetoric from the politicians, only to be subsequently repudiated by those same politicians.

When called on, the UDA was ready and willing to do what politicians asked of it. Thus, it gave its full backing to the strike called by the leaders of the UUP and DUP on the Day of Action, 3 March 1986, and was closely involved in the planning and execution of the strike, which included the setting up of hundreds of road blocks across the province to ensure that it was effective. The problem was that the two party leaders, who had little involvement with either the planning or the execution of the Day of Action, made public promises that there

would be no road blocks or other interference with those wanting to go
to work. In the event, those attempting to go to work were faced with
numerous barricades on the major thoroughfares. Some were manned
by hooded men prepared to use violence to discourage motorists from
proceeding further. There were widespread complaints that the police
were ineffective in dealing with intimidation. The RUC for its part
strongly criticised the broken promises of the two party leaders. There
were also a number of attacks on business premises that attempted to
stay open during the strike. Part of a factory in Lurgan was destroyed by
petrol bombs. During rioting in Protestant parts of Belfast as the strike
drew to a close, the police came under attack from snipers. When
violence also marred the anniversary rally against the Agreement in
November 1986, the Unionist party leaders resolved to exclude the
paramilitaries from the next mass protest on 11 April 1987. The Day of
Defiance, against a new public order law which Unionists attributed to
Dublin's influence through the Anglo-Irish Conference, was a flop. In a
striking demonstration of the UDA's influence on the streets, a march
on a police station in East Belfast attracted a crowd of only 350. The
UDA had advised shops and businesses to stay open during the protest.
Afterwards, McMichael called on Molyneaux and Paisley to resign as
party leaders.[51]

Although the UDA leadership was dissatisfied with the
ineffectiveness of their campaign against the Anglo-Irish Agreement it
was also critical of the Unionists' failure to put forward a constructive
alternative to the Agreement. In June 1986 the UDA announced that it
was drafting its own proposals for the establishment of an administration in Northern Ireland free of any input from Dublin[52] and on 29
January 1987—as the UPRG—published a booklet entitled *Common
Sense*.[53] A draft had been completed in September 1986 and then
discussed among the rank and file of the UDA. As the chairman of the
UPRG was John McMichael and it also included Andy Tyrie and
Tommy Lyttle among its seven members, the document had the full
backing of the UDA's leadership from the outset. In the context of
existing Unionist attitudes towards a political settlement, it was a
remarkable document, as remarkable as *Beyond the Religious Divide* had
been in its day. The centrepiece of the proposals was the establishment
of devolved government in Northern Ireland on a power-sharing basis.
The mechanism chosen to create power-sharing was deliberately
designed to avoid the institutionalisation of sectarian divisions. Places
on the executive were simply to be in porportion to the number of votes
the parties received. In illustrating how this might work in practice, it
gave an example of how portfolios on the Executive might be
distributed on the basis of the 1982 Assembly election results. On this
basis, the portfolio for the Administration of Justice went to the

SDLP![54] However, the document elsewhere expressed the hope that once the issue of the constitution had been settled, political divisions in Northern Ireland would be based 'on social and economic doctrine rather than Unionist versus Irish Nationalist or Catholic versus Protestant'.[55]

A written constitution, embodying the principle of accommodation between the communities, was as important a part of the document as the actual mechanism chosen for power-sharing. The document proposed that the Secretary of State for Northern Ireland should consult the parties with a view to the election of a conference to draw up a new constitution for Northern Ireland. It would require the support of two-thirds of voters in a referendum for the constitution to be implemented and thereafter to be amended. It was accepted by the UPRG that Northern Ireland would remain part of the United Kingdom in terms of any constitution that might be agreed among the parties. Indeed, the document argued that the process by which the constitution came into effect would help to remove uncertainty about the province's future by underwriting Northern Ireland's position within the United Kingdom.

> The fact that Northern Ireland's 'status' within the United Kingdom could not be changed without the consent of at least two thirds of those voting in a referendum would raise the siege on 'Ulster Protestants' and create a new atmosphere of security and stability conducive to reconciliation and political development. A Northern Ireland existing by consent would remove the need to constantly defend the psychological border.[56]

Common Sense warned that 'the pragmatic alternative to co-determination is to fight a bloody civil war and let the victor dictate the rules by which we will live' and concluded by declaring that 'the most dangerous thing to do, and unfortunately the most politically popular, would be to do NOTHING'.[57]

In spite of its rejection of an Irish dimension, and of the Anglo-Irish Agreement, *Common Sense* was warmly welcomed by representatives of the SDLP. Austin Currie described it as 'a very constructive document',[58] while wryly noting the nature of the organisation that produced it. The response of Unionists was more muted but far from dismissive. The main opposition to the document came not from traditional Loyalists but from the Campaign for Equal Citizenship, proponents of the total integration of Northern Ireland into the United Kingdom. They were opposed, in principle, to devolved government and to any mechanism such as power-sharing that marked Northern Ireland out as different from any other part of the United Kingdom. Despite their vociferous opposition, the influence of *Common Sense* on the main body of Unionists was considerable. It had become apparent that the Unionist campaign against the Anglo-Irish Agreement was making little headway and that a fresh approach was needed. In recognition of the impasse they had arrived at, the two party leaders appointed their deputies, Peter Robinson of the DUP and Harold McCusker of the UUP, and the chief executive of the UUP, Frank Millar, as members of a Task Force, which was given the job of assessing how best to enlist the support of Unionists in continuing the campaign against the Agreement. They were also asked to examine whether there was a consensus among Unionists on an alternative to the pact that could be put to the British Government. This initiative amounted to an acknowledgment firstly, that some of the tactics that had been employed in the campaign had proved unpopular among Unionists and, secondly, that one reason why the campaign had made little impact on British opinion was because it appeared to be wholly negative.

The section of the report of the Task Force dealing with alternatives to the Agreement and entitled 'An End to Drift', was published in July 1987. This proved to be a more radical document than either of the two party leaders had anticipated. Its debt to the proposals put forward by the UPRG was quite apparent. Referring to *Common Sense* the report commented:

> Many, in addition to the UDA would clearly be prepared to contemplate SDLP participation in the government of Northern Ireland *provided* the SDLP agreed to forfeit the role of the government of the Irish Republic as custodians of the nationalist interest.[59]

At the same time, the report recorded the authors' incredulity when they were confronted by a group demanding the restoration of devolution in Northern Ireland on the basis of majority rule. In this roundabout and somewhat diffident manner, the three politicians were indicating their endorsement for power-sharing, though they shied away from actual use of the term. Their diffidence was understandable in view of the attitudes of their party leaders. It was evident that Molyneaux remained sympathetic to integration, while Paisley made his position plain by continuing to condemn power-sharing in unequivocal language. However, the two party leaders did accept the report's recommendation that they should enter into talks with the British Government to explore the possibility of negotiating an alternative to the Agreement. These began in the summer of 1987, but, in the circumstances, with little expectation of a positive outcome of any kind. The irony that the UDA was more willing to compromise in order to achieve a political settlement than were the constitutional parties of Unionism was largely lost on British opinion.

Other aspects of the UDA's activities cast a rather different light on the organisation. In February 1987, the UFF placed incendiary devices in a number of stores in Dublin and Belfast. Those in Belfast appeared to be a response to the outcome of a court case in which three UDA men had been convicted of attempting to extort £150,000 from a chain of supermarkets.[60] In the same month, the UDA's assistance in the distribution of free EEC food to pensioners and those on supplementary benefit received considerable publicity.[61] The UDA's controversial involvement in organising the hand-outs was the product of its commitment to community politics as a way of embedding the organisation into Protestant working-class communities, particularly in the urban areas. To this end, the UDA had established the Ulster Community Action Group, paralleling Sinn Fein's involvement in such activities in Catholic areas.

Building a base in the Protestant community is particularly important to the UDA since it can draw on few external sources of support. Sporadic contacts between the UDA and a variety of neo-fascist organisations in Britain and on the continent of Europe reflect the UDA's international isolation rather than any ideological affinity with the extreme Right or sympathy with racism. Indeed, the bitter recognition that Loyalists have few friends anywhere in the world has underpinned the UDA's perception of the conflict as a prolonged siege, but it is by no means resigned to living in a permanent state of siege. The UDA's perception of itself as in the frontline and bearing the brunt of the conflict on the Loyalist side makes it disinclined to accept the notion that Loyalists should simply settle for the containment of the conflict and learn to live with uncertainty over Norther Ireland's political future. *Beyond the Religious Divide* and *Common Sense* address the central problems of Northern Ireland's lack of legitimacy as a political entity, the first focusing on the external dimension of the problem and the second on the internal dimension. That the two approaches do not easily meld together is more a reflection of the inherent difficulty of reconciling internally acceptable arrangements with prevailing international norms than of muddled thinking or confusion on the UDA's part. This difficulty is, however, compounded by a further one.

There clearly is a fundamental conflict between the UDA's commitment to political accommodation, which dates from the late 1970s, and the impact of the organisation's violent activities. The latter plays a significant role in the polarisation of Northern Ireland society. Just as the Provisional IRA appears blind to the perception of Protestants that attacks on members of the UDR and the RUC are directed against them as a community, so the UDA appears not to recognise how attacks on Republicans are perceived by the Catholic community. The selectivity of Loyalist attacks is far from evident to Catholics, not least because of instances of mistakes in identifying members of Republican paramilitary organisations. UFF claims to have killed a member of the Provisional IRA are all too frequently followed by statements from the RUC that the victim had no known links with any paramilitary organisation. Catholics tend to assume the worst about the motivation for such attacks. Further, for elements in the rank and file of the UDA, such as those involved in the intimidation of Catholic workers at Shorts' aircraft factory in the summer of 1987, the distinction between Republican and Catholic is largely seen as a cosmetic one and in practice ignored. Regardless of the leadership's commitment to accommodation, the UDA still remains an organisation that Catholics, whatever their political convictions, first and foremost fear.

The different facets of the UDA's activities from social welfare to sectarian assassination and from promoting reconciliation to preparation for civil war underline the danger of simplistic classification of the organisation, whether as vigilantes or terrorists. Like the Provisional IRA, the UDA is the product of uncertainty about the future of Northern Ireland. However, in the Provisionals' case, the external uncertainty helps to sustain their inner conviction in the inevitability of a united Ireland, provided they fight for it. No such inner conviction in the inevitable triumph of Loyalism or in the appropriate means to secure it sustains the UDA. A significant consequence of the internationalisation of the Northern Ireland conflict has been to enhance the Loyalists' sense of beleaguerment because of the overwhelming weight of international opinion in favour of a united Ireland. It has fostered a desire for self-reliance among Loyalists, epitomised by the UDA in both its positive and negative aspects.

5.

THE BRITISH DIMENSION

FROM an international perspective, much the most important aspect of the British dimension to the conflict is the nature and justification of British rule in Northern Ireland. Crisis management, the term used in the report of the New Ireland Forum,[1] provides the most succinct description of British policy towards Northern Ireland since the onset of the Troubles. Aside from its reactive character, its other most consistent feature has been the desire of the British Government to keep the problem of Northern Ireland at arm's length and to ensure that the conflict does not infect the rest of the body politic. Within these parameters, there have been some significant shifts in British policy over the last two decades.

Three principal phases of policy can be identified in the period from October 1968 to October 1979. Until 1972 the objective of British policy was the restoration of order through reform within the existing constitutional framework. The reaction to the introduction of internment in August 1971 was the principal reason for a change in the scope of British policy. After the imposition of direct rule on the province and the suspension of Northern Ireland's Parliament at Stormont in March 1972, the objective of policy was more ambitious. It was to achieve a political settlement of the conflict through the creation of a new constitutional order in Northern Ireland. It led to the establishment of a power-sharing Executive which collapsed as a result of the Ulster Workers Council strike in May 1974. The British Government attempted to rescue elements of this settlement from the wreckage through a Constitutional Convention in 1975. But it failed to establish any measure of consensus across the sectarian divide, so the British Government finally gave up its attempt to reconstruct devolved government. The third phase of policy, which can be dated from the end of 1975, involved the adoption of direct rule as a long-term *policy*. International pressure, especially from the United States, was instrumental in bringing about its demise. A British Government White Paper in November 1979 explicitly repudiated the policy as 'not satisfactory as a continuing basis for the government of the Province'.[2] It was produced for a new initiative aimed at putting pressure on the four main political parties in Northern Ireland to agree on the parameters of an internal settlement involving devolution.

The period from the launch of the Atkins initiative in October 1979 to the signing of the Anglo-Irish Agreement on 15 November 1985 is much more difficult to characterise in terms of phases of policy. Indeed, its most obvious feature is that different, and sometimes sharply conflicting, strands of policy were pursued simultaneously. While it is reasonable to regard the Anglo-Irish Agreement as the logical outcome of the Anglo-Irish process initiated at the Dublin summit in December 1980, the initiation of the process did not prevent the British Government from persisting with its efforts to achieve an internal settlement. At the same time, the Government continued to uphold policies in the security field that owed their origin to the abandoned *policy* of direct rule and fitted in logically with that approach. Different strands of policy appeared dominant at different times. Only the signing of the Anglo-Irish Agreement itself has entrenched the Anglo-Irish process as the predominant element in the Government's policy. While the creation of devolved institutions still remains one of the main objectives of the Government, that aim is now being pursued within the framework of the Agreement. Similarly, the influence of the Anglo-Irish process has been brought to bear on security policies. The result is that Government policy has appeared much more coherent since the Anglo-Irish Agreement in November 1985.

From this brief overview of British policy towards Northern Ireland, a number of further conclusions can be drawn. Firstly, the shifts in policy bear no relation to changes in government in Britain. Each of the principal phases in the first 11 years of the Troubles spanned periods of both Labour and Conservative rule. Bipartisanship on policy towards Northern Ireland has prevailed through most of the Troubles. There has been more conflict over policy towards Northern Ireland within the political parties than between their parliamentary leaderships. Northern Ireland has not been a significant issue in any British general election since the start of the Troubles. One consquence of the way policy towards Northern Ireland has developed has been a shattering of the alignments that existed before the Troubles between the main political forces in the province and the major parties in Britain. The close association of Conservative and Unionist on the one hand, and of Labour and anti-Unionist on the other, has disappeared. Indeed, at the time of the 1987 general election in Britain, Unionists were hoping the the Conservative Government would be defeated, while one prominent constitutional nationalist politician indicated his preference for the return of Thatcher on the eve of the poll.[3] Secondly, until the signature of the Anglo-Irish Agreement in November 1985, the long period of Conservative rule under Margaret Thatcher which began in 1979 brought no greater consistency or coherence to British policy than had existed during the politically more volatile 1970s. These features of policy towards Northern Ireland give it more in common with foreign than with domestic policy.

Prior to the Troubles institutional arrangements and established practices guided relations between Northern Ireland and the rest of the United Kingdom. Northern Ireland affairs had been an obscure departmental responsibility of the Home Office. The explanation for the low profile of the province before 1968 is to be found in the nature of Northern Ireland's relationship to the United Kingdom. From the creation of Northern Ireland as a political entity under the 1920 Government of Ireland Act to 1969, the province enjoyed a degree of autonomy that effectively placed it outside the domestic British political system, despite the fact that Northern Ireland elected twelve MPs to Westminster. From the outset a parliamentary convention was established that the House of Commons did not debate internal Northern Ireland affairs as these were deemed to be solely the responsibility of the Northern Ireland Parliament. This arrangement meant that it was possible for Ulster Unionist MPs at Westminster to vote with the Conservatives to oppose welfare legislation introduced by Labour Governments while the Unionist Government ensured that Northern Ireland benefited from these measures by securing the passage of equivalent legislation through the Northern Ireland Parliament at Stormont.

In the context of the complex web of relationships that united the British Empire, the arrangement was not seen as bestowing an inferior status on the province. Indeed Unionists by and large regarded the province's autonomy as a safeguard for Northern Ireland's membership of the United Kingdom. This was reinforced by the terms of the 1949 Ireland Act passed by Westminster in response to the establishment of a Republic in Southern Ireland. The Act guaranteed Northern Ireland's constitutional status as follows:

> Parliament hereby declares that Northern Ireland remains part of His Majesty's Dominions and of the United Kingdom and affirms that in no event will Northern Ireland or any part thereof cease to be part of His Majesty's Dominions and of the United Kingdom without the consent of the Parliament of Northern Ireland.[4]

As Buckland puts it, the Act 'showed just how far constitutional security was rooted in the 'soil' of devolution'.[5] From an external perspective Northern Ireland appeared to be an integral part of the United Kingdom politically. In fact, as far as the outside world was aware, Northern Ireland did not exist as a political entity in its own right. Consequently, events in the province attracted little external interest since they inevitably appeared to be wholly peripheral to the political direction or stability of the United Kingdom. Thus, the minor emergency of the IRA's Border campaign between 1956 and 1962 made virtually no impression at all on opinion outside of Ireland.

The paradox was that external illusions that Northern Ireland was a normal part of the United Kingdom depended on the province's rigid separation in practice from the British political system. They could not be sustained if the British Government intervened directly and visibly in Northern Ireland's affairs. However, the interests of the British political parties made such intervention unlikely. The great merit of the partition settlements of the 1920s from their perspective was that partition had solved the 'Irish Question', in the sense that Irish affairs no longer exercised a destabilising influence on politics at Westminster. For this reason, no party wanted the issue brought back into the centre of politics. However, despite this constraint on British action, Unionist fears of Westminster intervention grew during the 1960s. They were partly a reaction to the election of a Labour Government in 1964 and to the fact that Harold Wilson had personally expressed his support for the concept of a united Ireland. In reality, Wilson's attitude was much more a reflection of his cultivation of the Irish vote in Britain than of any intention to disturb the constitutional relationship of Northern Ireland to the United Kingdom. Another reason for Unionist anxiety was the realisation that the comfortable obscurity in which the province had conducted its affairs was threatened by the spreading influence of television. In particular, the grievances of the minority were beginning to attract attention in Britain. For example, in 1965 a pressure group called the Campaign for Democracy in Ulster was formed with the support of a number of backbench Labour MPs. It wanted an inquiry into how Northern Ireland was governed. A further factor in the situation was the weakness of Northern Ireland's economy as a result of the decline of traditional industries. This increased the province's dependence on subsidies from the British Treasury.

The Unionist Government under Terence O'Neill, who had become Prime Minister of Northern Ireland in 1963, responded to these pressures by embarking on a strategy of reform, to modernise the economy. O'Neill recognised that to achieve this aim it would be necessary to attract foreign investment to the province and that this could not be done if the image Northern Ireland presented to the outside world was that of a society deeply divided on sectarian lines. Overcoming the divisions through the building of bridges between the two communities became one of the Government's priorities. This was reflected at a symbolic level in the Prime Minister's visits to Catholic schools and homes. A more concrete step was the Government's decision to recognise the Northern Ireland Committee of the Irish Congress of Trade Unions. Another sign of the melting of traditional antagonisms was O'Neill's meeting with the Irish Prime Minister, Sean Lemass, at Stormont Castle in January 1965. The new style of government produced a strong reaction from some Protestants. Their champion was a Free Presbyterian clergyman, Reverend Ian Paisley, who had been waging a campaign against the ecumenical movement since the early 1960s.

Among Catholics as well as some liberal Protestants there was dissatisfaction that the Government's rhetoric of reform had not resulted in more substantial changes, especially in some of the blatantly sectarian practices of local government. The dissatisfaction grew when lobbying by pressure groups failed to move the Government. It was reflected in the formation of the Northern Ireland Civil Rights Association (NICRA) in February 1967. Its demands included one person one vote in local government, allocation of council housing on a non-discriminatory points system, and the repeal of the Special Powers Act. What made NICRA different from the previous pressure groups was that it planned to campaign for these demands through mass protest action on the model of the civil rights movement in the United States. It calculated that attracting the attention of the outside world to the existence of discrimination against Catholics in Northern Ireland in this way would cause acute embarrassment to the Government and force it to make concessions.

A civil rights march in August 1968 passed off peacefully despite the threat posed by Loyalist counter-demonstrations. However, because of the danger of a confrontation between the two groups, the Government banned the holding of a civil rights demonstration in Londonderry in October. The ban was ignored leading to a violent confrontation between a section of the marchers and the police. International television coverage focused on the savagery of police attacks on the demonstrators. The impact on mainland British opinion was considerable especially as what the demonstrators were protesting against appeared indefensible according to British standards. The Labour Government which had supported O'Neill's strategy of reform, put pressure on the Northern Ireland Prime Minister to meet NICRA's main demands. A package of reforms followed in November. It appeared to be generally well received in the province and for a brief moment it seemed as if a slide towards disorder might be averted. However, there was further violence in January 1969 when demonstrators on a cross-country march were ambushed and attacked by Loyalists at Burntollet bridge near the village of Claudy. Their assailants included off-duty part-time policemen in the B-Specials. Not merely did the regular members of the RUC fail to protect the marchers but later that day the police entered the Catholic district of the Bogside in Londonderry and ran amok. O'Neill resigned in April. In the same month British troops were dispatched to the province in aid of the civil power, though not as yet for the purpose of controlling demonstrations or patrolling the streets. This was in response to bomb attacks on electricity supply lines and waterworks. During the summer of 1969 the traditional parades of the Orange Order became the main focus of inter-community tensions, stretching the resources of the local security forces and prompting speculation of imminent British intervention. When prolonged rioting followed the Apprentice Boys' parade in Londonderry on 12 August, the Unionist Government asked for the assistance of British troops. On 14 and 15 August British troops began patrolling the streets of Londonderry and Belfast.

The implications were profound. According to Buckland, it meant that 'the affairs of Northern Ireland ceased to be the sole prerogative of Northern Irishmen' and that 'the longer the conflict continued the more it had international ramifications'.[6] By the same token, the British Government had acquired unavoidable political responsibility for the domestic affairs of Northern Ireland. In the process, the illusion in the outside world that Northern Ireland was politically as well as con-stitutionally an integral part of the United Kingdom was destroyed. This was evident in the meaning that now became attached to the notion of British intervention in the province. Of longer term significance, the reverse of intervention, British withdrawal, also acquired a definite and clearly understood meaning. Britain was now faced internationally with having to defend the existence of Northern Ireland as a separate political entity with a status that appeared similar to a dependency, notwithstanding Northern Ireland's involvement in the British political system through the election of MPs to Westminster. The awkwardness of the position was reflected in the Downing Street Declaration, a joint statement issued by the British and Northern Ireland Governments on 19 August. It began:

> The United Kingdom Government reaffirm that nothing which has happened in recent weeks in Northern Ireland derogates from the clear pledges made by successive United Kingdom Governments that Northern Ireland should not cease to be a part of the United Kingdom without the consent of the people of Northern Ireland....[7]

The Declaration went on to cite the specific terms of the 1949 Ireland Act quoted above. The paragraph ended with the bald assertion: 'The border is not an issue.'[8] Further paragraphs emphasised the commitment of the two Governments to the principle of equality of treatment for all citizens, while the Northern Ireland Government specifically undertook 'to take into the fullest account at all times the views of Her Majesty's Government in the United Kingdom'.[9] Taken as a whole, the Declaration underlined the determination of the British Government to limit the extent of its involvement in the affairs of Northern Ireland through a policy of reform within the existing constitutional framework. It hoped that reconstruction of the local security forces, which had been discredited as a result of the violent events of 1968 and 1969, would permit the early withdrawal of British troops and that political stability could be restored through changes to encourage political participation by the minority within the context of Northern Ireland's devolved government.

These hopes were to be disappointed. The welcome that British troops received in Catholic areas when they first appeared on the streets of Londonderry and Belfast was not just because they offered protection from Loyalist mobs but because nationalists recognised that British intervention constituted a political defeat for Unionism. Further, as long as British troops remained in Northern Ireland, nationalists had a guarantee that their grievances could not be marginalised. British responsibility meant British vulnerability to international criticism. In these circumstances, it is not surprising that a policy, the ultimate aim of which appeared to be the restoration of the constitutional *status quo ante*, should have encountered resistance among nationalists and that it should have facilitated the re-emergence of physical force Republicanism. After the civil rights movement's agitation for reform had succeeded in precipitating British intervention, there was a tendency for opinion in the Catholic community to become increasingly radicalised and dismissive of reforms, though this was not a universal reaction, especially in the first months of the reforms that accompanied British intervention. In particular, the Ulster Defence Regiment (UDR), established in 1970 as a replacement for the almost wholly Protestant B-Specials, initially attracted a significant proportion of Catholic recruits. However, such countervailing tendencies did not prevent the further polarisation of the society as the result of political violence. When the Unionist Government led by Brian Faulkner introduced internment on 9 August 1971, thirty-four people had already died in political violence that year. Internment simply made matters worse. Another 139 people died by the end of the year.[10]

The escalation of violence and adverse international reaction to internment put pressure on the British Government to extend its intervention in Northern Ireland. The events of Bloody Sunday, when thirteen unarmed demonstrators were shot dead by British troops on 30 January 1972 after an illegal civil rights march in Londonderry, made the pressure irresistible. On 24 March the British Prime Minister, Edward

Heath, announced that Westminster was taking direct charge of government in Northern Ireland and that in addition, Northern Ireland's Parliament at Stormont was being suspended. When direct rule was imposed, it was not intended as a long-term solution in itself, let alone as a step towards the political integration of Northern Ireland into the United Kingdom. The purpose of direct rule was to clear the decks for a political settlement. In fact, the broad outlines of the settlement Britain envisaged were apparent even before Bloody Sunday made a new political initiative inevitable. In an article in *Fortnight* in November 1971, Tom Hadden accurately predicted that its main elements would be proportional representation in elections, power-sharing in government between representatives of the two communities, and an All-Ireland Council.[11] However, while the aim of direct rule was to establish devolved government in Northern Ireland and not to draw the province into the domestic British political system, the machinery of government it entailed, the appointment within the British Cabinet of a Secretary of State for Northern Ireland and the establishment of the Northern Ireland Office as a department of the British Government, meant the abandonment of the notion that Northern Ireland could exist as a fully autonomous political entity unencumbered by the visible involvement of Westminster. Devolved institutions would at best share Britain's responsibility for government in the province. Further, since such a structure could not camouflage the fact that Northern Ireland was not a normal part of the United Kingdom in political terms, it would require both internal and external legitimisation.

Although direct rule failed to stem the escalation in the level of political violence, the British Government did eventually succeed in putting together the settlement it sought. With the Sunningdale Agreement of December 1973 a political settlement was achieved which embraced a majority of Unionists, the SDLP, and the Republic of Ireland. It represented a radical attempt to satisfy both Catholic interests and nationalist aspirations without removing the guarantee to Unionists that Northern Ireland would remain a part of the United Kingdom as long as that was the wish of a majority of people in the province. Catholic interests were to be safeguarded through power-sharing, while the Council of Ireland catered for nationalist aspirations. The proposals for the Council of Ireland involved a delicate balancing act. In one respect, they could be regarded as strengthening Northern Ireland's position within the United Kingdom by providing a basis on which both the Republic and nationalists in the North could accept the legitimacy of Northern Ireland's political institutions. On the other hand, the Council's 'executive and harmonising functions'[12] could be seen as providing a mechanism by which there would be a gradual accretion of political authority to an all-Ireland institution that would eventually lever the province out of the United Kingdom. Whatever the long-term implications of the creation of a Council of Ireland, in simply providing formal recognition of the legitimacy of nationalist aspirations, it underlined the minority's equality of status under the Sunningdale Agreement. This was important in the context of the British Government's efforts to counter any impression that existed in the outside world that the position of Catholics in Northern Ireland was analogous to that of natives under colonial rule.

However, by the same token, the proposals for the Council of Ireland were a threat to what remained of the Protestant position as the dominant community. Such a threat appeared particularly dangerous to a community that felt its security was already in jeopardy as a result of the continuing campaign of violence by Republican paramilitaries. A Protestant backlash quickly developed, principally over the Council of Ireland. A Westminster general election in February 1974 provided voters in Northern Ireland with an early opportunity to give their verdict on the Sunningdale Agreement. Candidates supporting the Agreement were routed, undermining the legitimacy of the power-sharing Executive, which had been in office for little more than a month. The Executive collapsed altogether after the UWC strike in May, which forced the resignation of its Unionist members. It seems unlikely that the Executive could have survived for very long in any event, given the hostility it faced among Loyalists for, unlike the Anglo-Irish Agreement, the functioning of the Sunningdale package required positive Unionist consent.

In the recriminations that followed, nationalists placed much of the blame for the fall of the Executive on the lack of resolution of the Secretary of State for Northern Ireland, Merlyn Rees. More recently, attention has focused on the role played by the British security services, MI5 and MI6 during this period and on allegations that elements of the security services, intent on destabilising the Wilson Government, were prepared to undermine the power-sharing experiment in Northern Ireland to this end.[13] After the fall of the Executive, direct rule filled the political vacuum in the absence of anything else. It was not yet the British Government's conscious policy preference. Rees interpreted the Ulster Workers Council strike as a manifestation of Ulster nationalism, which suggested that the British Government's first thoughts were of withdrawal and the establishment of an independent Northern Ireland.[14] In the event, a much more modest option was followed, though in the spirit of allowing the people of Northern Ireland to fend for themselves. A White Paper published in July 1974 proposed the establishment of a Constitutional Convention to see whether the political parties in Northern Ireland could reach agreement among themselves on a form of government acceptable to both communities.[15] But the elections to the Convention, which were held in 1975, under-lined the extent of sectarian polarisation. Even power-sharing without any Irish dimension was opposed by a majority of the members elected. The failure of the Convention[16] resulted in the adoption of a *policy* of direct rule.

The change in British policy was interlinked with developments in security policy and in policy on the treatment of political offenders. In November 1975, in line with the recommendations a year earlier of the Gardiner Committee which had been set up to review the functioning of the Emergency Provisions Act, the Government announced that the granting of special category status to prisoners convicted of politically motivated offences would cease from 1 March 1976. A month later, on 5 December, internment was ended, removing a major grievance of the Catholic community. The new policy entailed dealing with paramilitary organisations through the ordinary processes of law as far as was practicable. In particular, it meant reliance on the courts, though admittedly special courts operating without the benefit of juries. The Government also closed down the incident centres which had been set up in February 1975 to provide a channel of communication with the Provisional IRA in the context of the ceasefire. It henceforth became the settled policy of government not to negotiate with 'terrorists'. Together, these decisions added up to a policy of criminalising the Provisional IRA and other organisations engaged in political violence.

The policy of criminalisation was closely linked to a change in security policy. A review of security policy in the first half of 1976 put the seal on the change, the main elements of which were a policy of police primacy and increased reliance on locally recruited security forces or Ulster-isation, as it was dubbed.[17] The reduction in the British army's role fitted in logically with the emphasis being placed on the ordinary methods of law enforcement. Taken together, criminalisation, police primacy, and Ulsterisation presupposed a gradual return to normality in the province to enable British troops to be withdrawn. In political terms, the policies required conditions of relative political stability that could not be achieved while there was speculation that Britain was contemplating withdrawal from Northern Ireland. A further requirement of political stability as it appeared was that the British Government should refrain from political initiatives since they tended to create uncertainty and to increase the level of tension between the communities. The only policy that could meet these requirements after the failure of the Convention was a long-term commitment to direct rule by the British Government. The new policy was popularly justified as 'the least unacceptable solution'.

To begin with, the policy achieved considerable success both in

Northern Ireland and in Britain. It provided a framework of political certainty that facilitated the expression of the widespread desire within both communities in Northern Ireland for a reduction in the levels of political violence and intercommunity tension. This was reflected in the emergence of the Peace People, a decline in the membership of Loyalist paramilitaries, and a virtual end to sectarian 'tit for tat' killings. The result was a sharp fall in 1977 in the number of fatalities arising out of the Troubles. A strike against security policy in May 1977 divided Unionists and was a failure. There was more or less universal support in the British media for the Government's characterisation of the problem of political violence in the province as one of terrorism. But securing international legitimisation of the policy of direct rule was to prove more difficult, even though concern in the West over the appearance of terrorism in seemingly stable liberal-democracies helped the Government's case initially, as did the publicity which the Peace People received.

In the period leading up to the general election in May 1979, competition between the main British parties to attract the critical votes of the small Ulster Unionist contingent in the House of Commons led to a Government measure increasing Northern Ireland's representation in the House of Commons from 12 to 17, a step sought by the Unionists as compensation for the loss of the province's devolved institutions. For its part, the Conservative Party proposed in its manifesto for the 1979 general election that 'in the absence of devolved government, we will seek to establish one or more elected regional councils with a wide range of powers over local services'.[18] The promise was closely in line with the growing integrationist tendency of the Ulster Unionist Party's parliamentary leadership and readily fitted in with the existing framework of policy. The inter-party competition for Unionist support at Westminster was distracting attention from the fact that the *policy* of direct rule itself was running into difficulties. American pressure on Britain over the policy was intensifying as a result of lobbying by the SDLP and the Irish Government. It was evident that the Provisional IRA was far from being a spent force. A growing scandal over police interrogation methods was eroding confidence in the progress of the return to normality and beginning to cause the Government considerable international embarrassment as a result of investigation of the allegations of ill-treatment by Amnesty International. Finally, the policy of criminalisation was being challenged in the prisons by the refusal of a growing number of political offenders to accept the ending of special category status and their treatment as ordinary criminals.

In spite of these difficulties, the speed and manner of the new Conservative Government's abandonment of the policy was surprising.

It gave the clearest possible signals that it was launching its new political initiative in response to American pressure. There was to be a conference of Northern Ireland's four main parties to discuss devolution within broad guidelines laid down by the British Government and, although the prospects for agreement among the parties were very poor, the Government explicitly cut itself off from any retreat by repudiating the policy of direct rule.[19] The initiative infuriated the leadership of the Ulster Unionist Party, which saw its hopes of integration dashed. The party boycotted the conference. At the same time, the Government tried to restrict consideration of an Irish dimension to ensure the participation of the Democratic Unionist Party (DUP). In the process it alienated the SDLP, although eventually the party did agree to participate in the conference. The Government hoped to put pressure on the parties to narrow their differences by threatening to impose its own settlement if the parties could not reach agreement themselves. The tactic failed as the threat never appeared credible. In any case, the parameters within which the Government hoped that agreed proposals for devolution would emerge provided no clear answer to the problem of the external legitimisation of Northern Ireland's constitutional position, which was one of the main reasons why the policy of direct rule had run into difficulties in the first place.

Much more relevant to this problem was the stance of the Republic of Ireland towards Northern Ireland as a political entity. The policy of British Governments since the fall of the power-sharing Executive in 1974 had been to exclude the Republic from the political affairs of Northern Ireland, while continuing to promote co-operation on security and in other fields. Both Labour Secretaries of State for Northern Ireland, Merlyn Rees and Roy Mason, showed considerable hostility to the Republic's quest for political influence in Northern Ireland and rejected the idea that a solution could be found through Dublin's involvement.[20] This was the lesson that they derived from the UWC strike. The Conservative Government initially adopted the same attitude, though the possibility of movement was foreshadowed by the Government's desire to improve bilateral relations with the Republic in the context of the two countries' membership of the EEC. However, there was no outward change in the Government's stance on Northern Ireland at a summit meeting between Haughey and Thatcher in May 1980, though by this time the Atkins initiative was faltering. The decisive shift in the British Government's position came at the Dublin summit in December 1980.[21] The communiqué after the summit referred in vague terms to giving consideration to 'the totality of relationships'[22] between the two countries. The initial step to this end was the modest one of commissioning joint studies for a further meeting. The British Government hoped that the deliberately ambiguous language of the communiqué and the inclusion of Northern Ireland alongside a range of other bilateral matters would limit the extent of the Loyalist backlash to its change of policy, the essence of which was that Britain accepted that the Republic had a political role to play in the settlement of the conflict.

At the time of the summit a hunger strike of Republican prisoners was in progress and a common explanation given for the change of policy was that Britain needed the Irish Government's goodwill in the context of the prisons issue. Another explanation was that it was an attempt by the Government to restore its authority in Northern Ireland after the failure of the Atkins initiative by impressing on Unionists that the British Government could go over their heads if they were not more amenable to compromise. A further explanation was that the British Government initiated the Anglo-Irish process in order to pre-empt an international campaign by the SDLP to demand the withdrawal of the constitutional guarantee to Unionists as the way to end the deadlock among the Northern Ireland parties. Each of these explanations has a degree of plausibility. In sum they underlined the extent to which the Government had got into difficulties over its policy on Northern Ireland. While the Dublin summit exacerbated the situation within Northern Ireland, leading to increased tensions between the communities, it was very well received in the outside world and especially in the United States, where it was interpreted as a step that might eventually lead to a united Ireland. This stood the Government in good stead in 1981, the year when ten Republican prisoners died in the H-blocks on hunger strike.

The hunger strike was a severe challenge to Britain's international standing over the issue of Northern Ireland. In particular, the mass mobilisation of opinion in Catholic areas behind the prisoners' demands destroyed the credibility in the outside world of the Government's representation of those engaged in political violence in Northern Ireland as terrorists comparable to the Red Army Faction in West Germany or other miniscule violent groups within democratic societies on the continent of Europe.[23] While the strike was in progress it took priority over other areas of policy. In its aftermath, there was considerable relief that the strike had not done even greater damage to Britain's position and particularly that President Reagan had resisted pressure for American intervention. While there was a summit in November 1981 between the British and Irish Prime Ministers and publication of the joint studies commissioned the previous year, a change of government in the Republic and the new Government's pre-occupation with domestic affairs due to its precarious position in the Dáil had reduced the impetus behind the Anglo-Irish process. In addition, from Britain's perspective, FitzGerald's constitutional crusade had temporarily placed the onus for partition on the Republic, reducing the need for the British Government to take any action. The political impact of the strike on Catholic opinion in Northern Ireland was not yet fully apparent.

In September 1981 James Prior, the leading critic within the Cabinet of Thatcher's economic policies, was appointed to the Northern Ireland post. His dispatch to Northern Ireland was widely interpreted as punishment for dissent. Policy on Northern Ireland fell victim to the political ambition of a new Secretary of State for Northern Ireland and to posturing by the Prime Minister. Prior's determination to make a mark in his new job to answer his humiliation was reflected in the speed with which he pressed for a fresh initiative for an internal settlement in Northern Ireland. Although by no means hostile by ideological disposition to the involvement of Dublin, Prior was forced to sacrifice the Irish dimension to get the initiative off the ground. His rationalisation for a fresh initiative was that it would provide a means of rallying moderate opinion in the two communities after the traumatic experience of the hunger strike.[24] The scheme Prior devised, 'rolling devolution', allowed political progress to be made in advance of full agreement among the parties by permitting devolution to take place in stages. Transfer of responsibility could take place in any area if the political parties could reach agreement that it should be controlled locally. But an obvious flaw was that it did not tie in with the Anglo-Irish process, providing the SDLP with a pretext for adopting an abstentionist position in relation to the Assembly, the engine of devolution under Prior's scheme. The simultaneous hostility of integrationists in the Ulster Unionist Party towards the Assembly reduced the political price paid by the SDLP for its hostile attitude towards the initiative. To make matters worse, the British Prime Minister's Parliamentary Private Secretary let it be known that Thatcher did not think much of the scheme and this contributed to its rough passage through the House of Commons.[25] Right-wingers who did not like Prior's liberal attitudes felt free to snipe at the Bill. Their criticism reflected the general ideological competition within the Conservative Party rather than any coherent set of objections to the policy.

The White Paper for 'rolling devolution'[26] was published shortly after Argentina invaded the Falkland Islands at the beginning of April 1982. Irish criticism of the sinking of the *Belgrano* a month later led to a sharp deterioration of relations between Britain and the Republic, further complicating policy towards Northern Ireland. However, there was no attempt to reappraise policy towards Northern Ireland in the light of this development. Posturing took the place of policy-making with the British media publicising the British Prime Minister's fury with the Irish Government and Charles Haughey, in particular. The hostility towards the Republic and the Irish in general that was aroused by the Irish Government's neutrality over the conflict in the South Atlantic was exacerbated by bomb attacks in London in which the Provisional IRA killed eleven soldiers in the Household Cavalry and in the band of the Royal Green Jackets. There were demands at the Conservative Party Conference in October for the disenfranchisement of Irish voters in Britain, demands which the Government actually agreed to consider.[27] Later that same month voters in Northern Ireland went to the polls to elect the Assembly provided for under Prior's scheme. The success of Sinn Fein in winning more than 10 per cent of first preferences came as a profound shock to British public opinion.[28]

The initial impact of the Assembly elections was to make government policy in Northern Ireland more susceptible to Unionist influence. The belief that the SDLP's abstentionist policy in the elections had contributed to Sinn Fein's success had made the SDLP unpopular both in the British press and at Westminster.[29] By contrast, the Unionist parties were able to use the Assembly to put pressure on Prior to adopt a tougher security policy since his standing would have been damaged even further if the Assembly had collapsed as a result of Unionist protests over government failures in this field. A series of incidents in November and December led to speculation that the security forces had been officially authorised to adopt what were dubbed 'shoot to kill' tactics. At the time, the Government appeared willing to claim the credit for a change in policy.[30] But that attitude did not last once the Government began to grasp the political implications of Sinn Fein's challenge to the SDLP's claim to represent the minority; it would be difficult to sustain its claim to be acting as an intermediary between the two communities if it appeared that one of the communities supported a violent campaign against British rule in any form. The reason this mattered was that, for much of international and indeed British opinion, Britain's role as an intermediary constituted the principal, if not only, justification for the British presence in the North.

A new avenue for policy had been opened up by the change of government in the Republic in November 1982. This had brought to power Garret FitzGerald who, unusually for an Irish politician, was popular in Britain. However, the prospect of rapid progress over Northern Ireland in this context had been complicated by an initiative which was launched by the SDLP and which the main parties in the Republic had supported. This was the establishment in May 1983 of the New Ireland Forum. Its purpose was to create a consensus among constitutional nationalists in their stance towards the political future of Northern Ireland. The Forum issued its report in May 1984. While Prior, responding on behalf of the British Government, rejected the three options outlined in the report, he made it clear that the door was open to negotiations between the two Governments over Northern Ireland. The conciliatory tone of his response fuelled Irish expectations that political progress would be made over the question of Northern Ireland at the summit between the British and Irish Prime Ministers due in November 1984. The summit acquired added significance after the Provisional IRA almost succeeded in assassinating the British Prime Minister at the Conservative Party Conference at Brighton in October. In the event, not merely did no significant agreement emerge from the summit but in the dismissive manner in which the British Prime Minister repeated the Government's rejection of the Forum options at the press conference that followed the summit, the impression was given that the British Government placed little value on the Anglo-Irish process itself.

Although the British Government acted quickly to reverse the impression that Thatcher had given at the press conference, the un-favourable international reaction to the outcome of the summit intensified the pressure on Britain to reach an agreement with the Republic on Northern Ireland. The pressure from the United States, where there had been widespread support for the New Ireland Forum proposals, was particularly strong. As early as March 1985 there were clear signals in the British press that a wide-ranging agreement with the Republic over Northern Ireland was being contemplated by the British Government. Such kite-flying was probably intended to test whether there would be an adverse reaction in the UK mainland to concessions to the Republic. On 15 November 1985, less than a year after the debacle at Chequers, the British and Irish Prime Ministers, Margaret Thatcher and Garret FitzGerald, signed the Anglo-Irish Agreement[31] at Hillsborough in Northern Ireland. The essence of the Agreement was the institutionalisation of the Republic's role in Northern Ireland. This went as far as could be reconciled with the claim that there had been no derogation from British sovereignty over Northern Ireland and that could be defended as leaving intact the constitutional guarantee that there would be no change in the province's status without the consent of a majority of the people of Northern Ireland. In the Dáil, FitzGerald penetratingly described the Republic's input as 'beyond a consultative role necessarily, [but] because of the sovereignty issue, falling short of an executive role'.[32]

The constitutional guarantee was reiterated in Article 1 of the Agreement, alongside a commitment that if in the future a majority of people in Northern Ireland wished there to be a united Ireland, effect would be given to their desire. The centrepiece of the Agreement was the establishment of an Intergovernmental Conference concerned with Northern Ireland and relations between the two parts of Ireland. Under

Article 2 of the Agreement, the British Government accepted the right of the Irish Government to 'put forward views and proposals on matters relating to Northern Ireland within the field of activity of the Conference in so far as those matters are not the responsibility of a devolved administration in Northern Ireland'. The Article further provided that 'determined efforts shall be made through the Conference to resolve any differences'. Article 3 laid down that there would be 'regular and frequent ministerial meetings' and provided for the creation of a Secretariat to service the Conference. Article 4 described the Conference as a framework for 'the accommodation of the rights and identities of the two traditions in Northern Ireland' echoing the language of the New Ireland Forum. It also spelt out the support of both Governments for devolution, subject to the consent of the two communities in Northern Ireland. The main issues that would be dealt with by the Conference were described in Articles 5 to 10, underlining its wide scope and alluding to some of the substantive proposals being considered by the two Governments. Article 11 provided for a review of the workings of the Conference after three years or earlier if requested by either Government. Article 12 referred to the possibility of establishing an Anglo-Irish Parliamentary body, while Article 13, the final part of the Agreement, laid down the procedure by which the Agreement would come into force.

The international political significance of the Agreement was underlined by a joint statement of support from President Reagan and the Speaker of the House of Representatives, Tip O'Neill. Similar statements were also issued by the Governments of the member states of the EEC and by Canada, Australia, New Zealand, and Japan. Approval of the Irish Dáil and Seanad followed, while the British House of Commons gave its support to the Agreement by the massive majority of 473 votes to 47 after a debate in the last week of November. In December the Agreement received further endorsements from the European Parliament and from both Houses of Congress in the United States. On 21 December the two Governments registered the Agreement at the United Nations as a binding international treaty. This impressive international underpinning of the Agreement, the result of the strenuous diplomatic efforts of both Governments, stood in marked contrast to the overwhelming hostility of Protestants in Northern Ireland to the Agreement, vividly shown by the huge scale of the demonstration against the Agreement outside Belfast City Hall on 23 November. Indeed, since such opposition was predictable, an obvious implication of the British Government's readiness to enter into the Agreement was that it attached more importance to securing external legitimisation of its position in Northern Ireland than to whether Unionists consented to giving the Republic a role in the North.

The Government's priority was in large part a reflection of how far the conflict in Northern Ireland had become internationalised and of its recognition of this reality.

Much of the early debate on the Agreement centred on the interpretation of Article 1. The British Government placed considerable stress on the fact that the Irish Government had endorsed the proposition that the existing status of Northern Ireland could not be changed without the consent of a majority in Northern Ireland, while Unionists complained that the declaration by the Irish Government was of no value since the Agreement did not explicitly define what that status was and since Articles 2 and 3 of the 1937 Constitution remained in force. The debate was a largely sterile one, for outside the very particular context of a challenge to the Agreement in the Republic's courts, the precise legal meaning of the Agreement in this respect is of little practical significance. The acceptance of the boundaries of the United Kingdom as including Northern Ireland is already implicit in many previous agreements entered into by the Republic, including its accession to the European Economic Community. What mattered was the Republic's political legitimisation of Northern Ireland's status in the context of the Agreement. However, Unionists had little reason to welcome this legitimisation of their position precisely because it was limited to the context of the Agreement, which they believed had effectively altered the political status of Northern Ireland within the United Kingdom. The Agreement did indeed underline that Northern Ireland was different politically from any other part of the United Kingdom, but it was no more than magnifying a difference that was already present in the terms of the constitutional guarantee itself. Northern Ireland had never been more than a conditional part of the United Kingdom.

The paucity of concrete measures that accompanied the establishment of the institutional framework for Anglo-Irish co-operation on Northern Ireland belied the immense political significance of the Agreement. It was never designed to be a quick fix. The Agreement entailed an ongoing commitment by the British and Irish Governments to accept constraints likely to test their political resolve on an almost continual basis. The slow implementation of measures agreed to in principle reflects the difficulties both Governments have encountered in practice. An example is the Irish Government's delay in ratifying a new extradition treaty with Britain because of concern over the administration of justice not just in Northern Ireland but in Britain itself. Because the Agreement provides the Republic with the means of seeking redress for the grievances of the minority, it also by implication puts the Irish Government in a position of sharing responsibility for the conduct of British rule in the North. This responsibility without power enhances the risk of friction between the two Governments over particular episodes or issues. However, provided the disagreements between the two Governments do not call in question the value of the Agreement itself or threaten its existence, such difficulties are likely to be regarded by both Governments as an acceptable price to pay for the benefits that have accrued to Britain and the Republic from the Agreement.

The most fundamental of these benefits is that the functioning of the Agreement largely insulates the domestic political systems of the two countries from Northern Ireland's Troubles, reducing the danger that opinion in either the UK mainland or the Republic will be magnetised by the protagonists in the conflict. In Britain's case this was strongly underlined by the failure of Unionist protests against the Agreement to evoke a sympathetic response. Indeed, the more violently Loyalists protested against the Agreement, the stronger was the desire of British opinion that the province be kept at arm's length and the tighter the grip of the Agreement became.[33]

To the dismay of Unionists there has been no backlash against the Agreement in Britain itself and on the grounds that it permits a foreign state to intrude into the internal affairs of the United Kingdom. Given the strength of patriotic xenophobia in Britain in the 1980s as well as the antipathy that Provisional IRA bombing campaigns targeted there have aroused towards the Irish, the absence of such a backlash requires explanation. Part of the answer is to be found in the clear understanding of British public opinion that Northern Ireland is not part of the British nation or community, even if formally part of the United Kingdom. This understanding is most obviously reflected in the consistency with which British opinion has supported the withdrawal of British troops from Northern Ireland and in its lack of identification with Unionist opposition to a united Ireland. Even before troops were sent to Northern Ireland, a Gallup poll in May 1969 recorded substantial approval for a policy of encouraging unification between the two parts of Ireland.[34] That troops should begin to be withdrawn was the most popular in a list of options as early as November 1971, shortly after the introduction of internment.[35] In June 1974, the month after the fall of the power-sharing Executive, this option was favoured by 59 per cent of respondents.[36] The message of other and subsequent polls has been similar in character. In a survey for the *Sunday Times* in December 1981, 63 per cent of respondents said that they would vote against Northern Ireland remaining part of the United Kingdom if there were a referendum on the issue on a United Kingdom-wide basis, while 54 per cent of respondents favoured withdrawal of troops either immediately or within five years in a poll conducted for *New Society* in September 1981.[37] The Anglo-Irish Agreement appears to have made little difference to opinion. In a poll conducted for the *Daily Express* in February 1987 61 per cent of respondents were in favour of the with-drawal of troops, while only 29 per cent were in favour of Northern Ireland remaining part of the United Kingdom.[39]

Popular sentiment in favour of withdrawal has received little support in the editorial columns of the British press, though the *Daily Mirror* has supported withdrawal at different times as has the *Sunday Times*.[39] At a political level, support for withdrawal has by and large been confined to a minority on the far left of British politics, though there has also been some support for it in the Liberal Party. In particular, at the Liberal Assembly in Harrogate in 1983, a resolution was passed calling for the withdrawal of British troops, their replacement by European or United Nations forces, and the establishment of an All-Ireland Council to work for a united Ireland, though it was carried by only a small majority against the advice of the party leadership.[40]

At its conference in 1981, the Labour Party made Irish unity the long-term objective of its policy, but accepted that it could only be achieved with the consent of a majority of people in Northern Ireland.[41] By couching Labour's support for the constitutional guarantee in a new form, the party hoped to head off the challenge presented by the growth in support on the Left of the party for Sinn Fein. It was with some relief that the party leadership endorsed the approach of the Anglo-Irish Agreement, which was supported by an overwhelming majority of Labour MPs in the House of Commons vote. However, Labour spokesmen have caused some embarrassment to the Government by suggesting that the Agreement represents a step towards a united Ireland.[41] Opinion at Conservative Party Conferences has reflected more accurately than the other parties the anti-Irish feelings that have been engendered in Britain by the conflict in Northern Ireland. However, such attitudes have not resulted in any greater support for the Unionist case on Northern Ireland, since Ulster Protestants are themselves seen as Irish by most people in Britain. Indeed, it is evident from the responses given to other questions that hostility towards the Irish rather than any sympathy with the claims of Irish nationalism, let alone Republicanism, constitutes the principal motivation behind public support for the withdrawal of troops.[43]

The strength of support for withdrawal also reflects the absence of any obvious British stake in the retention *per se* of the constitutional link with Northern Ireland. The circumstances in which the Labour Government was advised in 1949 that 'it has become a matter of strategic importance to this country that the North should continue to form part of His Majesty's Dominions'[44] are no longer relevant in the strategic environment of the 1980s. Even an upgrading of the role of conventional defences and greatly reduced reliance on nuclear deterrence could not restore the importance that the defence of the Atlantic sea lanes and Ireland's role in that context had 40 years ago. It is notable that opponents of British rule in Northern Ireland have paid far more attention to the strategic issue as an explanation for Britain's continued presence than have Ministers in defending Britain's role in Northern Ireland. If a persuasive strategic case existed for the retention of the link, it would clearly be to the advantage of the British Government both domestically and internationally to advertise the fact. A positive British strategic interest in the Union is also difficult to reconcile with the frequency of the Government's declarations of its readiness to see a change in the status of Northern Ireland if that is the wish of its inhabitants. The one context (mentioned in Chapter 1) in which strategic considerations have been alluded to by Ministers has been in reference to the possible consequences of British withdrawal from Northern Ireland in circumstances of continuing conflict in the North.

The emphasis given by Republicans and by sections of the British Left to the strategic argument is an indirect acknowledgment that the maintenance of the Union cannot be explained by any economic interest on Britain's part in the retention of Northern Ireland within the United Kingdom. The scale of British subventions to Northern Ireland, approximately £1 billion in 1985-86,[45] underlines the extent to which the province has become a burden on the British exchequer. The weakness of strategic and economic explanations for the retention of Northern Ireland within the United Kingdom and the absence of strong ties of sentiment between mainland opinion and the people of the province lead Anthony Kenny to suggest that the only argument that remains for maintaining the Union is a moral one. In *The Road to Hillsborough* he argues that 'the Union must be preserved because, for the foreseeable future, the alternative to preserving it would be a catastrophe for the inhabitants of the province'.[46] This not merely elevates crisis management into an end in itself, but appears to accept that the containment of the conflict will continue to be the essential basis of British policy in the future. While Kenny is realistic in implying that the Anglo-Irish Agreement has not fundamentally changed Britain's role within Northern Ireland, the explanation of the British presence in terms simply of a disinterested desire to avert bloodshed is unpersuasive. It is also distinctly double-edged from the perspective of Unionists, since presumably there is an upper limit to the sacrifice that might reasonably be expected of any country in acting as an intermediary between hostile communities.

Britain's departure from Palestine in 1948 is an analogy that has been taken up by British advocates of withdrawal from Northern Ireland.[47] But the analogy with Palestine breaks down because a majority of people of Northern Ireland do not want Britain to leave. That is Britain's difficulty. The question why Britain stays in Northern Ireland is misleading so long as it implies that Britain has an overriding motive for remaining in Northern Ireland that is independent of the wishes of the province's inhabitants. The Anglo-Irish Agreement has underlined that Britain has no wish to encourage Unionists in their desire to remain British[48] and that Unionist wishes are seen for the most part as an obstacle to what Britain wants. That is an end to a situation in which Britain attracts not merely criticism, but, as the Liberal Party leader, David Steel, put it on a visit to Belfast in 1984, 'odium in many parts of the world'.[49] Quite how deeply such international disapproval is felt in Britain is apparent in Kenny's analysis of the Anglo-Irish Agreement.

> But even if, in the worst case, the Hillsborough agreement were to be brought down, it would have achieved, irreversibly, something of historic significance. It has shown the world that the problem of Northern Ireland is not caused by the presence of British administrators and British soldiers. No one who has followed events since Hillsborough can believe that the province's troubles would end by a simple withdrawal of British power.[50]

This view takes too little account of the reality that the Agreement owes much of its international popularity to the fact that it is interpreted as being the first step towards a united Ireland and a British withdrawal.

What remains to be explained is why the principle of consent by itself has proved so effective in sustaining a British commitment to the province. Part of the answer is to be found in the nature of British political culture. The idea of consent, loyalty to the Crown, and an ethnocentric notion of kith and kin have played an important role in the actual definition of who the British are as a community in the absence of the usual emphasis on the state or on territoriality as the basis of national identity. By implication, the political rights and obligations of being British are not confined to a state with fixed boundaries. Consequently, defence of the rights of free British subjects, wherever they be, against the imposition of alien rule has much the same power to arouse patriotic feeling in Britain as does defence of the national territory in other countries. The principle of consent is too closely bound up with the justification of such rights to be wantonly discarded even in the case of a 'pestilent province'.[51] This represents an important, if generally concealed, constraint on British policy towards Northern Ireland.

Policy towards other territorially defined parts of the United Kingdom such as Scotland and Wales constitutes, in principle, the closest analogy with British policy in Northern Ireland. At first sight, the question of the desirability of devolved institutions in Northern

Ireland seems to have been considered by government totally independently of official attitudes towards devolution for Scotland or Wales. The most 'integrationist' phase of British policy in Northern Ireland, reliance on unadorned direct rule, took place for the most part during the tenure of a Labour Government committed to devolution in Scotland and Wales, while the centralist Thatcher Administration has persistently sought to bring about devolution in the case of Northern Ireland. But given the lack of enthusiasm in Britain for the option of the integration of Northern Ireland into the United Kingdom, the establishment of Scottish and Welsh Assemblies would quite obviously deal a blow to integrationist aspirations in Northern Ireland, since it would make it still more difficult for them to achieve their aim of bringing about the disappearance of Northern Ireland as a separate political entity by dissolving it into a centralised United Kingdom state. But could Northern Ireland's fate as a political entity serve as a precedent for Scotland and Wales? The effect that a British decision simply to abandon Northern Ireland might have on the strength and, more importantly, character of Scottish and Welsh nationalism constitutes a possible additional argument against the option of unilateral withdrawal.

A slightly less obvious comparison than that of policies towards different regions of the United Kingdom is one between British rule in Northern Ireland and the treatment of contested British dependencies outside of the British Isles, particularly the cases of the Falkland Islands, Hong Kong, and Gibraltar. The fate of these territories under the Thatcher Government forms a particularly instructive parallel with policy towards Northern Ireland. It also highlights very clearly in what circumstances the conflict in Northern Ireland might pose a threat to the stability of the whole of the United Kingdom. In each case, the issue of the consent of the inhabitants has been at the very heart of the problem, an obstacle in the case of dependent territories to Britain's desire to divest itself of potentially costly imperial responsibilities in a post-colonial age.

Shortly after the Conservatives came to power in May 1979, the Foreign Secretary, Lord Carrington, recommended the opening of negotiations with Argentina over its claim to the Falkland Islands, but the Prime Minister insisted they be postponed until after the settlement of the Rhodesian issue. The solution favoured by the Foreign Office was a leaseback arrangement whereby Britain would continue to administer the islands but under Argentinian sovereignty. In the event, when the Foreign Secretary's deputy, Nicholas Ridley, clumsily raised the possibility of leaseback in the House of Commons in December 1980 after a visit to the islands, he received an extremely hostile reception from all sides of the House to the effect that such a transfer of sovereignty would be contrary to the wishes of the islanders. The Government was forced to declare that there could be no coercion of the islanders over the issue of leaseback. This blow to the possibility of a negotiated settlement was one of the factors that led to Argentina's invasion of the islands in April 1982. It took a victorious war to recapture the islands to expunge the humiliation. The consequence has been that the 1,800 inhabitants of the Falkland Islands have been given a veto over any change in their status, regardless of the cost to Britain of a continuation of the *status quo*.[52]

The Thatcher Government was more successful in its handling of the issue of Hong Kong. The fact that under the 1898 Peking Convention part of the territory automatically reverted back to China in 1997, the eagerness of the Chinese Government to demonstrate its capacity to accommodate different social systems within the country's borders for economic reasons, and the recognition by Hong Kong Chinese that the racial issue constituted an obstacle to the sympathy of metropolitan opinion were all factors that helped to bring the negotiations over the future transfer of Hong Kong to China to a successful conclusion in September 1984. The issue of the consent of the inhabitants of the territory to the agreement was handled by the establishment of an Assessment Office to test the acceptability of the arrangements for the transfer agreed between the two Governments. On the basis of some 2,500 submissions from local organisations and individuals, it concluded that the terms were acceptable to a majority of the inhabitants *largely because they regarded the transfer of the territory to China as inevitable*.[53]

No agreement has yet been reached with Spain over Gibraltar, the subject of patriotic fervour in Britain in the 1960s, when Franco challenged the status of the territory. The first indication that Britain might be willing to discuss the issue of sovereignty with Spain was the somewhat ambiguously worded Lisbon Agreement in 1980 which linked the possibility of negotiations on the whole problem to a lifting of the Spanish blockade of the territory. And negotiations began in 1985 after Spain finally ended all restrictions on movement between Spain and Gibraltar in response to Britain's explicit agreement to negotiate on the issue of sovereignty. The obvious contrast is with Britain's refusal since the war in 1982 to enter into negotiations with Argentina over the issue of sovereignty over the Falkland Islands, notwithstanding the weight of world opinion behind Argentina's demand for talks. Admittedly, at every stage in its talks with Spain the British Government has insisted that it will honour the wishes of the inhabitants of Gibraltar in any settlement. However, the absence of opposition in the House of Commons to the principle of talks with Spain on Gibraltar's sovereignty clearly limits their effective political leverage.

The Falklands case provides the parallel with the conflict in Northern

Ireland that must cause the most concern to the Foreign Office. In particular, were the Unionists in Northern Ireland to be Falklandised as a result of Republican atrocities directed either at them or at members of the British establishment and were public opinion in Britain then to demand the elimination at any cost of the Republican threat to Northern Ireland's status as part of the United Kingdom, the political pressure on the Government to adopt a policy such as Brian Crozier's 'strategy for victory'[54] entailing hot pursuit across the Irish Border, internment, capital punishment, and interrogation in depth, might prove irresistible. The consequences for the country's relations with the United States and with Europe would clearly be catastrophic. Indeed, in such circumstances, the strategy's inevitable failure would pose a lethal threat to the political stability of the United Kingdom as a whole. Such magnetisation of British public opinion by the conflict has been a lingering hope of Unionists since the Troubles began. The Falklands war itself emphasised that British opinion gave a greater priority to the defence of a tiny British colony in the South Atlantic than to that of a part of the United Kingdom and therefore intensified Unionist bitterness, while also raising hopes that such patriotic fervour might one day be harnessed to their cause. These hopes were finally dashed by the Anglo-Irish Agreement and the total absence of any sympathetic response in Britain to Unionist protests against it. The ironic role of the Falklands factor was that it so wrapped the Prime Minister in the flag as to make her politically invulnerable to patriotic criticism of the Anglo-Irish Agreement. The Hong Kong and Gibraltar cases are most obviously relevant to Unionist anxieties that the British Government will seek to use the Anglo-Irish Agreement to lever the province into a position where a majority can be induced to acquiesce in a united Ireland. Such anxieties tend to produce an accentuation of the sectarian divide as, in the last resort, the solidarity of the Protestant community is seen as the most reliable barrier to the construction of consent to a united Ireland. It seems extremely unlikely that such anxieties can be fully allayed whatever the British Government does, given the fact that sections of British political opinion as well as international opinion see the Agreement in precisely this light, in other words, as a stepping stone to Irish unity.

The impact on Northern Ireland of Unionist opposition to the Agreement has meant that the Agreement's objectives of peace, reconciliation, and stability have had a rather hollow ring within the province itself. In the months following the Agreement there was a marked rise in sectarian tensions, reflected in widespread incidence of intimidation and an increase in the level of political violence of all kinds. Notwithstanding the slow implementation of measures under the Agreement, it has benefited constitutional nationalism politically, helping the SDLP to expand its representation in the House of Commons from one to three.[55] The other side of the coin has been a decline in electoral support for violent Republicanism as represented by Sinn Fein. This relatively modest shift in opinion among the minority is by no means all the British Government has gained from the Agreement inside Northern Ireland. Part of the political background to the Agreement was the gradual erosion of Britain's role as an effective buffer between the sectarian factions in Northern Ireland. As a result of the failure of successive British political initiatives, the British state came to appear less as a positive political presence within the province, standing above the centrifugal forces of sectarianism, than as a weak intermediary unable to impose its will and too vulnerable to pressure to seem neutral. For this reason, the Agreement was significant not just as a recognition that British policy needs the involvement and support of the Republic of Ireland, but, paradoxically, also as a reassertion of British authority in the province.

However, the change wrought in Britain's role in Northern Ireland by the Agreement should not be exaggerated. The parameters of British policy remain much the same. Crisis management is still the most apposite description of how Britain governs the province. Notwithstanding the partial sharing of responsibility with the Republic, the burden of governing Northern Ireland has not diminished. Indeed, because of the constraints on British policy under the Agreement, it has grown in some respects. In particular, the Agreement has reduced the legitimacy of the role played by the British Government in Northern Ireland among Unionists. At the same time, there is very little prospect of a change in that role through the establishment of political institutions and processes with the requisite widespread support in both communities. The difficulty does not only lie in Unionist opposition to operating within the framework of the Agreement. For all the gains made by constitutional nationalism under the Agreement, the SDLP remains unwilling to accord the police more than qualified legitimacy and its commitment to Northern Ireland's continued existence as a political entity remains at best muted. In short, Britain is no closer to finding an answer to the problem of Northern Ireland's lack of *internal legitimacy*. Indeed, the priority given by government to damage limitation in its handling of affairs in the province is an acknowledgment of the improbability of such a breakthrough. The Agreement has been helpful in the *external legitimisation* of Britain's role, though it has by no means eliminated the embarrassment Britain suffers internationally as a result of its presence in Northern Ireland. Britain's most important initiative since the Troubles began, the Anglo-Irish Agreement, is very much less than a solution to the conflict. At most, it holds out the prospect that what happens in Northern Ireland matters less.

6.

THE SOUTH AND THE NORTH

THE view that Southern irredentism is one of the principal causes of political violence in Northern Ireland dominates Unionist interpretations of the Northern Ireland conflict. Thus, Unionists see the South's claim to the North, enshrined in the country's 1937 constitution, as providing much of the inspiration for the Provisional IRA's campaign of violence. They also see it as the essential basis of Southern policies towards the conflict in Northern Ireland.[1] Article 2 of the 1937 constitution asserts that 'the national territory consists of the whole island of Ireland, its islands and the territorial seas', though this is coupled with the acceptance in Article 3 that in practice the sovereignty of the state is limited to 26 counties, 'pending the re-integration of the national territory'. While Unionists stress the practical import of these Articles, they constitute for the South an expression of the symbolic importance of the goal of unification rather than a statement of the practical significance of the issue in the Republic.

While the aspirational nature of the goal has not precluded strategies aimed at the actual achievement of unification, thereby confirming Unionist fears of Southern intentions, these have been pursued within limits that rule out both the use of physical force and giving the goal of unification a priority over policies for the South itself. If an overriding priority were given to the objective of Irish unity, failure might detract from the legitimacy of the Southern state by demonstrating its powerlessness to achieve the goal. Such an outcome would be profoundly disturbing for Southern society because of the role nationalism has played in the development of its consensus. As a symbol or aspiration, the goal of unification has served to underwrite *both* the legitimacy of the Southern state *and* the illegitimacy of partition, without obvious risk to the Republic's own stability. The low priority for unity at the level of practical policy also reflects the Southern public's low expectation that the goal can be achieved in the medium term.[2] This was very evident both during the 1983 referendum campaign on an amendment to the constitution prohibiting abortion, which was passed, and during the 1986 campaign on a proposal to remove the constitutional bar to divorce, which was defeated. In neither case did the issue of how Protestants in Northern Ireland might react to the outcome of the voting carry any weight with the Southern electorate.

The Republic's policy towards Northern Ireland has undergone several shifts in the course of the last two decades, a period that has encompassed seven general elections in the South and as many changes in the country's political leadership. In summary, they were as follows. The Republic's initial reaction to the breakdown of law and order in the North was to place the blame on partition and to seek international intervention in the conflict. This strongly nationalist phase of policy came to an end with the dismissal in May 1970 of two members of the Government over charges of gun-running. After a period during which the Government attempted to return to the policy of functional co-operation it had pursued towards the North prior to the Troubles, the imposition of direct rule in Northern Ireland paved the way to a new phase of policy and the opening up of a dialogue over Northern Ireland with the British Government. This culminated in the Sunningdale Agreement and the establishment of a power-sharing Executive in Northern Ireland. After the collapse of the Executive, there followed a period during which the main priority of Southern policy was the defence of the Republic's own stability.

This phase was superseded by a diplomatic quest to influence British policy in response to growing dissatisfaction of constitutional nationalists in Northern Ireland with the policy of direct rule. International pressure on the British Government to grant a role to the South in the evolution of its policy towards Northern Ireland was eventually successful and led to the initiation of the Anglo-Irish process in 1980. This new dialogue broke down as a result of British reaction to the Republic's neutrality during the Falklands conflict, but was resumed after Garret FitzGerald's victory in the Republic's general election of November 1982. It eventually resulted in the Anglo-Irish Agreement of November 1985. In Opposition Fianna Fáil voted against the Agreement but after the party's victory in the Republic's general election of February 1987, it readily accepted the new arrangements in Government. The result is that there is now a general consensus among the Republic's main political parties on policy towards Northern Ireland.

The onset of the Troubles in Northern Ireland in 1968 and 1969 constituted a fundamental challenge to Southern rhetoric on the issue of partition at a time when the grievance of partition appeared to be losing its salience in the Republic's politics. The reversal of policies of economic protectionism that went back to the 1930s, the 1965 free trade agreement with Britain, and the prospect of membership of the European Economic Community contributed to a change in the approach of the Irish Government to the issue of partition during the 1960s. In place of the attempt that had been made in the late 1940s and during the 1950s to mobilise international opinion against Britain over partition, the emphasis switched to a quest to improve North-South relations through functional co-operation. This was the context of the historic meeting at Stormont between the Taoiseach, Sean Lemass, and the Prime Minister of Northern Ireland, Terence O'Neill in January 1965. O'Neill's commitment to reform in the North was a further factor easing the way to a change of policy in the South. The influence of the new approach was also reflected in the unanimous recommendation of a parliamentary committee on the Constitution in 1967 that the wording of Article 3 of the constitution should be amended to be less offensive to Unionists in the North.[3] However, the Government failed to act on the recommendation, which would have required a referendum.

The first serious incidence of mass unrest in the North occurred on 5 to 7 October 1968 in Londonderry (or Derry as nationalists refer to the city). The Taoiseach, Jack Lynch, who had succeeded Lemass as the Republic's Prime Minister in November 1966, reacted to the riots in a speech on 8 October in which he identified as the root cause of the dissension in the North 'the partition of our country against the wishes of the overwhelming majority of the Irish People'[4], though this was tempered by references to the need for internal reforms in Northern Ireland. Inevitably his speech provoked a hostile response from Northern Unionists, threatening the new détente between North and South. Following talks later that month between the Taoiseach and leaders of Catholic opinion in the North in which they indicated that they were seeking Westminster intervention to promote internal reforms, Lynch himself placed greater emphasis on reform within Northern Ireland and on developing cross-border co-operation at a meeting of the national executive of Fianna Fáil in November. Despite further violence in the first half of 1969 and despite the resignation of O'Neill in April, the instability in Northern Ireland was not an issue in the South's general election in June, although it was already apparent that there were divisions within Fianna Fáil over what approach to take to the crisis in Northern Ireland. The main challenge to Fianna Fáil in the election came from a resurgent Labour Party emphasising its commitment to socialism. In the event, an increase in the Labour vote did not translate into gains in seats and Fianna Fáil was re-elected with a comfortable overall majority, despite a fall of over 2 per cent in its share of first preference votes.

The tensions between the communities as the summer of 1969 approached gave rise to widespread anxiety that the traditional Loyalist parades would spark off civil disturbances and that the province's security forces would be severely stretched. The anxiety filtered through to the Irish Government which sent a message to the British Government expressing the fear that the Apprentice Boys parade in Londonderry on 12 August, in particular, would provoke further violence. However, despite many similar predictions of trouble, the Northern Ireland Government declined to ban the parade. The march led to a general breakdown of law and order in the city and disturbances in other parts of the province in reaction to the events in Londonderry. On the evening of 13 August, the Taoiseach broadcast to the Republic on the Troubles in Northern Ireland, declaring that 'the Irish Government can no longer stand by and see innocent people injured or worse'.[5] He explained that the Irish army had been directed to set up field hospitals close to the Border to provide treatment for those who had been injured in the riots and who were unable or unwilling to seek help in Northern Ireland.

Lynch also announced that the Irish Government had requested the British Government to apply to the United Nations for the dispatch of a peacekeeping force to Northern Ireland. He said that the employment of British troops would be neither acceptable to nationalists, nor successful in restoring the peace. In the event, British troops were deployed on the streets of Londonderry the following day, 14 August. None the less the Irish Government persisted with its attempt to get a United Nations peacekeeping force sent to the province despite the British Government's rejection of the idea. A letter was sent from Ireland's Permanent Representative at the United Nations to the President of the Security Council on 17 August, requesting an urgent meeting of the Council. It met on 20 August to consider the request. The British representative spoke against placing the issue on the Council's agenda on the grounds that events in Northern Ireland were an internal matter as the province was an integral part of the United Kingdom and therefore consideration of the Irish request would be contrary to Article 2(7) of the United Nations Charter. The British response highlighted a major drawback of the Republic's attempt to internationalise the issue. Since an appeal to the principle of domestic jurisdiction constituted Britain's best defence of its actions in Northern Ireland in a formal international setting, pressing Britain over the issue in a context such as the United Nations ran the risk of eliciting a stronger commitment by Britain to the Union as a way of underpinning its claim that the matter was indeed an internal question.

In the event, after the Irish Minister for External Affairs, Patrick Hillery, had been permitted to address the Security Council, a proposal by the Zambian representative that the Council adjourn was carried, thus avoiding a vote on the substance of the British contention but also effectively shelving the Irish initiative. On 5 September the Republic's Permanent Representative wrote to the Secretary General of the United Nations asking for the situation in Northern Ireland to be included on the agenda of the General Assembly. An accompanying memorandum put forward the view that unless the causes of unrest in the North were tackled there could be serious consequences for the whole island. The outcome was similar to that in the Security Council. On 17 September the General Committee of the Assembly decided to defer whether to recommend the inclusion of the item on the agenda of the next session of the General Assembly, while on 20 September the General Assembly took note of this decision. That was the end of the Republic's attempt to internationalise the conflict through the machinery of the United Nations, at least at a formal level. In his account of the Security Council's deliberations on the issue, Andrew Boyd suggests that the Irish Government was fully aware of what the likely outcome of its approach to the United Nations would be and that its real purposes had been impressing opinion at home and gaining a platform to air its views on the conflict so as to increase external pressures on the British Government to force reforms on the Unionists.[6]

Lynch's other initiative was to establish a Northern sub-committee within the Cabinet consisting of three Ministers from Border constituencies and the Minister for Finance, Charles Haughey, who had relatives in Northern Ireland. The original purpose of the sub-committee was simply to collect information, but after the Cabinet agreed to provide funds of £100,000 from the exchequer for the relief of distress, it became the vehicle for the expenditure of this money. Some of the money was spent on the establishment of a Propaganda Corps to mount a publicity campaign against partition. This included the financing of a paper, *The Voice of the North*, which campaigned against the existing leadership of the IRA and gave support to the establishment of the Provisional IRA.[7] Some of the money was also used in an attempt to import arms with the purpose of supplying them to Northern nationalists. In the context of the time this was less surprising than it appears now.

The Government had not yet developed a clear view of events in the North, let alone formulated a consistent set of policies on how it should respond to what was happening. An invasion of Northern Ireland had even been considered as an option at one point. The threat of a pogrom against Catholics in Northern Ireland appeared so real in the closing months of 1969 that public opinion supported the turning of a blind eye to paramilitary activities connected with the defence of the North's nationalist ghettoes. Nationalist politics in Northern Ireland were themselves in a state of flux and it was natural that Ministers in the Republic most closely interested in their development should wish to exercise a measure of influence over their future direction. The minority's need for arms appeared to provide them with that opportunity. However, once it appeared that the threat to Catholics from Loyalist mobs had been greatly exaggerated, revelation of the involvement of Ministers in the machinations of paramilitary organisations was bound to cause a political scandal.

On 6 May 1970 the Taoiseach sacked two members of the Northern sub-committee from his Cabinet, Charles Haughey and Neil Blaney. A third Cabinet Minister, Kevin Boland, resigned in protest at the sackings. Haughey and Blaney were later charged with conspiracy to import arms and ammunition into the Republic. The case against Blaney was dismissed on the ground of insufficient evidence before it came to trial. Haughey was acquitted after a sensational trial. The arms crisis shook but did not bring down the Government. Fianna Fáil rallied to the support of the Taoiseach, Jack Lynch. In the aftermath of the arms crisis, policy on Northern Ireland reverted to an emphasis on functional co-operation as a way of bringing the two parts of Ireland together. In particular, Lynch took the initiative in launching negotiations between North and South on cross-border co-operation during 1971. The Taoiseach also emphasised the need for reform in the Republic so as to reduce Unionist fears of a united Ireland, while the Government continued to make representations to the British Government through diplomatic channels over issues causing concern in the minority community in the North. However, it found the Conservative Government, which had been elected in June 1970, for the most part unreceptive to both its pleas and its warnings.

This low-key approach by the Republic to the conflict was brought to an end by the introduction of internment in Northern Ireland in August 1971. Its effect on Southern opinion mirrored its radicalising impact on Catholic attitudes in the North. There was a sharp deterioration in relations between Britain and the Republic as a result of the Irish Government's orchestration of international protests against British policy in Northern Ireland and its support for passive resistance in the province.[8] The climate was further soured by a scandal over methods of interrogation being employed in Northern Ireland and by the Irish Government's decision to initiate proceedings against the British Government under the European Convention on Human Rights. However, the nadir in relations between the two countries was reached in February 1972 when the British Embassy in Dublin was burnt down by a mob in the protests that followed Bloody Sunday. An easing of the tension began within weeks of this episode as a result of the strong signals from the British Government that a major political initiative on Northern Ireland was under consideration.[9] The imposition of direct rule on 24 March 1972 to clear the way for the creation of a new political dispensation in Northern Ireland went beyond Dublin's expectations and brought about a marked improvement in relations. The change in the relationship was underlined in October 1972 by the issue of a discussion paper in which the British Government formally acknowledged for the first time the existence of an 'Irish dimension' to the problem.[10] By this was meant that the British Government accepted the principle that the Republic had a legitimate interest in the conflict in Northern Ireland. In effect, Britain had acceded to the Republic's claim to be the 'second guarantor'[11] of the minority in Northern Ireland. The new relationship was also cemented by steps taken by the Republic, including the enactment in December 1972 of emergency legislation directed at the activities of Republican paramilitaries and the passage by referendum in the same month of an amendment to the constitution deleting the reference in the 1937 Constitution to the special position of the Catholic Church. The former was hastened by explosions in Dublin that killed two people and injured 127.

By the time that the British Government published its constitutional proposals for the province in a White Paper in March 1973[12], there had been a change of government in Dublin as a result of a general election in the Republic. Fianna Fáil had been defeated by a coalition of Fine Gael and Labour. The new Government was hurriedly consulted on the contents of the White Paper shortly before publication. The White Paper included a proposal to establish a Council of Ireland, an idea that went back to the 1920 Government of Ireland Act. This was taken a stage further in the Sunningdale Agreement of December 1973. The Agreement was in the form of a joint communiqué issued after a conference of the British and Irish Governments and the prospective members of the Northern Ireland power-sharing Executive. The communiqué outlined in detail what the institutional arrangements for the functioning of the proposed Council of Ireland would be. The problem of extradition, which was a source of friction between North and South, was addressed by an agreement to establish a joint law commission to recommend the most effective means of ensuring that the Border was no longer a barrier to the prosecution of politically motivated crimes of violence. The communiqué also included a declaration by the Irish Government that it 'fully accepted that there could be no change in the status of Northern Ireland until a majority of the people of Northern Ireland desired a change in that status', while for its part the British Government indicated that 'if, in the future, the majority of the people of Northern Ireland should indicate a wish to become part of a united Ireland', it 'would support that wish'.[13]

At the time, the Sunningdale Agreement was a triumph for the Republic of Ireland. It underscored British acceptance of the legitimacy of the idea of a united Ireland, a notion central to the nationalist consensus in Southern society. At the same time, the practical limitations on the functioning of the proposed Council of Ireland, including the unanimity rule on decision-making by the joint Council of Ministers, were as much a protection for the South from unwanted intrusion of the North into its affairs as they were a safeguard for Unionists. However, the fragility of the whole arrangement soon became apparent. An early embarrassment for the Irish Government was a challenge to the constitutionality of the Agreement by Kevin Boland, who claimed that its acceptance of the principle that the status of Northern Ireland could not be changed without the consent of a majority in Northern Ireland was in conflict with Articles 2 and 3 of the 1937 Constitution. The Government's successful but politically damaging defence relied on the technicality that the communiqué embodying the Sunningdale Agreement had no standing in law and that consequently the issue of a conflict with the constitution did not arise. In Northern Ireland, where hostility towards the Sunningdale Agreement had become the very effective rallying cry of opponents of the newly inaugurated power-sharing Executive, the episode reduced still further the value that Unionists placed on the Republic's assurances.

The collapse of the power-sharing Executive and with it the Sunningdale Agreement was a traumatic period for the Republic. Shortly after the UWC strike began, 31 people were killed and 150 injured by car bombs in Dublin and Monaghan. In the wake of the fall of the Executive, there was discernible disenchantment in the Republic with all shades of opinion in Northern Ireland. The mood of disillusionment was captured by the Taoiseach, Liam Cosgrave, when he declared that violence in the North was killing the South's desire for unity.[14] The change in mood was reflected in the altered priorities of the Government's policy towards Northern Ireland. Defence of the security of the state was given clear precedence over the pursuit of the goal of Irish unity. The South's loss of confidence as a result of the failure of Sunningdale was reflected in preoccupation with potential threats to the state through the mid 1970s. A large rise in the number of bank robberies due to 'fund-raising' by paramilitary organisations, and incidents such as the kidnapping of a Dutch businessman, Tiede Herrema, in October 1975 and the assassination of the British Ambassador in Dublin in July 1976 increased fears of a spill-over of the North's Troubles into the South, and damaged the Republic's reputation of political stability. As in Britain, the public's fear of violence emanating from Northern Ireland overrode its concern that the measures being adopted by the Government to meet the threat represented an erosion of civil liberties.

While opinion in the Republic was inclined to blame lack of

resolution on the part of Britain's minority Labour Government for the failure, the lesson that much of British political opinion drew was that the involvement of the Republic through the Council of Ireland had wrecked the power-sharing experiment. These perspectives were to play a part in the evolution of the two Governments' policies towards the conflict. However, of more immediate concern to the Irish Government than judgments about the past was discerning what Britain's next step would be. To the very considerable alarm of the Irish Government, it appeared that the British Government was contemplating withdrawal and the establishment of an independent Northern Ireland. In 1983, Merlyn Rees, who had been the British Secretary of State for Northern Ireland in the mid 1970s, revealed that the Irish Government had actually sought assurances from the British Government in 1974 that it would not withdraw from Northern Ireland.[15] The story caused considerable embarrassment in Dublin and brought denials that the British Government had been approached in quite the terms described by Rees. The embarrassment was understandable. From the perspective of Irish nationalist ideology, to demand that Britain stay in a part of Ireland was clearly heretical in any circumstances.

Uncertainty over British intentions persisted into 1975 and 1976 because the obvious question the Constitutional Convention prompted was how the British Government would respond to its readily predictable failure. Throughout this period of flux the British Government showed little interest in consulting Dublin, although the Irish Government for its part continued to support the principle of power-sharing and persisted with the commitments it had entered into on security under the Sunningdale Agreement. By contrast, to the Irish Government's considerable annoyance, the British Government entered into indirect negotiations with the Provisional IRA. But the British Government's eventual adoption of direct rule as a long-term policy finally ended the doubts over its intentions. From the Irish Government's perspective, the dispelling of uncertainty was the new policy's only merit. Dublin continued to be excluded from any influence on policies in Northern Ireland, while the influence of constitutional nationalists also waned. By contrast, that of Unionists grew both as a result of the Government's anxiety to avoid a repeat of the 1974 UWC strike and as a result of the position at Westminster where the Government depended on the votes of other parties in the House of Commons to stay in office and was keen to improve its odds of survival.

It was against this background of nationalist weakness that a new strategy emerged in which the Irish Government and the SDLP, particularly in the person of John. Hume, looked outside the British Isles to the United States and to Europe to secure diplomatic support for the constitutional nationalist case as a way of exerting pressure on the British Government. An important feature of the strategy was the care with which this case was distinguished both from traditional anti-partitionist opposition to the British presence in Northern Ireland and from any association with support for the activities of Republican para-militaries. The strategy achieved its most significant diplomatic break-through on 30 August 1977 when President Carter issued a policy statement on Northern Ireland. The statement promised American economic assistance for Northern Ireland following the achievement of a settlement commanding widespread support in Northern Ireland and which enjoyed the support of the Irish Government. Criticism of Britain's policy of direct rule and of the exclusion of the Republic from a role in Northern Ireland was implied rather than stated.

The circumstances in which the statement had been issued underlined the continuity of the Republic's policy towards Northern Ireland. In June 1977 the Coalition Government of Fine Gael and Labour had been crushingly defeated by Fianna Fáil in a general election. By that time much of the groundwork for Carter's statement had already been laid. Lynch, who was Taoiseach again, carried the initiative through to a successful conclusion. However, the larger purpose of the diplomatic effort was not achieved in the short term. The intervention of the American Administration brought no change in British policy towards Northern Ireland. All Lynch received in talks with the British Prime Minister, James Callaghan, in September 1977 was an assurance that Britain was not contemplating integration as a solution to the conflict. However, both the Irish Government and the SDLP persisted in their diplomatic campaign for a political initiative. By the time of the British general election of May 1979 the international pressure on Britain to alter course was substantial.

The announcement in October 1979 by the new Secretary of State for Northern Ireland, Humphrey Atkins, that a constitutional conference of Northern Ireland's main political parties would be held, signalled Britain's change of course. However, the initiative was unsatisfactory from the perspective of the Irish Government and the SDLP since the conference's terms of reference specifically included rejection of an Irish dimension. A formula was none the less found that made it possible for take part in the conference in these circumstances resulted in the resignation of the leader of the SDLP, Gerry Fitt. His successor was John Hume, who insisted that any settlement had to have an Irish dimension. A formula was none the less found that made it possible for the SDLP to participate in the conference despite its stance on this issue. Shortly after Fitt's resignation, Jack Lynch resigned as Taoiseach and leader of Fianna Fáil in December 1979. His successor was Charles Haughey, one of the Cabinet Ministers Lynch had sacked in 1970 over gun-running allegations. Haughey's election by Fianna Fáil TDs in a closely contested leadership ballot owed more to his cultivation of the grass roots of the Fianna Fáil party in the years after the arms trial than to any dramatic change in Fianna Fáil on attitudes towards Northern Ireland, although disenchantment with British policy in Northern Ireland was a factor in the readiness of the party to elect such a controversial figure.

The change of leadership in the South was reflected in tougher, more uncompromisingly nationalist rhetoric on the issue of Northern Ireland. At Fianna Fáil's annual conference in February 1980, Haughey described Northern Ireland as a failed political entity and was wildly applauded when he called for 'a declaration by the British Government of their interest in encouraging the unity of Ireland, by agreement and in peace'.[16] The speech was a clear indication that the Republic would not countenance the notion of an internal settlement to the conflict in Northern Ireland and that Haughey intended relations between London and Dublin to be the main vehicle for his policy towards Northern Ireland. The first step in this direction was a summit in London with the British Prime Minister, Margaret Thatcher, in May 1980. Little emerged out of this meeting. The character of the second summit held in Dublin in December 1980 was altogether different, as was the context. By this time, the Atkins initiative had finally ended in failure as the British Government had predictably backed off imposing a settlement. Furthermore, a hunger strike of Republican prisoners was in progress. Against this background, there were talks not merely between the two Prime Ministers but between senior Cabinet Ministers on both sides. The communiqué issued after the talks spoke of 'the further development of the unique relationship between the two countries' and registered the two Governments' agreement to establish joint studies, 'covering a range of issues including possible new institutional structures, citizenship rights, security matters, economic co-operation and measures to encourage mutual understanding'.[17] These were to enable consideration to be given to 'the totality of relationships within these islands'.[18] It was this last phrase that particularly alarmed Unionists.

However, in the Republic, Haughey's difficulty was in convincing sceptics both in the press and in the Opposition that the vague language of the communiqué justified his description of the outcome of the talks as historic.[19] He did not help his case by overstating what the British Government had agreed to. Even after the Anglo-Irish Agreement, the view has persisted that Haughey greatly exaggerated the summit's significance.[20] While this remains a fair comment on some of the inflated rhetoric that emerged from the summit such as the Irish Foreign Minister's claim that there had been measurable progress towards Irish unity, it overlooks the wider international context of the summit. Internationally, the Dublin summit was interpreted as a major new initiative by the British Government over Northern Ireland and warmly welcomed as such. Bereft of the option of an internal settlement by the failure of the Atkins initiative, Britain was effectively locked into the Anglo-Irish process as its only means of countering international criticism of direct rule.

Paradoxically, however, in initial stages the Anglo-Irish process created more difficulties for the Irish Government than for the British. In the course of 1980, one of the kites that Haughey had flown was the possibility of defence co-operation between the two countries as a *quid pro quo* for progress towards Irish unity. Although there was no mention of defence in the communiqué after the Dublin summit, its open-ended language did nothing to dampen speculation of a deal along these lines. The speculation was fuelled further by speeches by politicians in both Britain and the Republic. However, the prospect was not greeted with enthusiasm by public opinion in the Republic, where the threat that such a deal posed to the country's policy of neutrality provoked considerable hostility and underlined the limits the public placed on the aspiration to a united Ireland. In the ensuing debate in the Dáil on neutrality, Haughey was forced to retreat to the position that limited the strategic offer to Britain to a review of the country's defence arrangements after reunification.[21] Shortly afterwards, the second hunger strike by Republican prisoners in Northern Ireland aroused considerable hostility towards the British Government in the Republic, reducing the political value to the Irish Government of the achievements of the Dublin summit. At the same time, the desire to safeguard the Anglo-Irish process inhibited the Irish Government's criticism of the British Government's handling of the prisons dispute. The impact of the hunger strike on Southern opinion was reflected in the results of the Republic's general election in June. Two Republican prisoners were elected on the issue in Border constituencies, contributing to the narrow defeat of the Fianna Fáil Government.

The new Taoiseach was Garret FitzGerald, heading a minority Coalition Government of Fine Gael and Labour. From the outset, the new Government's prospects of survival looked slim, given the seriousness of the country's economic problems and the need for cutbacks in expenditure to reduce the growth of the country's immense burden of foreign debt. In these circumstances, it was not surprising that the conduct of the Government's Northern Ireland policy became increasingly politicised. FitzGerald exploited his reputation as a reconciler in contrast to the hardline attitudes associated with his predecessor and shifted the emphasis from reaching agreement with the British Government to accommodating Unionists. To this end, he launched a constitutional 'crusade'[22] in the Republic in September 1981 to persuade public opinion of the need for substantial changes in the Republic's constitution to enhance its acceptability to Northern Protestants. FitzGerald wanted to excise the territorial claim to Northern Ireland from the constitution and to remove articles of a confessional character in areas such as divorce. If successful, it was FitzGerald's stated intention to hold a referendum on a new constitution. However, he made it clear that he regarded the attitude of Fianna Fáil as an obstacle to his campaign for a more pluralist society in the South, putting Fianna Fáil on the defensive politically over policy towards Northern Ireland.

FitzGerald's crusade provoked a wide-ranging debate in the Republic as well as attracting favourable publicity in Britain and Northern Ireland. Reconciling the two traditions in Ireland formed one of the main themes of the communiqué issued after the summit between the British and Irish Prime Ministers in November 1981.[23] The communiqué also recorded the two Governments' agreement to establish an Anglo-Irish Intergovernmental Council, providing for regular meetings at ministerial and official level. They also agreed to the publication of the joint studies commissioned by the previous summit, with the exception of a paper on security matters, in order to reassure Unionists that the matters discussed did not represent a threat to the constitutional status of Northern Ireland. Publication also had the effect of deflating the claims that Haughey had made about the studies prior to his departure from office. In January 1982 the Government was defeated on its budget proposals. There was a small shift of opinion against the Government in the ensuing general election in February. A minor factor assisting Fianna Fáil was that Provisional Sinn Fein failed to hold the vote that candidates supporting the Republican prisoners' campaign won in June 1981. The result was that the minority Coalition Government was replaced by a minority Fianna Fáil Government with Haughey Taoiseach once again.

The circumstances in which Haughey came to power in 1982 could hardly have been less propitious for the development of the Anglo-Irish process. The capacity of the Irish Government to exert pressure on Britain over Northern Ireland had been considerably weakened as a result of the inter-party political competition over policy on the North. It had begun with Haughey's inflation of the results of the Dublin summit and had permeated FitzGerald's crusade. The fact that the origins of the Republic's two main parties lay in different degrees of nationalism provided a ready-made ideological basis for such competition. The Government's precarious hold on power further reduced the Republic's leverage. A few days before the general election, FitzGerald wrote a confidential letter to the Secretary of State for Northern Ireland in which he argued that the rolling devolution proposals Prior was then putting forward 'would be certain to be un-acceptable to the minority in Northern Ireland and hence unworkable' and warned of 'a very serious setback' if he proceeded.[24] When the proposals were published as a White Paper on 5 April,[25] the Fianna Fáil Government presented its objections to the scheme in terms almost identical to those in FitzGerald's letter. However, the common ground between the parties on this issue was not reflected in public debate in which they continued to emphasise the differences in their approach to the North. Neither the White Paper itself nor the Irish Government's attacks on it received much attention in Britain. A few days earlier on 2 April Argentina had invaded the Falkland Islands.

Initially, the Republic supported Britain over the issue. Ireland was then a member of the Security Council and voted in favour of a resolution of the Council calling for an Argentinian withdrawal. Further, as a member of the EEC the Republic agreed to the adoption of economic sanctions against Argentina. However, there was an abrupt change in the Irish Government's position with the outbreak of hostilities in the South Atlantic. After the sinking of the *Belgrano* on 2 May, the Irish Government sought a meeting of the Security Council to call for a ceasefire and withdrew its support for the EEC sanctions. The Republic's policy of neutrality was invoked to explain the change. In particular, the Government drew a distinction between supporting Britain while a diplomatic solution was still being sought and backing Britain in a war. The change was more obviously a response to the wave of anti-British feeling prompted by the large loss of life resulting from the sinking of the *Belgrano*. In turn, the Irish Government's stance and the rhetoric that accompanied it provoked a wave of anti-Irish feeling in Britain. In this atmosphere there could be no question of summits between the two Prime Ministers. It was the end, for the present, of political dialogue between the two countries over Northern Ireland.

In November, Haughey's minority Government was defeated in the Dáil on a vote of confidence. Fianna Fáil lost seats to Fine Gael in the ensuing general election on 24 November and when the Dáil met in December, Garret FitzGerald was elected Taoiseach at the head of a Coalition Government of Fine Gael and Labour with a clear overall majority. The return of FitzGerald to power and the prospect of a period of political stability in the Republic did not lead to an immediate revival of the Anglo-Irish process. The British Government was still committed to its own initiative for an internal settlement, though by this time, Prior's plans for rolling devolution had run into considerable difficulties. Sinn Fein had won 10 per cent of the vote in elections to a Northern Ireland Assembly in October. The constitutional nationalist party, the SDLP, had fought the elections on an abstentionist basis and had no intention of giving its support to the scheme, while the

Government also faced opposition to its plans from integrationists within the Ulster Unionist Party. The British Government's reaction to these setbacks to its policy, especially the apparent toughening of security policy, had further alienated nationalist opinion in the North. The threat this posed to the SDLP alarmed the new Irish Government and in an interview in January 1983, FitzGerald warned of the danger of a civil war in Northern Ireland.[26]

The concern in the South over the rise of Sinn Fein presented the SDLP with the opportunity to press its call for the holding of a council for a New Ireland to formulate concrete constitutional proposals for a settlement of the Northern Ireland problem. The rationale the SDLP gave for this initiative was that it would force nationalists to address the practical implications of their aspirations for Irish unity and that nationalists could thereby allay some of the fears of Unionists. Of more immediate importance to the SDLP was constraining inter-party competition in the South over Northern Ireland in order to renew pressure on the British Government. In March 1983 the main Southern political parties announced their agreement to the establishment of a council in accordance with the SDLP's proposal. They decided to call it the New Ireland Forum. The first meeting of the Forum was held at the end of May. The lack of consensus in the South on policy towards Northern Ireland was underlined by the divergences in the party leaders' opening speeches. The Forum was still deliberating when there was a renewal of the Anglo-Irish process in the shape of a summit between the two Prime Ministers at Chequers in November. It was a reflection of the political momentum that had already been generated by the New Ireland Forum that both sides recognised that no decisions of substance could be made before its report had been issued.

The report of the New Ireland Forum was finally published on 2 May 1984. Even before its publication, the Republic had launched a diplomatic offensive in the United States and in Europe to put pressure on Britain to respond positively to the report. The credibility of the exercise depended on the three Southern parties and the SDLP agreeing to a common position. This was achieved with some difficulty and the tenuous nature of the consensus was emphasised by the different interpretations placed on the report's conclusions by the leaders of Fine Gael and of Fianna Fáil in the press conference that followed publication. In its interpretation of history and in its analysis of British policy, the report stuck closely to nationalist orthodoxy.[27] However, considerable emphasis was placed within this basic framework on the need to accommodate the two traditions in Ireland and for respect for the 'unionist identity',[28] in particular. A unitary state was presented as the 'particular structure of political unity which the Forum would wish to see established'.[29] The report also set out, without explicit recommendation, two other options, a federal/confederal state and joint authority. The status of these two options formed the nub of the disagreement between FitzGerald and Haughey after the publication of the report. The argument tended to obscure a paragraph in the report in which the parties in the Forum declared their readiness 'to discuss other views which may contribute to political development'.[30]

In the debate on the report in the House of Commons in July, the Secretary of State for Northern Ireland, James Prior, made much of this paragraph as the basis for progress, while explicitly rejecting the three constitutional models presented in the report. The rejection was softened by Prior's acknowledgment that a close relationship between the United Kingdom and the Republic was desirable and by his declaration that the dangers of doing nothing were greater than the risks of seeking a political advance.[31] In the months that followed, expectations of an agreement between Britain and the Republic grew. They were strongly encouraged by the Irish Government. For example, the Irish Minister for Foreign Affairs, Peter Barry, referred to the possibility of a settlement as a result of Britain's response to the report of the New Ireland Forum in a speech to the United Nations General Assembly in September.[32] The main focus of the expectations was a summit between Thatcher and FitzGerald at Chequers in November. In the event, the communiqué issued at the end of the summit merely indicated that the two Governments were in agreement on a number of general principles. Much worse for the Irish Government followed. At her press conference after the summit, the British Prime Minister replied to a question on the three options of the Forum report by a description of each of the options followed by the words 'that is out'.[33] She was also dismissive of the thesis of Catholic alienation presented in the Forum report. The press conference was universally interpreted in Ireland as a humiliating rebuff not just for FitzGerald but for the whole cause of constitutional nationalism. The summit was widely referred to in the Irish press as a 'debacle'.[34] The tone of the coverage was reflected in the heading the *Sunday Press* gave to its report of the SDLP's reaction: 'Anger, fear, loathing and bitterness sweep the North.'[35] By contrast, Enoch Powell called on Unionists to rejoice.[36]

The exaggerated reaction in the Republic to the British Prime Minister's remarks, which by contrast attracted little attention in the British press, was in part a reflection of the significance and authority that Irish opinion had come to attach to the report of the New Ireland Forum and in part a belief that what the British Prime Minister had said constituted a rejection of the Anglo-Irish process as a whole. It was quickly made clear by the British Government that this was not intended. Indeed, with the benefit of hindsight, it is apparent that the summit had in reality greatly strengthened the Irish Government's bargaining position, such was the adverse international reaction to the brusque manner in which Margaret Thatcher had dismissed the options of the New Ireland Forum report. That opinion outside the British Isles saw the report as a most conciliatory document was not merely a response to the report's explicit condemnation of paramilitary organisations, but showed the extent to which world opinion shared the report's nationalist assumptions. The respective reputations of the two Prime Ministers reinforced the impression of British unreasonableness. During 1985 a reversal of roles took place in the attitudes of the two Governments towards the prospects of an agreement. From early in the year it was the British Government that was holding out the likelihood of a settlement,[37] while the Irish Government, which had appeared so confident of a breakthrough in 1984, was now deliberately lowering expectations of a deal. At the same time, the Irish Government sought diplomatic support for its position. In May the Taoiseach made several speeches in the United States and had a meeting with the Canadian Prime Minister, while the Minister for Foreign Affairs, Peter Barry, lobbied the Australian Government during a visit there in the same month.[38]

There were two meetings between FitzGerald and Thatcher on the margins of summits of the EEC during the first half of 1985. In retrospect, it appears that these meetings were significant in removing the remaining obstacles to agreement. After a final Ministerial meeting in London on 6 November, the Anglo-Irish Agreement was signed at a summit of the two Prime Ministers at Hillsborough on 15 November 1985. It was by any standards a momentous diplomatic achievement for the Republic. But while the Coalition Government was given credit in the South for its negotiation of the Agreement, there appeared to be little appreciation of quite how significant the Agreement was. This was partly because its centrepiece was the establishment of a framework rather than a specific set of reforms. Indeed, in the latter respect, the Agreement failed to live up to its advance billing. By contrast, the role afforded to the Republic through the Intergovernmental Conference went considerably further than had been expected. If this did not get the recognition it merited, it was also partly because of the unrealistic expectations that had arisen out of the New Ireland Forum.

From the outset Haughey insisted that Fianna Fáil should oppose the Agreement. Consequently, the party voted against the ratification of the Agreement in the Dáil. The Agreement was none the less approved by a clear majority in the Dáil of 88 votes to 75. In fact, the issue proved damaging to the Opposition, with opinion polls indicating that the Agreement enjoyed the support of a substantial majority of the public.[39] Even more serious for Fianna Fáil were the defections from its ranks as a result of its stance on the Agreement. The departure of Mary Harney was instrumental in the creation of a new political party, the Progressive Democrats, which rapidly attracted a substantial level of public support and a nucleus of five TDs, four of whom were defectors from Fianna Fáil, though economic policy rather than the party's position on the North formed the principal basis of its appeal. The basis of Haughey's opposition to the Agreement was that the Irish Government's affirmation that a change in the status of Northern Ireland required the consent of a majority of the people of Northern Ireland, enshrined the legitimacy of the Unionist position in an international treaty. It was a somewhat ironic claim because part of the Unionists' case against the Agreement was that it amounted to a change in the status of Northern Ireland without the consent of the people of Northern Ireland. Another difficulty for Haughey was that he had previously affirmed the principle of consent himself in negotiations with the British Government. However, Haughey did not pursue his constitutional objection to the Agreement to the extent of seeking a test in the courts of its compatibility with Articles 2 and 3.

By the time of the general election in the Republic in February 1987, Fianna Fáil was playing down its opposition to the Agreement. Indeed, policy towards Northern Ireland only became an issue in the campaign after Haughey mildly stated that Fianna Fáil would pursue its constitutional objections to the Agreement through political and diplomatic action. However, this was sufficient for the other parties to raise doubts as to whether the Agreement would survive a Fianna Fáil victory. Contrary to expectations at the start of the campaign, the party narrowly failed to win an overall majority in the Dáil and Haughey became Taoiseach at the head of another minority Government. But with the emergence of the Progressive Democrats as a strong force with fourteen seats and 12 per cent of first preference votes and an ideologically divided opposition, the Government's survival prospects seemed much better than they had been in 1982. Another significant feature of the election results was the performance of (Provisional) Sinn Fein, which attracted only 1.9 per cent of the vote. In the admittedly different context of elections to the European Parliament, Sinn Fein had won nearly 5 per cent of the vote in the South as recently as 1984. One of the aims of the Agreement, the political marginalisation of Republican paramilitary organisations, was being achieved.

Haughey chose the occasion of his visit to Washington in March for St Patrick's Day to make clear his Government's full support for the Anglo-Irish Agreement. In fact, the Fianna Fáil Government has behaved as if the party had never opposed the Agreement. No attempt has been made to act on Haughey's promise to renegotiate the terms of the Agreement, while the Minister for Foreign Affairs, Brian Lenihan, has been notably accommodating in his attitude towards the British

Government's efforts to draw the Unionists into discussions on the establishment of devolved government in Northern Ireland, despite the Taoiseach's record of opposition to the whole notion of an internal settlement of the conflict.[40] As a consequence, conflict among the parties in the South over policy towards Northern Ireland has markedly diminished. The debate has been confined to the narrow issue of how well the Government is discharging its duties and responsibilities under the Agreement. As long as there is a broad consensus among the South's main parties on the functioning of the Agreement, the North's Troubles seem unlikely to threaten the Republic's political stability, even if there were to be a spill-over of violence across the Border. This is because the Agreement has established a context in which the Republic is able to enjoy the benefits of partition in the shape of the retention of its own consensual political institutions, without incurring the damage to their legitimacy that would flow from being forced to jettison their normative basis, which lies in the aspiration of nationalists to the unity of the island. In particular, the Agreement provides a mechanism whereby the South's commitment to Northern nationalists can be discharged without imposing an unacceptable burden on Southern society.

One of the unintended consequences of the Forum exercise was to make Southern opinion much more aware of just how impossibly large the economic costs of unity were likely to be, ironically partly as a result of the calculations done by economists working on behalf of the Forum itself.[41] An editorial in the *Irish Times* with the striking title, 'Do we really want all those Protestants?', published shortly after the report of the Forum came out, suggested what some of the political costs of a unitary state might be.

> It means, for example, Paisley in the Dáil, shouting about Old Red Socks; he and his clerical colleagues ranting about the Romanist content of any and every Bill. It means ritual denunciation and derision of the Irish language every time there is an education estimate or anything about education. It means that neutrality will be shouted down. It means that Dáil Éireann would be in uproar for a long time to come. And who would be Taoiseach? The Unionist bloc would have a big say in defining that, and there would be a large Unionist bloc for a long time to come. After that, Labour might have its day.[42]

It was a discouraging prospect for such a conservative society. The editorial went on to emphasise that the two parts of Ireland had developed vested interests in maintaining the Border after more than sixty years of partition.[43] However, these doubts about the practicality of ending partition stopped short of questioning the basic legitimacy of the nationalist case for a united Ireland. Partition was still seen as wrong.

The ambiguity of Southern attitudes towards partition is accommodated rather than resolved by the Anglo-Irish Agreement. Outwardly, the Republic is afforded a status in relation to Northern Ireland virtually equal to that of Britain itself. However, the Agreement's effective operation is dependent on the British Government recognising that it is in its own interests to sustain this impression. Any implication that the Republic had been drawn into an arrangement whereby the South lent British rule a measure of international legitimacy in return for a largely ineffective consultative role would have profoundly destabilising consequences in the Republic. In such a situation the consensus on the Agreement would crumble. There would be a danger of polarisation between those wishing to abandon the aspiration to unity and those who were willing to sacrifice the country's stability in pursuit of the claim enshrined in Articles 2 and 3 of the 1937 Constitution. It is because the issue has the potential capacity to fracture Southern society that the North matters so much to the Republic.

7.

THE AMERICAN CONNECTION

OUTSIDE of the British Isles the country most deeply involved in the Northern Ireland conflict is the United States. Viewed from Northern Ireland the American dimension has assumed increasing importance in the conflict as is shown by the attention all parties in Northern Ireland lavish on American opinion. By contrast, the conflict in Northern Ireland is not a high political priority in the United States itself. Indeed, it is striking how little attention is devoted to Northern Ireland even in the specialist literature on the Irish in America.[1] It is consequently far easier to trace the effect of American actions and pronouncements on Northern Ireland than it is to gauge the impact of events in Northern Ireland on the opinions of Americans in general or even of those assumed to have a special interest in the situation, the Irish-Americans.

In the 1980 census Americans were asked to identify their ethnic origin or heritage group with the intention of defining all Americans for the first time by self-chosen heritage groups. On this very loose basis 43.7 million Americans out of a population of 226.5 million (19 per cent of the total) identified themselves as Irish.[2] These figures can be contrasted with the estimates that Andrew Greeley gives in *The Irish-Americans* that Irish Protestants constitute 5.2 per cent of the American population and Irish Catholics 4.8 per cent or with the 1970 census which put the number of Americans of Irish ancestry at 13.3 million or 6.7 per cent of the total population.[3] Since the publication of the details of the 1980 census, a figure of over 40 million Irish-Americans is the one that is most commonly used in political discourse. However, neither this figure nor the one of 20 million it displaced bears any relationship to the numbers that might be mobilised politically over the issue of Northern Ireland. But in so far as the figure derived from the 1980 census has tended to inflate expectations as to the potential influence of Irish-Americans, it is not without political significance. The available evidence suggests that in practice only a very small proportion of Irish-Americans take any special interest in events in Northern Ireland. For example, the largest and oldest Irish-American organisation, the Ancient Order of Hibernians, claims a membership of only 80,000.[4] According to Paul Artherton, 'in moments of candour most knowledgeable Irish-Americans will admit that the potential number of people interested in Northern Ireland can be counted in hundreds of thousands rather than millions'.[5] Lawrence McCaffrey has argued that 'since 1921 the links between the Irish in Ireland and the American Irish have become tenuous' and that the 'Irish cultural empire' in the United States has disintegrated, a development he attributes to a variety of factors including a decline in Irish emigration to the United States and the economic and social mobility of Irish-Americans.[6]

By 1980 the numbers emigrating to the United States from Ireland had slowed to a trickle. In that year, the number of legal immigrants from the Republic of Ireland was 982 and from Northern Ireland 410.[7] But during the recession of the 1980s there was an increasing flow of illegal immigrants to the United States from the Republic of Ireland and this immigration became a significant issue in bilateral relations between the Republic and the United States. Estimates of the number of illegal Irish immigrants in the United States range between 50,000 and 100,000. Despite the new wave of immigration during the 1980s the number of Americans who were born in Ireland is diminishing almost to the point of insignificance outside states such as New York, Massachusetts, and Pennsylvania where the Irish connection remains particularly strong. The upward mobility of Irish-Americans has been reflected in a movement from the ghetto to the suburbs with the consequent disappearance of the Irish-American neighbourhood outside of the Northeast and a few large urban centres in other regions of the country.[8] The precise extent and meaning of Irish assimilation into the American mainstream remains a matter of dispute and counter-vailing tendencies can be pointed to, in particular, the increased opportunities, as a result of cheap air fares, for Irish-Americans to return as tourists to their roots in Ireland and the attempt by some to reconstruct the values and lifestyles of the neighbourhood. What matters at a political level is that the American connection remains a potent factor in the Northern Ireland conflict notwithstanding the narrowing of the base of Irish-American nationalism and the fading of Irish identity outside of census returns.

American interest in partition between the end of the civil war in Ireland in the 1920s and the onset of the Troubles in 1968 remained largely dormant. The main exception was a brief flurry of activity in Congress in the early 1950s stimulated by de Valera's anti-partitionist campaign over the passage of the 1949 Ireland Act. In particular, in 1950 the House of Representatives passed an amendment to the Foreign Aid Appropriation Bill to withhold all aid to Britain as long as Ireland remained partitioned, although at a subsequent stage in the legislative process it was rejected by a large majority.[9] In a similar vein, during the course of the 1952 presidential election, the Republican Vice-Presidential candidate, Richard Nixon, proposed using the lever of economic aid to put pressure on Britain to end partition.[10] Irish-American interest in Northern Ireland was re-invigorated by the civil rights marches in 1968 and 1969 and the disturbances that followed in their wake. A Friends of the Northern Ireland Civil Rights Association was established with branches in cities across the United States. With their help and that of other Irish-American organisations, Bernadette Devlin toured the United States in August and September 1969, raising $200,000 for the Civil Rights Association, although that fell well short of the seven figure target she had set herself.[11]

Another organisation created specifically in response to the Troubles was the American Committee for Ulster Justice. The announcement of its formation was contained in a large advertisement in the *New York Times* in December 1971, a few months after the introduction of internment.[12] Its newsletter of June 1972 contained a classic statement of the Republican perspective in an American context.

> The violence in N.I. is the final chapter in Ireland's seemingly eternal struggle against British colonialism. The United States, which itself was the first colony of Britain to successfully initiate its independence, must look with sympathy on the fight of the people who of all the nations on earth are most identified with the historical movement of national liberation and political independence.[13]

The newsletter concluded with a plea for American involvement at a diplomatic level:

> The United States need not involve itself in any military solution in Northern Ireland, but rather the influence of friendly persuasion should be used to convince the United Kingdom that the only permanent solution lies in a free united and independent Ireland.[14]

Lobbying for United States intervention at a governmental level is an important strand of activity by Irish-American organisations. Other Irish-Americans have favoured a direct approach.

By far the most important organisation to be established in the first years of the Troubles was the Irish Northern Aid Committee (Noraid). It was founded at the beginning of 1970 by Michael Flannery, a member of the North Tipperary brigade of the IRA during the 1920s. Flannery had joined the IRA in 1917 at the age of fifteen. He was among those who fought on after the Treaty with Britain. After their defeat in the civil war he was arrested and jailed in the South for two years and, after breaking with de Valera over the latter's acceptance of constitutional politics, underwent a spell of internment before he emigrated to the United States in 1927. In America he joined Clann na Gael, which was continuing to raise money for the Republican cause. For Flannery, the violence that followed the civil rights marches constituted a resumption of the struggle of his youth. His case is not unique. Those who emigrated to the United States in the 1920s—and their sons and daughters—figure prominently in descriptions of supporters of Noraid.[15]

From the outset Noraid was very closely identified with the Provisional IRA. Its formation followed a meeting in Ireland between Flannery and representatives of the newly established Provisional IRA in December 1969. Flannery himself has stated that Noraid was created in response to the Provisionals' pleas for help.[16] It remains the most militantly Republican of all Irish-American organisations. Its main activity is fund-raising. For example, considerable sums of money are collected from the sale of tickets to annual testimonial dinners attended by prominent politicians sympathetic to Noraid's view of the Northern Ireland conflict. Collections in Irish bars, dinner-dance benefits, and direct mail solicitation also raise money for the organisation. It is frequently asserted, especially by the British and Irish Governments, that money raised by Noraid finances the purchase of arms for the Provisional IRA. There is strong circumstantial evidence to support this proposition, though direct proof, at least in the public domain, is harder to come by. Noraid claims that the money it raises is devoted exclusively to welfare for the families of prisoners. The money is sent in the first place to An Cumann Cabhrach, Sinn Fein's prisoner relief organisation in Dublin. Most of the money is then transmitted to Green Cross in Belfast and is distributed to the families of Provisional IRA prisoners.

According to Noraid it raised approximatley three million dollars for this purpose up to the end of 1986. Under the American Foreign Agents Registration Act of 1938, Noraid is required to disclose any remittances it makes to Ireland. To meet the requirements of this law, Noraid registered under the Act in January 1971, naming initially the Northern Aid Committee, Belfast, as its foreign principal. Subsequently, Noraid filed with the Justice Department six-monthly returns on the moneys transmitted to Ireland. However, this measure of compliance with the law by no means satisfied the Federal authorities. Two issues, in particular, concerned these authorities: the transmission of funds to Ireland not included in the returns made to the Justice Department, and Noraid's relationship with the Provisional IRA. These issues were fought in the courts. In 1981 a District Court Judge concluded that Noraid was 'an agent of the IRA providing money and services for other than relief purposes' and ordered Noraid to register the IRA as its foreign principal.[17] Through appeals to higher courts Noraid delayed compliance with the order until the middle of 1984. It reluctantly complied then under a compromise whereby it was permitted to state that the identification of the IRA as its foreign principal was the result of a court order. While these appeals were being made Noraid stopped filing returns on the money being transmitted to Ireland.

Despite the limitations of Noraid's six-monthly returns to the Justice Department, they do provide a partial indication of the general scale of its fund-raising, and, more clearly, of its ups and downs. The high point of its fund-raising effort was in the first six months of 1972 when $312,000 were transmitted to Ireland.[18] This coincided with reaction to Bloody Sunday. Another peak in Noraid fund-raising coincided with Bobby Sands's hunger strike. In the first six months of 1981 £250,000 was raised, though less than half this amount was actually registered as having been transmitted to Ireland at this time, due to the dispute with the Justice Department. The low point occurred in the second half of 1977 when $39,000 were sent to Ireland.[19] It forms the trough of a general period of decline in Noraid fund-raising in the late 1970s. In an interview in the first half of 1979 Flannery acknowledged the fall in contributions to Noraid but attributed it to a depression in the building industry in New York.[20] This explanation provides more of an indication of the social milieu of many of Noraid's supporters than of the actual reasons for the decline. The main centre of Noraid's activities is the city of New York where the organisation's headquarters are located. Nationwide there are approximately 126 chapters of Noraid. While these are to be found in every region of the United States, much of Noraid's network is concentrated in the Northeast. Since the hunger strike, Noraid claims that it has raised approximately $300,000 a year.[21]

Allegations that money raised by Noraid is used to buy arms for the Provisional IRA take two main forms. The first is that a proportion of the declared money sent to Ireland is used for that purpose by its Irish recipients, which is possible as An Cumann Cabhrach does not publish accounts detailing how the money is dispersed. Secondly, it is alleged that Noraid raises funds additional to those it declares and that a proportion of this money is retained in the United States where it is used directly for arms purchases, while the rest is sent to Ireland by couriers. Public evidence suggesting a link between Noraid fund-raising and arms purchases by the Provisional IRA in the United States emerged during the trial of Noraid's founder, Michael Flannery, and four other Irish-Americans in Brooklyn during 1982 on charges of conspiring to smuggle weapons to the Provisional IRA. Among

Flannery's co-defendants was a former treasurer of the Flatbush branch of Noraid in New York City. In his testimony, Flannery admitted providing $17,000 for the purchase of arms for the Provisional IRA. He claimed that the money did not come from Noraid but from a secret IRA fund he kept in his home, made up of contributions from individuals who had specifically requested that their donations should go directly to the Provisional IRA. None of the accused sought to deny their involvement in the attempt to smuggle arms to the Provisionals. The defence case was that the accused were under the impression that arms shipments to the Provisional IRA had been sanctioned by the Central Intelligence Agency because of fears that the Provisionals might otherwise turn to the Soviet Union for support. It was claimed that one of the middlemen in the arms deal had links with the CIA. Despite the tenuous nature of evidence presented by the defence all five accused were acquitted. Even clearer evidence of a connection between Noraid fund-raising and Provisional IRA arms purchases emerged during the 1983 trial of Andrew Duggan and Gabriel Megahey in Brooklyn on gun-running charges. In that trial, Michael Hanratty, a former electronics purchaser for the Provisional IRA, testified for the prosecution that some of the money sent by Noraid to Ireland was returned by courier to the United States for arms purchases.[22]

Assessing the level of Noraid's financial contribution to the Provisional movement over and above the sums declared in its returns to the Department of Justice is difficult. No official estimates have been published of the contribution that Noraid makes to financing the Provisional movement and the more careful researchers emphasise the uncertainty that exists in official agencies.[23] Warren Richey in a series of articles on the Noraid connection published in the *Christian Science Monitor* in 1985 quoted a spokesman for the RUC as estimating that 'at least half of what is raised in America stays in the US for the purchase of weapons'.[24] A slightly different perspective is provided by Brigadier Glover's report for British army intelligence on future terrorist trends in Northern Ireland, dated November 1978 and leaked to the press during 1979.[35] He estimated the Provisional movement's total annual income at £950,000. Out of this total Glover estimated the level of overseas contributions at £120,000 (13 per cent) with Noraid accounting for well over half the total, a contribution 25 per cent above the amount it declared in its returns to the United States Department of Justice. Glover estimated the annual expenditure of the Provisional movement on prisoners' dependants at £180,000. He also estimated money raised from Green Cross in Britain and Ireland at £30,000 annually. These figures suggest that, at the time when Glover prepared his report, all overseas contributions *could* in principle have been absorbed in the budget for prison welfare work. From the perspective of the British Government (and that of the Irish and American Governments, for that matter) there is no real distinction to be drawn between income for one purpose rather than another if it frees other money for the Provisional IRA's campaign of violence. Indeed, it was Flannery's intention at the outset that by raising funds for the families of prisoners Noraid should help ensure that the Provisional IRA was able to sustain its campaign and that it would not peter out as the IRA Border campaign between 1956 and 1962 had done.[26] However, by no means all of Noraid's contributors and supporters take this view and some do attach importance to the difference between support for prisoners' families and financing Provisional IRA operations.[27] Further, where the distinction between different forms of expenditure obviously does matter is that it makes it more difficult for governments to prevent the flow of funds into the Provisional movement's coffers.

However, at the time Glover prepared his report Noraid fund-raising was close to its nadir. Consequently, his figures almost certainly under-estimate Noraid's contribution as a proportion of the Provisional movement's income. Glover also included a section in his report on external support for terrorism other than finance in which he concluded that the United States had become 'PIRA's main weapons source'.[28] The figure given in Warren Richey's articles is that the American connection accounts for roughly half of the Provisional IRA's arms.[29] The importance of the United States as a source of weaponry for the Provisionals was most dramatically demonstrated by the interception of a large shipment of arms in September 1984. Seven tons of guns and ammunition bound for the Provisional IRA were seized by the Irish authorities from an Irish fishing trawler, *Marita Ann*, after their transfer from an American trawler, *Valhalla*, which had sailed from Boston. Putting all the factors together it is possible to suggest that a likely figure for the American contribution to the Provisional movement, including arms purchases in the United States, would be between two and three times the amount Noraid says it has transmitted through the course of the Troubles or, in other words, a figure of between six and nine million dollars in the period from 1970 to 1986. But whatever the precise amount actually is, it is clear that in relation to the Irish-American population of the United States it is very small indeed and does not begin to bear comparison with, for example, the contributions made by American Jews for a variety of causes to Israel. However, while a sum of less than ten million dollars is tiny in the context of the United States, it represents a very significant contribution in the context of the Northern Ireland conflict. In short, the relationship is an asymmetrical one. It is part of the explanation why there is more interest in the American connection in Northern Ireland than there is in the United States.

Very closely associated with Noraid in the weekly newspaper the

Irish People, which operates out of the same office in New York, though legally it is a separate organisation and has successfully fought through the courts an action aimed at forcing it to register under the Foreign Agents Registration Act. The *Irish People* reproduces material first published in *An Phoblacht/Republican News*, though it does so selectively. Articles referring to Sinn Fein's stance on foreign policy issues, especially where it involves criticism of United States policy in the Third World, are usually omitted. It also carries news of the activities of Irish-American organisations in relation to Northern Ireland in the United States and coverage of Irish sports events. The *Irish People's* perspective is by no means identical with that of Sinn Fein. In particular, the social conservatism and anti-Communism of the *Irish People* set it apart from the trends of radicalisation, secularisation, and politicisation that have shaped Sinn Fein ideology since the late 1970s.

The figure in the Provisional leadership most closely associated with Noraid and the American connection is Joe Cahill, a founding member of the Provisional IRA and identified ideologically with the old guard within the Provisional movement. He is a treasurer of Sinn Fein and one of three trustees of An Cumann Cabhrach. Despite being deported from the United States in 1971, Cahill has continued to make fund-raising trips to America. His passport actually turned up in the house of one of the defendants in the 1982 gunrunning trial involving Flannery. In May 1984 he was apprehended in the United States travelling under a false passport and deported for a second time. Strongly anti-Communist in outlook, Cahill is an advocate of giving priority to military activity and of attacking targets in England,[30] though, crucially for the radical leadership of Sinn Fein, he also backed the dropping of abstentionism in relation to the Dáil in 1986. It is a combination of views that makes Cahill particularly suitable as a go-between with Noraid. How far Noraid exercises a political influence on the Provisionals as a consequence of the importance of its fund-raising to the movement is difficult to gauge, although it can be inferred that the American connection is a restraining influence on the radicalism of Sinn Fein. The conservatism of its American supporters is widely recognised within the ranks of Sinn Fein and is occasionally alluded to in Sinn Fein meetings. The American connection also places a premium on a high profile for the Provisional IRA's campaign, since this is how the Provisionals' effectiveness tends to be judged by contributors to Noraid.[31] Noraid itself generated headlines in 1983 and 1984 during tours of Northern Ireland by its supporters that became the focus of violent incidents. When Noraid's publicity director, Martin Galvin, began to address a Belfast rally in August 1984 in defiance of an exclusion order, a man was shot dead by the RUC with a plastic bullet in the disturbance resulting from police efforts to arrest Galvin.

The main organisation lobbying for American diplomatic intervention over Northern Ireland is the Irish National Caucus with offices in Washington. It was founded in 1974, originally as an offshoot of Noraid.[32] An important figure in the Caucus from its inception was Dr Fred Burns O'Brien who fell out with the Provisional leadership in 1979.[33] Under the directorship of Father Sean McManus the Caucus also gradually became estranged from the leadership of Noraid.[34] While there appears to be a considerable overlap between membership of the Caucus and Noraid, by the late 1970s the position of the Caucus was clearly distinct from that of Noraid. The Caucus takes the view that violence in Northern Ireland, whether from Republican paramilitaries, Loyalist paramilitaires, or the security forces, constitutes a sympton of partition for which British withdrawal and a united Ireland are the cure. Caucus literature carries a logo of the dove of peace superimposed on a shamrock and strongly emphasises that the Caucus is a non-violent organisation which sends none of the money it raises in the United States to Ireland.[35] The Caucus has concentrated its campaigning on human rights issues. Among the issues it has highlighted are police interrogation methods, prison conditions, the use of plastic bullets, allegations that the security forces operate a 'shoot to kill' policy, and, most successfully of all, discrimination against Catholics in employment.[36] At the initiative of the Caucus, the Ad Hoc Congressional Committee for Irish Affairs was established in September 1977 under the chairmanship of Congressman Mario Biaggi, a conservative Democrat representing the Bronx in New York. Although an informal body without any standing in Congress it has maintained a membership of well over a hundred Congressmen, a majority of whom are Democrats, mostly representing districts in the urban centres of the Northeast. Like Biaggi, many of the members of the Ad Hoc Committee are not themselves Irish-Americans.

Altogether separate from the Ad Hoc Committee, but also within the American legislative process are the Friends of Ireland, established in 1981 and associated with leading Irish-American politicians such as Senator Edward Kennedy and the former Speaker of the United States House of Representatives, Tip O'Neill. The main features of the Friends' position on Northern Ireland are opposition to fund-raising for the Provisionals in the United States, support for constitutional nationalism as represented by the SDLP and the Irish Government, and a commitment that the United States Government should provide generous economic aid for Northern Ireland after a political settlement. They played the leading role in getting Congressional approval for American aid to Ireland following the Anglo-Irish Agreement in November 1985. The origins of the Friends of Ireland can be traced back to a joint statement by Senator Edward Kennedy, Speaker Tip O'Neill,

Governor Hugh Carey, and Senator Patrick Moynihan on St Patrick's Day 1977. It condemned the Provisional IRA and called on Americans not to give the Provisionals money or encouragement. The four Democrats, who became known as the Four Horsemen, repeated the same message on St Patrick's Day 1978 but their 1978 statement also strongly criticised the lack of political progress under direct rule and violations of human rights by the security forces. On a practical level, the Four Horsemen have supported the Ireland Fund, established in 1976 to provide an alternative to Noraid fund-raising. The Fund has channelled money from its headquarters in Boston into projects throughout Ireland with the support of the Irish Government. However, claims that the Ireland Fund in its first years drew the bulk of donations away from Noraid[37] need to be treated cautiously since the Fund has operated in a very different social milieu from the Irish bars in which Noraid makes its collections. Other factors, such as the fall in violence in Northern Ireland after 1976, provide a more convincing explanation for the decline in Noraid fund-raising in the late 1970s. In 1987 the Ireland Fund merged with an older fund-raising organisation, the American-Irish Foundation, set up after President Kennedy's visit to the Republic in 1963, to form the American-Irish Fund.

Much less welcome to the British Government than their opposition to Noraid were the efforts of the Four Horsemen to end the American Government's policy of non-involvement in the Northern Ireland conflict. At a meeting with the Secretary of State, Cyrus Vance, in June 1977, they pressed for a statement from President Carter. After negotiations involving both the British and Irish Governments, President Carter issued a statement on Northern Ireland on 30 August 1977, which condemned violence, expressed support for a peaceful settlement involving the Irish Government, and promised American help with investment in the event of such a settlement. Carter's own interest in the issue appears to have been slight, although prior to his election in November 1976, Carter had met with leaders of the Irish National Caucus and of the Ancient Order of Hibernians and indicated his belief that the American Government should speak out on the issue of human rights in Northern Ireland while supporting peace and the unification of Ireland.[38] At the time, President Carter's statement made little or no impact on British policy towards Northern Ireland. But the novelty of the declaration was that it treated the situation in Northern Ireland as a legitimate concern of American foreign policy. Its importance in raising the issue into a realm of inter-state relations that transcended non-governmental influences from the United States on Northern Ireland was not immediately recognised. A key figure in the development of the American connection to this higher level was John Hume of the SDLP.

It was Hume who had suggested that the four leading Irish-American politicians should issue a joint statement on St Patrick's Day 1977.[39] The origins of Hume's links with leading Irish-American politicians can be traced back to November 1972 and a meeting with Senator Edward Kennedy in West Germany.[40]. The meeting was at Kennedy's request. In the early years of the Troubles he had been fiercely critical of British policy. In October 1971 shortly after the introduction of internment, Kennedy introduced a resolution calling for the immediate withdrawal of British troops and the establishment of a united Ireland. An identical resolution was introduced in the House of Representatives by Hugh Carey, than a Congressman representing Brooklyn. A thread that ran through Kennedy's criticisms of British policy was that Northern Ireland was Britain's Vietnam. Though he toned down the stridency of his criticism after the imposition of direct rule, which he welcomed, he still pressed the analogy with Vietnam, comparing Bloody Sunday with the My Lai massacre in an article in the Summer 1973 issue of *Foreign Policy* entitled 'Ulster is an international issue'.[41] However, he drew back from his advocacy of the immediate withdrawal of British troops while raising the possibility of a United Nations peace-keeping force, a Common Market force, or a reconstituted Northern Ireland police force as alternatives. The influence of Hume, and of the Irish Government, which had sharply criticised Kennedy for his stance in 1971, is clearly apparent in the position he adopted on a political settlement. He advocated that the American Government should convey to Britain its suppport for

> effective and even-handed peace-keeping arrangements and for the fair implementation of the power-sharing arrangements to be established in the legislative committees and the executive departments of government once the new Northern Ireland Assembly is elected.[42]

He also argued that 'no British settlement in Ulster can ignore the Republic's rightful role'.[43] At the same time he condemned the flow of funds and arms from the United States to Northern Ireland. In short, the article anticipated many of the positions taken by the Four Horsemen and later by the Friends of Ireland. It also provides a clue as to why the American connection was not more important during this period. British policy after the imposition of direct rule was running on parallel lines. In fact, after the Sunningdale Agreement Kennedy suggested that William Whitelaw deserved the Nobel Peace Prize for his achievement.

There were other reasons why the American connection had little impact on British policy prior to 1977. In the first place, the Nixon and Ford Administrations resisted all Congressional pressure for American involvement at a governmental level. Secondly, the Nixon Administration, in particular, acted on British requests to step up action by the Federal Bureau of Investigation against groups involved in gunrunning to Northern Ireland.[44] For example, in September 1971 Joe Cahill was deported from the United States on, in the words of the State Department, 'information made available by the British government'.[45] Thirdly, Irish-American responses to the conflict required no alteration in what was then the main goal of British policy, the negotiation of a political settlement among the parties in Northern Ireland. It was only after the fall of the power-sharing Executive and the failure of the Constitutional Convention in 1975 that the context of British policy altered in a way that gave enhanced importance to the American connection.

With the adoption of direct rule as a long-term policy in 1976 and its associated strategy of the criminalisation of political violence, the American connection loomed much larger. Stemming the flow of funds to the Provisional movement from the United States became more important, especially in the light of reorganisation within the Provisional IRA that shifted the emphasis from the achievement of a rapid victory to sustaining the campaign of violence over a protracted period. Further, the breach with constitutional nationalism over the policy of direct rule provided the SDLP and the Irish Government with the incentive to use the American connection as a lever to change British policy. Thus, President Carter's statement of August 1977 was an important first step in undermining the British Government's position, notwithstanding the mild nature of the actual content. It created a precedent for further American involvement in the conflict at a governmental level. For the British Government, much worse was to follow in 1979.

The lack of a British response to their initiative and a burgeoning scandal over police interrogation methods in Northern Ireland prompted the Four Horsemen to issue a statement harshly critical of British policy on St Patrick's Day, 1979. It referred to evidence of 'official brutality and violations of human rights' in police interrogation centres in Northern Ireland, while urging the British Government to consider a confederation of the two parts of Ireland as providing the possible framework of a solution.[46] The toughness of the statement drew praise from the Irish National Caucus. The following month during a visit to Ireland, including Northern Ireland, the Speaker of the House of Representatives, Tip O'Neill, launched a strong attack on British policy. His speech made a considerable impact in Britain, partly because it was delivered in the midst of the 1979 general election campaign. O'Neill accused Britain of treating the problem of Northern Ireland as a 'political football'.[47] What he had in mind was the way the two main parties had bid for the votes of the small Ulster Unionist contingent at Westminster in the finely balanced parliamentary situation prior to dissolution. O'Neill called for 'an early, realistic, and major initiative on the part of the incoming British government'.[48] The likelihood of such an initiative seemed small. The Conservatives had fully supported the policy of direct rule and their election manifesto contemplated no fundamental change in policy. In the absence of devolved government it proposed the establishment of 'one or more elected regional councils with a wide range of powers over local services'.[49]

During the first few months of Conservative rule there was no indication that the Government was contemplating a change in direction. Then in the month of August 1979 there were two major setbacks to government policy. The first was an announcement at the beginning of August by the American State Department that it was suspending the sale of arms to the RUC. The decision was a triumph for Mario Biaggi and the Ad Hoc Congressional Committee for Irish Affairs. In July Biaggi had tried to attach an amendment banning arms sales to the RUC to a State Department funding bill. As a *quid pro quo* for withdrawing the amendment Biaggi was promised an investigation into the RUC's order for 3,000 pistols and 300 rifles by the chairman of the House of Representatives Foreign Affairs Committee. It was the prospect of hearings that would invoke the reports of Amnesty International and the Bennett Commission into the maltreatment of suspects in RUC interrogation centres and the fact that Tip O'Neill had come out against the sale that persuaded the State Department to pre-empt further Congressional action by suspending arms sales to the RUC, pending its own review. What made the Carter Administration particularly vulnerable to pressure over the issue was its general commitment not to supply arms to countries violating human rights. Although the weaponry was not of great importance in itself, the suspension was an alarming development for the British Government.

Historically, American Presidents had successfully resisted far greater domestic political pressure over the Irish question than Carter faced.[50] It was a measure both of the weakness of the Presidency in this period and of Carter's domestic political position that the Administration failed to resist this pressure. It was also an instance of how the Administration's emphasis on human rights in the conduct of foreign policy drew the United States into involvement in the domestic policies of other states. Inevitably this emphasis increased the Administration's vulnerability to domestic ethnic pressures since any ethnic group's grievance over its status in other lands could readily be represented as an issue of human rights. A disturbing aspect of the State Department's decision, from the Irish Government's perspective, was the way that its own use of the American connection through the efforts of the Four Horsemen was becoming entangled with the lobbying of more radical groups such as the Ad Hoc Committee and the Irish National Caucus. The Irish Government distrusted both the Ad Hoc Committee and the Caucus as organisations subject to Provisional influence, particularly in their advocacy of British withdrawal. The difficulty was that once the proposition was accepted that the Northern Ireland conflict was a legitimate concern of American foreign policy, it was impossible to decree that only those who worked with the Irish Government should have the right to put forward proposals for consideration by the American Government. Further, the Four Horsemen themselves became sucked into a competition with other groups to establish their credibility over the issue. In this competition, the State Department's decision constituted a tremendous boost for the Ad Hoc Committee and its associate, the Irish National Caucus.

Less than a week after the suspension of arms sales to the RUC, the Governor of New York, Hugh Carey, announced at a press conference that the Secretary of State for Northern Ireland, Humphrey Atkins, and the Irish Foreign Minister, Michael O'Kennedy, had agreed to what he called a 'peace parley' in New York in September.[51] It later transpired that Humphrey Atkins had agreed to consider the possibility, but had not formally accepted Carey's invitation. After a meeting with the Prime Minister, Atkins turned down the invitation on the grounds that it had become clear that Carey envisaged the talks as a forum for negotiations on Northern Ireland's future. The episode did not enhance Atkin's political reputation. By contrast, Carey's quixotic initiative drew praise from a *New York Times* editorial which called for a new political initiative and declared: 'It is not American meddling but American compassion that has prompted Governor Carey to attempt the unconventional to end the intolerable.'[52]

On 27 August the second major jolt to British policy occurred. A bomb planted by the Provisional IRA killed Lord Mountbatten and three others on a boat in the Irish Republic and, in a separate incident, eighteen British soldiers were killed at Warrenpoint in an IRA ambush. These events brought to the surface considerable discontent within the military over security policy, particularly the emphasis on police primacy, and over the prospect of an indefinite continuation of direct rule.[53] The combination of military dissatisfaction and, more importantly, the British Government's fear that a contest for the Democratic Presidential nomination might increase still further the Carter Administration's vulnerability to Irish-American pressure, prompted an abrupt change in British policy. The centrality of the American connection to the British Government's initiative was underlined by the fact that conditions in Northern Ireland for the launching of negotiations among the parties could hardly have been less propitious. Paisley had topped the poll in elections to the European

Parliament in June and tensions were rising as a result of the crisis looming in the prisons. Significantly, the first indication that the British Government was indeed about to launch a fresh initiative came in a statement to that effect on 16 September from the British Ambassador to the United States, Sir Nicholas Henderson. Ironically the statement came the day after a major speech by the newly elected leader of the Ulster Unionist Party (UUP), James Molyneaux, in which he had ruled out the possibility of devolved government within the next five years and had argued that his party should concentrate on improving direct rule. Two days later, in a partial denial of the Ambassador's statement, Atkins said that 'no action of any kind could be expected before late October or November at the earliest'.[54] In the event, the new initiative was launched by Humphrey Atkins on 25 October. Throughout the launch the British Government made no secret of its desire to impress American opinion. The day after announcing the proposal for a conference Atkins briefed American journalists in London, while the Prime Minister described the initiative in an interview with the *New York Times* on 13 November. She explained that 'she would not permit the squabbling political parties to block her political initiative', threatening that 'she would impose a solution'.[55] With cues like these, editorials and political columnists in the British press gave prominence to the American connection in their analysis of the initiative.[56]

As it turned out British fears of the power of the Irish-American lobby during 1980 proved unfounded. The seizure of American diplomats as hostages by Iran in November 1979 and the Soviet invasion of Afghanistan in December 1979 overshadowed other foreign policy issues in American politics and there was no question of Northern Ireland having any impact either on the Presidential primaries or the election itself. The Democratic Party platform included a call for an end to 'the division of the Irish people' with a solution based on 'consent of all the parties to the conflict'[57] while a vigil outside the Republican Party convention by the Irish National Caucus attracted some publicity. However, none of the candidates took up the issue. During the primaries Reagan had responded to a request by the Irish National Caucus to outline his position on Northern Ireland with a statement that ruled out American interference and, in strongly condemning terrorism, he warned Americans not to give money that might end up in the hands of gunrunners.[58]

Where the American connection did make an impact during 1980 was in the Republic of Ireland in what was dubbed the Donlon affair. Sean Donlon had been the Irish Ambassador in Washington since October 1978. In that capacity he had been outspoken in his criticism of Irish-American organisations with associations with the Provisionals. He placed both the Irish National Caucus and Mario Biaggi's Ad Hoc

Congressional Committee in that category and had accused Biaggi of 'serving the interests of terrorism'.[59] This position was in accordance with the stance taken by successive Irish Governments. However in July 1980 the news leaked that Charles Haughey intended to remove Donlon from his post in Washington, fuelling speculation that there had been a shift in the Irish Government's attitude. The ensuing row persuaded Haughey to abandon his plans to move Donlon. He spelt out his attitude towards the various Irish-American groups in a speech in Cork in which he strongly condemned Noraid while commending the efforts of the Four Horsemen. He also said that the evidence of associations between Noraid and the Irish National Caucus cast grave doubt on the Caucus although he qualified his criticism by saying that the Caucus contained 'many fine people who are not aware of its undesirable associations'.[60] But he made no mention of Congressman Biaggi. The response of John Hume provides an interesting contrast to Haughey's speech. The SDLP leader declared:

> The removal of Ambassador Donlon would have done serious damage to the hard work of many people for many years in building up the most influential support that this country has ever had in the United States, culminating in the historic declaration on the Democratic platform in the presidential election. Senators Kennedy and Moynihan, Speaker O'Neill and Governor Carey have been solid and true friends of Ireland. In order that all shreds of suspicion be removed and this unfortunate affair closed, it is necessary that it be made clear that the activities of Congressman Mario Biaggi and the organisations with which he is associated enjoy no support whatsoever among any substantial section of Irish opinion.[61]

The significance of the Donlon affair was that it raised the issue of where the line was to be drawn between the accommodationist position of constitutional nationalism and the Republican fringes of constitutional politics represented by such figures as Neil Blaney, Kevin Boland, and Sean MacBride whom the Caucus was assiduous in cultivating. The distinction was not well understood in the United States.

In July 1980 the British Government retreated from its threat to impose a settlement without the agreement of the parties in Northern Ireland and the Atkins initiative petered out. At a summit meeting between Margaret Thatcher and Charles Haughey in Dublin on 8 December, the two Prime Ministers agreed to discussions on the 'totality of relationships within these islands'.[62] Although there was a very favourable reaction to the summit in the United States the new approach owed little to the American connection except in so far as it was a response to the failure of the Atkins initiative. With the election of Ronald Reagan as President in November, it seemed that the British Government no longer had reason to fear action by the American Administration.[63] In fact, the conservative electoral tide was reckoned to have diminished the influence of the Irish-American lobby in all its various manifestations.

The deaths of Republican prisoners on hunger strike in the Maze during 1981 received very extensive coverage in the media in the United States and the British Government's stance on the issue was fiercely criticised by all the different strands of Irish-American opinion. The most direct effect of the prisons crisis was the boost it gave to fund-raising by Noraid. After the death of Sands, longshoremen operated a 24-hour ban on the handling of British goods and there were pickets of Irish-Americans protesting against British policy outside many British consulates in the United States. However, there were a number of factors that limited the impact of the protests. In the first place, the existence of an Anglo-Irish dialogue on the wider constitutional question helped to shield the British Government from more generalised criticism of its policy on Northern Ireland. Secondly, the concern in the United States over the problem of international terrorism, highlighted by the Iranian hostage crisis, had a restraining influence on American reaction to the prisons crisis in Northern Ireland. Thirdly, President Reagan resisted both domestic pressure and an appeal from the Irish Government to involve his Administration in efforts to resolve the prisons crisis.

It might seem tempting to conclude that the lack of impact of the American connection at the inter-state level during 1981 demonstrated the hollowness and weakness of the Irish–American lobby. The fact that Reagan had been able to sustain a policy of non-involvement without any apparent difficulty throughout the crisis appears to bear this out. However, such a view takes too little account of the Reagan Administration's overall stance on the issue of Northern Ireland. Firstly, Reagan did not lift the suspension of arms sales to the RUC, despite appeals from the British Government to do so. Secondly, and more positively from the perspective of the Irish Government, the Reagan Administration reiterated Carter's commitment to aid Northern Ireland economically in the event of a political settlement.[64] The maintenance of the arms embargo was a clear indication of the continuing potency of the Irish-American lobby, while the pledge on aid linked to a political settlement showed that the American connection was still relevant at the level of inter-state relations. In fact, the hunger strike was a rather special case, because it touched on an area in which countervailing opinions to those of the Irish-American lobby existed, opinions about what was the appropriate response to terrorism.[65] It was one area in which Unionist delegations have been able to strike a chord with American opinion.

From the first years of the Troubles Unionists had gone to the United States to explain their point of view on the conflict, usually without receiving much attention. Ian Paisley, with links with fundamentalist Protestants going back to his association with Bob Jones University, visited the United States in the summer of 1969 and did receive extensive media coverage. But the main effect of his trip and subsequent attempts to influence American opinion appears to have been to make Americans more aware of the sectarian dimension of the conflict, reducing their sympathy with either side in the conflict rather than creating any sympathy for the Unionist viewpoint. The Scottish-Irish or Irish Protestant connection with its origins in eighteenth and nineteenth-century emigration is too remote from the circumstances of partition to have generated any sectional support for Unionism. In January 1982, in a major effort to reach American opinion, a number of leading Unionist politicians took part in a nation-wide tour of the United States. However, most of the publicity generated by Operation USA concerned the State Department's refusal to grant Ian Paisley an entry visa for the tour. The State Department's action followed intensive lobbying by the Irish National Caucus, though the aim of the Caucus was less to keep Paisley out of the United States than to persuade the State Department to reverse its stance on the exclusion of leading members of Sinn Fein. Similarly, in the late 1970s the UDA was cultivated by the Irish-American lobby, not because of any empathy with its position but because the UDA's support for an independent Northern Ireland could readily be used to back the Irish-American lobby's demand for a British withdrawal. Stressing that the UDA had a positive contribution to make to a settlement also provided useful cover for justifying the need for an input from Sinn Fein into negotiations about the future of Northern Ireland.[66]

While the problem Unionists faced in the United States was a general lack of sympathy for their political cause, the Irish Government's quite opposite problem was one of countering the influence of groups espousing the cause of Irish nationalism, but in a manner that Dublin disapproved of. The period after the hunger strike in 1981 was marked by skirmishing between the Irish Government and various Irish-American organisations over, for example, the symbolic issue of the election of the Grand Marshal of the main St Patrick's Day parade in New York. The election of Michael Flannery in 1983 and that of a conservative Republican supporter of Noraid, Peter King, in 1985 led to a boycott of the parade by the Irish Government in those years. Another figure who became influential in the Irish-American network in the 1980s was James Delaney, a Texan millionaire and conservative Republican, whose interest in Northern Ireland was stimulated by the death of Bobby Sands and the deaths of children from the use of plastic bullets. In 1983 he founded the Irish-American Unity Conference, the aim of which was to create an umbrella organisation for the numerous Irish-American groups that had proliferated across the country. In mid-1984 it claimed a membership of 46,000, making it one of the largest Irish-American organisations in the United States.[67] Noraid was among organisations affiliated to the Irish-American Unity Conference. At its first conference in July 1983, the Irish-American Unity Conference issued a manifesto in which it described the Northern Ireland problem as a threat to the Anglo-American alliance, called for British withdrawal by 1986, and demanded the outlawing of plastic bullets. It also proclaimed its support for *both* the Ad Hoc Congressional Committee for Irish Affairs and the Friends of Ireland. Delaney himself also praised the New Ireland Forum Report. Such apparently contradictory attitudes underlined the failure of the Irish Government to convince American opinion of the distinction between the accommodationist approach of constitutional nationalism and the anti-colonial Republican perspective that still tended to dominate Irish-American attitudes towards the conflict.

The Irish Government's efforts to shape American opinion were also made much more difficult in this period by a sharp divergence in attitudes towards the Irish-American network among the political parties in the Republic after Fianna Fáil lost office in November 1982. In Opposition Haughey emphasised the need for an unambiguous commitment to unification by the Irish Government as the way to galvanise Irish-American opinion and to put pressure on the British Government.[68] He made it clear that he did not agree with the strategy adopted both by the Irish Government and by John Hume of drawing a sharp distinction between support for constitutional nationalism and those ready to condone, if not endorse, the use of force to achieve a united Ireland. In 1984 Fianna Fáil registered as a foreign agent in accordance with American law in order to enable the party to raise funds in the United States. Fianna Fáil branches were founded in Washington and New York and, in addition, a Friends of Fianna Fáil organisation was established. In an interview with the *Irish Herald* in 1984, the secretary of the fund-raising committee, Paul Kavanagh, explained that the party would appeal to Irish-Americans who saw Haughey as the man to take on the British and who were concerned by threats posed to Ireland as a conservative Catholic democracy by the emergence of the Workers Party and Fine Gael's alignment with labour.[69]

Where the Irish Government did achieve a large measure of success was in securing American support for the proposals of the New Ireland Forum, though President Reagan dismissed speculation on the eve of his visit to the Republic that the American Government might itself launch an initiative on Northern Ireland.[70] However, there was a hostile response from the Administration to the British Prime Minister's brusque rejection of the Forum options in November 1985. Shortly afterwards, in a pointed message, President Reagan praised 'the Irish statesmen for their courageous and forthright efforts recently embodied in the report of the New Ireland Forum'.[71] Thatcher was strongly criticised for her remarks by the Friends of Ireland and by the *New York Times* and the *Washington Post*. When she met Reagan in late December at Camp David, she briefed him on the talks with FitzGerald and insisted at a press conference that contrary to the impression that had been created, there had been no breach with the Irish Government.[72] Her sensitivity to American opinion was further in evidence when she addressed a joint session of Congress in February 1985. Malcolm Rutherford headed his account of her speech in his column in the *Financial Times*: 'Dr FitzGerald and I',[73] conveying the emphasis she placed on the fact that the negotiations with the Republic to reach an agreement on Northern Ireland were continuing. In March, even before the appearance of speculation in the British press that there would be an agreement between Britain and the Republic over Northern Ireland, a prominent member of the Friends of Ireland, the Speaker of the House of Representatives, Tip O'Neill, was expressing confidence that there would be political progress over Northern Ireland and speculating on the possibility of American aid for Ireland as a result of a settlement.[74] His confidence was the result of a discussion he had had with the British Prime Minister on Northern Ireland.

The role played by American pressure in the achievement of the Anglo-Irish Agreement is perhaps not quite as clear cut as the role it played in prompting the British Government to launch the Atkins initiative in 1979, but the sequence of events leading up to the Agreement suggests that it was a significant factor. The reaction in the United States to the Agreement was overwhelmingly favourable from the President downwards. This was most clearly reflected in the easy passage through both Houses of Congress of resolutions in favour of the principle that the United States should provide aid to both parts of Ireland as a mark of its approval of the Agreement. It was also evident in the muted reaction of Irish-American organisations, such as the Caucus, which had been strongly critical of the Irish Government's stance over Northern Ireland. The extent of approval for the Agreement across the United States appeared to vindicate the Irish Government and its policy of working through the Friends of Ireland and ignoring the more radical pressure groups. They had been marginalised, at least in this context. In July 1986, President Reagan duly signed legislation providing for aid of $50 million to assist the economic and social development of both parts of Ireland. The following month Congress voted to provide an additional $35 million a year over the next two years. In September, the British and Irish Governments set up an International Fund to handle the money received from the United States and elsewhere as envisaged under Article 10 of the Anglo-Irish Agreement. By this time Canada had donated $10 million and New Zealand had also made a small contribution. The approval for British policy in Northern Ireland was of course much more important to the British Government than the actual sums of money involved.

Attitudes in the United States towards the Provisional IRA remained a major concern of the British Government. Government Ministers on visits to the United States repeatedly emphasised the damage done to Northern Ireland by donations to Noraid. Their efforts were largely misdirected in so far as very few Americans ever contributed to Noraid and those that did were unlikely to be influenced by representatives of the British Government. There was also particular anger over the attitudes American courts sometimes adopted towards the IRA. Two notable instances were Federal Judge John Curtin's praise for the 'excellent motives and reputation' of two leading members of Sinn Fein convicted of illegal entry into the United States in 1983 and Federal Judge John Sprizzo's ruling in an extradition case in 1984 that characterised the Provisional IRA's campaign as a form of guerrilla warfare.[75] But Sprizzo's ruling also upset the Reagan Administration which believed that judgments as to the character of political violence in any country ought to be made by the executive branch of government. The result of the case was that both Governments agreed to renegotiate their extradition arrangements to avoid the possibility of such embarrassment in the future. In June 1985 they signed a Supplementary Extradition Treaty. It amended the 1972 Extradition Treaty between the two countries by removing the protection of the political exception clause from a range of offences including kidnapping, hijacking, bombing, shooting, and possession of firearms. The clause had enabled individuals to escape extradition by pleading that their offences had taken place in the context of political disturbances, the issue at the heart of Sprizzo's judgment.

However, the new Treaty required ratification by the American Senate by a two-thirds majority. It ran into strong opposition from liberals oncerned about its implications for civil liberties and from the Irish American lobby. In May 1986 President Reagan made a public appeal for the Senate to approve the Treaty, making much of Britain's role in providing bases for the American air raid on Libya the previous month. It was eventually ratified in July 1986 after significant changes removing, for example, possession of firearms from the list of offences covered by the new Treaty, ensuring that an individual had the right to present evidence at an extradition hearing, and giving the courts the right to adjudicate on the question as to whether the individual would get a fair trial, if extradited. These had satisfied most of the liberal opponents of the original proposals. The scrutiny of the administration of justice in Northern Ireland by American courts could still prove embarrassing for the British Government.

The issue on which the more radical elements in the Irish-American lobby have had the greatest success has been that of discrimination in employment. In 1983 the Irish National Caucus launched a campaign against the awarding of contracts by the United States Air Force to Short Brothers, because of the firm's reputation for discrimination against Catholics. The Caucus was eventually defeated on this particular issue as a result of changes in the labour policy of Shorts, including the introduction of an affirmative action programme, and as a result of lobbying by the Irish Government and the Friends of Ireland in support of the contracts. None the less, the Caucus was successful in making a wider political issue of discrimination against Catholics. The issue was a central feature of the section on Northern Ireland in the Democratic Party's Presidential platform in 1984. It declared its support for 'a ban on all commercial transactions by the US government with firms in England and Ireland that practise discrimination in Northern Ireland on the basis of race, religion, or sex on an ongoing basis'.[76] This far-reaching proposal reflected the involvement of the Irish-American lobby in the primaries. The Irish-American Unity Conference supported the candidature of Senator Gary Hart because he advocated active involvement by the United States Government to help bring about a united Ireland.[77] After the Presidential election, the Irish National Caucus launched a new campaign over the issue of discrimination in Northern Ireland. In November 1984, the former Irish Minister for External Affairs and the chairman of the Irish National Caucus Association in the Republic of Ireland, Sean MacBride, gave his name to a set of principles designed to provide a code of conduct for American firms operating in Northern Ireland. Among the Northern Ireland figures sponsoring the principles was a prominent trade unionist, Inez McCormack.

There are nine MacBride principles. They include: 'increasing the representation of individuals from under-represented religious groups in the work force', 'the banning of provocative religious or political emblems from the workplace', 'special recruitment efforts should be made to attract applicants from under-represented religious groups', and 'the development of training programs that will prepare substantial numbers of minority employees for skilled jobs'.[78] They were closely modelled on the principles of American affirmative action programmes as well as the Sullivan principles, a voluntary code of conduct covering American investment in South Africa. It was the explicit intention of the Caucus to link the issues of South Africa and Northern Ireland as a way of broadening support for American action over Northern Ireland through the building of an ethnic coalition over the two issues. For example, the national director of the Caucus, Sean McManus, was among those arrested in protests outside the South African Embassy in Washington in December 1984. By the middle of 1985, the MacBride principles had been endorsed by the American trade union federation, the AFL-CIO and by the United States National Council of Churches. More importantly, the issue was being taken up by a number of state legislatures, where proposals were under consideration to make the investment of state pension funds in American companies with subsidiaries in Northern Ireland dependent on their adherence to the principles.

The campaign in support of the MacBride principles presented the Irish Government with a considerable dilemma. On the one hand, it was fearful that the effect of the campaign would be to deter American companies from investing in Northern Ireland and to promote disinvestment, especially as the principles appeared to incorporate the principle of positive discrimination. This was contrary to the principle of equality of opportunity embodied in Northern Ireland's Fair Employment Act, though this problem was eased by a clarification of the principles in 1986. On the other hand, the Irish Government was anxious lest opposition to the MacBride principles should lend credibility to the Caucus's persistent charge that the Irish Government was uninterested in the fate of the nationalist minority in Northern Ireland[79] and should give the impression that the Irish Government was satisfied with the record of the British Government on the issue of discrimination in Northern Ireland, which was far from being the case. The dilemma was reflected in the speeches made by the Irish Prime Minister, Garret FitzGerald, during his visit to the United States in May 1985. After initially denouncing disinvestment as a calculated strategy to wreck Northern Ireland's economy, FitzGerald later gave qualified approval to the principles themselves, but emphasised that they should not form a condition for existing or future investment.[80] John Hume has similarly attempted to explain that his opposition is to the campaign to secure compliance with the principles, not to the principles themselves.[81] Charles Haughey, who became Taoiseach following the Republic's general election in February 1987, has adopted a more ambiguous attitude towards the campaign. Apparently, he still takes the view that the Irish Government should do nothing to alienate Irish-American organisations, if it can possibly be avoided.

Massachusetts became the first state to adopt legislation requiring compliance with the principles in November 1985. New York, New Jersey, Connecticut, and Rhode Island have followed suit. It is under consideration in a number of other states, including California. The size of the vote in the New York State Assembly in favour of the legislation where it was passed by 138 votes to six[82] gives an indication of the difficulties the British Government faces in resisting this tide. The campaign has provided the main impetus for the British Government's announcement in September 1987 of radical anti-discrimination measures to be embodied in legislation in 1988.[83] These will bring labour practices in Northern Ireland into broad alignment with the MacBride principles, though stopping short of the introduction of positive discrimination. In the two years prior to the Government's announcement of fresh measures, there had been no new American investment in the province, though also no disinvestment.[84] The impact of the MacBride principles demonstrates the continuing significance of the Irish-American lobby, in spite of the Anglo-Irish Agreement. It provides a striking illustration of the ability of the lobby to wield influence through tailoring its proposals to accord with principles accepted by American opinion in other fields and to draw on the general disposition that exists in favour of a united Ireland. In this way, it has been able to overcome lack of interest in Northern Ireland outside periods of crisis and to make an impact quite out of proportion to the number of Americans actively involved in it. Indeed, the numbers involved in the Irish-American lobby are a poor guide to its political influence. Thus, the size of Irish-American organisations cannot explain the Ad Hoc Committee's success in recruiting members in Congress. While much of the membership of the Ad Hoc Committee is nominal and relatively few members of Congress play more than a passive role in its activities, the mere fact that so many members of Congress are willing to lend their names to its activities suggests that members calculate that there is an electoral benefit to be gained from membership of the committee, as the conflict is not of intrinsic importance to the United States.

A small illustration that suggests that this calculation might have a measure of validity is provided by the New York Senate race in 1980 between a conservative Republican, Alfonse D'Amato, and Congresswoman Elizabeth Holtzmann, a liberal Democrat. D'Amato made an election issue of Holtzmann's refusal to join the Ad Hoc Committee and after the election claimed that the Irish question had played an important part in his victory.[85] While the issue of Northern Ireland is in general far too peripheral to American politics to be the subject of detailed electoral analysis that could test the validity of a claim like this, it is sufficient that members of Congress believe that the issue has an electoral salience, however small, to sustain the Ad Hoc Committee's influence. What makes all the difference is the existence of a general disposition in favour of the proposition that a united Ireland is both desirable and inevitable that goes beyond the Irish-American community. Such a disposition is a consequence of Northern Ireland's perceived lack of international legitimacy as a political entity, to use the concept developed in the Introduction. Of course, those holding the view that Irish unity was desirable and inevitable would hardly explain their own attitudes in such terms. However, they probably would make reference to both the norm of self-determination and the issue of territorial integrity. Otherwise electoral considerations on their own could not explain the readiness of so many members of Congress to support the cause of Irish nationalism in one way or another. While conviction as to the rightness of the cause extends beyond the Irish-American community, however widely defined, its political exploitation within any locality depends on the existence of a sufficiently strong Irish-American network to translate it into more than the expression of a pious hope for a united Ireland. What makes the Irish-American lobby almost irrestible, once a campaign has got off the ground, is the absence of countervailing opinions that might temper support for the nationalist case. The issue of terrorism provides one possible exception to this proposition. But, in general, the capacity of the Irish-American lobby to draw upon a very wide range of relatively uncommitted support, without encountering significant opposition, constitutes striking evidence of the political resonance of international norms.

8.

EUROPEAN INTERVENTIONS

UNLIKE American involvement in Northern Ireland, European involvement has been almost entirely through formal institutional channels. It has operated at three main levels. Much the most important has been that through the European Economic Community (EEC) and its various institutions. Next in importance has been the role played by the Council of Europe, particularly through the European Convention on Human Rights. Bilateral relations between Britain and individual European states and the European diplomacy of the Republic of Ireland form the third and least important channel of European influence on the conflict, though the precise importance of diplomatic exchanges over the issue is difficult to evaluate as little information about them reaches the public domain. The three levels are best discussed separately because they are substantially different in form and independent of one another, although there have been instances of interaction between these levels of influence, an example being reaction in the European Parliament to decisions of the European Court of Human Rights.

The United Kingdom of Great Britain and Northern Ireland and the Republic of Ireland became members of the EEC on 1 January 1973. However, the prospect that the two states would join the Community had an impact on the situation in Northern Ireland well before 1973. The United Kingdom had first applied to become a member of the Community on 31 July 1961. The Republic's application followed next day. Even before then there had been speculation in the Republic as to the possible implications of European co-operation for Anglo-Irish relations and the question of partition, in particular. In a speech to the Dáil in 1954, the Minister for External Relations, Liam Cosgrave, put forward a view of European co-operation as having the potential to provide a context for transcending divisions within Ireland; this view was to be echoed in the debates about the implications of membership of the EEC:

> Isolation or aggressive policies tend to divide us more and more
> fundamentally from the majority of our fellow-countrymen in the

Six Counties. On the other hand, the more we direct our activities towards playing a part suitable to our means and geographical position in the solution of the great problems that confront Western Europe as a whole, the more it will become apparent to the people of the Six Counties also that their destiny is one with ours, just as ours is one with the peoples of Western Europe.[1]

Yet much of the appeal of European unity to the Republic was less its effect on partition than as 'a means of getting out of the straitjacket of British-Irish preoccupations and a relationship which, after three hundred years, had become stifling'.[2] From the Republic's perspective, membership of the EEC implied a less unequal relationship with the United Kingdom, notwithstanding the obvious dependence of the Irish application on Britain's own decision to seek membership of the Community.

The British applications prompted Unionist concern that membership of the EEC would lead to interference with local employment practices and the Safeguarding of Employment Act, and there was concern too over the economic implications for Northern Ireland as a peripheral region.[3] Terence O'Neill, who became Prime Minister of Northern Ireland in 1963, was less suspicious of where greater prospects for North-South co-operation in the context of EEC membership might lead than his predecessor, Lord Brookeborough, had been. He described those who saw Europe as the setting for a united Ireland as 'following the old time-worn course of self-delusion'.[4] In fact, the European Community had positive attractions for liberal Unionists committed to the modernisation of the province's economy and who hoped that economic change would break down sectarian divisions in the province. This viewpoint was expressed by the Minister of Commerce, Robin Bailie, in a debate at Stormont on the EEC in December 1971:

> Preoccupations with the hatreds and bitterness of yesteryear has no place in the mainstream of European thinking. We have to make up our minds whether we are going to be cornered in this cul-de-sac of history or get into the mainstream of European progress and thinking. I have no time at all for the Sinn Fein ideology or for its equivalent which is sometimes expressed in a narrow Ulster view.[5]

In the same debate Northern Ireland's Prime Minister, Brian Faulkner, answered the arguments of those who saw membership of the EEC as presenting the threat (or promise) of a united Ireland:

> When frontiers are no longer a barrier to the free movement of trade or a line of demarcation between different fiscal, social, or

economic systems they will remain primarily as a mark of people's continuing sense of national identity and loyalty. In such a context it would become even clearer than it is today how foolish as well as immoral it would be for any one to seek to remove frontiers against the will of the majority of the inhabitants. And if that were to be accepted the Border could at last recede from the forefront of many minds.[6]

He saw closer relations between Northern Ireland and the Republic of Ireland being balanced by closer relations between the Republic and the United Kingdom as a whole, concluding that the Community would require 'an acceptance that neither the Irish Sea nor the English Channel can represent the boundaries of our world'.[7]

These views were in line with the prevailing European perception that progress towards political union in general would flow out of growing economic interdependence that brought the peoples of Europe closer together. As this implied that political progress could only take place from the bottom up, it tended to allay Unionist fears that the EEC might seek any direct political role in relation to partition. It also implied that any political effects of membership on Northern Ireland would be long term in nature and would not take place through new political structures imposed from above. Britain's signature of the Treaty of Accession and entry into the Community coincided with the imposition of direct rule from Westminster and an intensification of the conflict in Northern Ireland. Consequently, there was a relatively muted reaction in the province to actual entry to the Community, although the British Government referred to the United Kingdom's and the Republic's prospective membership of the EEC in its October 1972 discussion paper on the province's future as a reason why 'any new arrangements for Northern Ireland should, whilst meeting the wishes of Northern Ireland and Great Britain, be so far as possible acceptable to and accepted by the Republic of Ireland'.[8]

In the Republic, the possible impact of membership of the EEC on relations between the two parts of Ireland also attracted attention. In his vision of a new federal Ireland, published in 1972,[9] Garret FitzGerald argued that membership of the European Community might prove to be 'the single most important factor influencing events in a positive direction in the years ahead'.[10] While he rejected the view that membership could act as a panacea, he saw such influence as membership might have as 'uniformly directed towards easing the path to a united Ireland'.[11] He put forward a number of arguments in support of this expectation. Firstly, he argued that membership of the Community would have a psychological impact on people in both parts of Ireland because more extensive contact with other Europeans would make internal differences in Ireland appear less significant. Secondly, he argued that common interests between North and South within the Community in relation to such matters as agriculture and regional policy, where there was likely to be a considerable divergence in interests between Great Britain and Northern Ireland, would draw the two parts of Ireland together. Thirdly, an economic rationale for partition in terms of a conflict of interest between North and South over the existence of protective tariffs would be removed. Fourthly, he saw the likely development of a common social policy within the Community as closing the gap between North and South in terms of social provision. Fifthly, he argued that the emotional impact of a transfer of power from Westminster to an Irish Federal Government would be lessened in a context in which much of the power exercised by Westminster had already been transferred to Brussels. Finally, he argued that the structure of European institutions strongly favoured small states and that the North might be attracted by the much larger representation it would secure in these institutions through being part of a united Ireland.[12]

Despite the obvious differences between FitzGerald's analysis and the political arguments advanced by liberal Unionists in favour of membership of the Community, both perspectives were basically derived from the same premise, the assumption that divisions between states and nations would become less significant with greater European integration. Consequently, as expectations of further progress towards integration within the Community diminished, the hopes that membership of the Community would transcend the Northern Ireland conflict and perhaps even change its terms tended to recede as well. For example, a 1982 study of Northern Ireland by the Institute for the Study of Conflict dismissed the relevance of the European dimension in the following terms: 'But since the EEC has so far been unable to promote any really significant political integration among its own members, it seems far-fetched to expect it to offer much in the search for a political solution in Northern Ireland.'[13] However by this time, it was already apparent that the Community had acquired a quite different political relevance to the conflict, one that few had envisaged during the debates on membership in the 1970s. These unexpected implications form the subject of much of the rest of this chapter.

The 1975 referendum on the British Labour Government's renegotiated terms of membership provided the opportunity for a debate within Northern Ireland on the advantages and disadvantages of membership and for a test of political opinion on the issue in the province. It was a low-key campaign in which relatively little attention was paid to the impact membership might have on Northern Ireland's position within the United Kingdom. By this time membership was already seen as having limited relevance to Northern Ireland's political

problems. The issue tended to cut across political divisions in the
province, though there was a discernible correlation between support
for power-sharing in Northern Ireland and support for continued
membership of the Community.[14] The small pro-power-sharing
Unionist Party of Northern Ireland supported continued membership,
as did the Alliance Party and the SDLP, though two of the SDLP's
leading figures, Gerry Fitt and Paddy Devlin, were opposed to
membership. Of the forty-seven anti-power-sharing Unionists elected
to the Constitutional Convention in May 1975, thirty-eight were
opposed to membership.[15] The most strident opposition to the
Community came from the leader of the DUP, Ian Paisley, who made
much of the Catholic character of the original six members of the EEC
and claimed that the Pope had referred to the Virgin Mary as the
'Madonna of the Common Market'.[16] The result of the referendum in
Northern Ireland, a narrow majority in favour of continued
membership, was a considerable surprise,[17] though the turn-out was
one of the lowest in the whole of the United Kingdom.

An opinion survey of Northern Ireland in 1978, which tested
attitudes towards the EEC, provides an interesting comparison with the
result of the 1975 referendum. The Northern Ireland Attitude Survey
asked respondents how they would vote in a hypothetical referendum
on United Kingdom membership of the European Community. The
result was very similar to that of the 1975 referendum with 49.3 per cent
of respondents indicating that they would vote to stay in the Common
Market.[18] A breakdown of the replies showed the remarkable extent to
which the issue cut across the sectarian divide with 54.9 per cent of
Catholics saying that they would vote to stay in as opposed to 47.2 per
cent of Protestants. In terms of party political affiliations. Alliance
Party supporters were most favourable to EEC membership, those of
the DUP least so. However, economic rather than political factors
dominated attitudes towards the Common Market and only 16.4 per
cent of Protestants and 26.7 per cent of Catholics agreed with a
proposition that membership of the Community made Northern
Ireland's political problems easier to solve.[19] Such responses were not
surprising given the extent to which expectations of a political
dimension to membership of the EEC had faded by the late 1970s.
Furthermore, in 1979 the British response to a European initiative in the
economic field struck a considerable blow against convergence between
North and South. The United Kingdom, unlike the Republic, decided
not to participate in the European Monetary System (EMS), a scheme
to limit exchange-rate fluctuations within the EEC. As a consequence,
parity between the Irish punt and the pound sterling was broken,
providing an added economic dimension to partition.

At first, the outcome of direct elections to the European Parliament in 1979 seemed merely to confirm the demise of any European political dimension by underlining the impenetrable nature of Northern Ireland's political divisions. In sharp contrast to the rest of the United Kingdom, there was a higher turnout in Northern Ireland in these first direct elections to the European Parliament than there had been in the referendum on membership of the Common Market in 1975. The explanation was not any increased interest in the EEC in Northern Ireland, but the fact that the elections to the European Parliament were treated as a contest of political leadership within the province and as a vote on the constitutional issue. Ian Paisley topped the poll with over 30 per cent of first preference votes. He interpreted his stunning personal triumph as a general mandate to speak for the province's Protestant population. John Hume of the SDLP also did well, polling 24.6 per cent of first preferences. The third candidate to be elected was John Taylor of the Ulster Unionist Party. The candidate of the pro-EEC Alliance Party performed poorly with less than 7 per cent of first preferences. Another significant feature of the result was the strong showing of Bernadette McAliskey standing as an independent Anti-Repression candidate. The polarisation of voting on sectarian lines demonstrated the dominant role the conflict in Northern Ireland had played in the voting.[20] What had taken place was certainly not any transcending of Northern Ireland's divisions in a 'neutral' European context but rather the 'localisation'[21] of the European dimension.

Prior to 1979, Northern Ireland had briefly been represented in the European Assembly by a moderate Unionist, Rafton Pounder, who was a member of the Conservative delegation to the Assembly in 1973 and 1974 until his defeat in the Westminster general election of February 1974. The absence of elected representatives from Northern Ireland in the Assembly and its reluctance to delve into contentious political issues outside its remit had kept the issue of Northern Ireland out of its deliberations. The direct election of the European Parliament drastically changed this, although formally consideration of the province's constitutional position went well beyond the scope of the Parliament. Paisley was the first MEP to broach the constitutional issue of Northern Ireland's international status directly in the European Parliament by raising the issue of the Republic's claim to jurisdiction over the North in February 1980. The following month the Irish MEP, Neil Blaney, who had been elected on a strongly nationalist platform, attempted to secure a full scale debate on the situation in Northern Ireland. His proposal that the Legal Affairs Committee of the Parliament should investigate violations of human rights in Northern Ireland was rebuffed.

The 1981 hunger strike proved to be a watershed in European perceptions of the Northern Ireland problem, though this was not immediately apparent in the deliberations of the European Parliament. Two Irish MEPs, Neil Blaney and Paddy Lalor of Fianna Fáil, initiated a debate on prison conditions in the Maze in May 1981. Their resolutions, which were strongly critical of British policy, were rejected in favour of an amendment put forward by the European Democratic Group that condemned terrorism while expressing concern over the hunger strike and the level of violence in the province. The amendment was carried by 107 votes to 68. The amendment also contained a clause 'recognizing that the European Community has no competence to make proposals for changes in the Constitution of Northern Ireland'.[22] However, in the same month, an informal working group of the Parliament was established under the Danish MEP, Niels Haagerup, to examine the Northern Ireland problem. A year later the European Parliament debated the use of plastic bullets in Northern Ireland, an issue that the Parliament had twice previously declined to discuss. A resolution calling for a ban on their use was passed by 110 votes to 43 with three abstentions. The inhibitions that had restrained the Parliament from delving into contentious political issues in relation to Northern Ireland were gradually disappearing. The development of a sense of European political identity within the Parliament was eroding the belief that a sharp distinction could be drawn between foreign and domestic affairs within the states of the Community or between Community affairs and political questions that were the responsibility of individual states. What put Northern Ireland at the fore of this process was the belief of many MEPs, reinforced by the hunger strike crisis, that the conflict in Northern Ireland constituted a blot on Western European civilisation and detracted from the European Community's developing political image in the outside world.

The next significant step in the development of European involvement in the conflict was a decision by the European Parliament in February 1983 that its Political Affairs Committee should conduct an inquiry into the political and economic problems of Northern Ireland. The decision shocked the British Government, which denounced the call for an inquiry as interference in the internal affairs of a member state and declared that no governmental assistance would be given to such an inquiry. The two Unionist MEPs attempted to block the establishment of the inquiry as outside the Parliament's remit and put down motions for investigations into the situations in Corsica, Sicily, and South Tyrol and into the position of Moslems in Greece, French speakers in Belgium, and Protestants in the Republic of Ireland in an effort to embarrass the Parliament into reversing its decision. However, the Bureau of the European Parliament overruled their objections and Niels Haagerup was appointed as rapporteur for the investigation. Despite the British Government's strictures on the inquiry, the Northern Ireland Office agreed to brief Haagerup on social and economic matters when he visited the province in September 1983. Unionist isolation in relation to European involvement was shown by the equivocal attitude taken by British Conservative MEPs towards the establishment of an inquiry.[23]

Haagerup's draft report on the situation in Northern Ireland was published on 12 December 1983.[24] It was a cautious document that was studiously moderate in its analysis of the conflict and in its political prescriptions. As such it was acceptable to a wide cross-section of opinion in the European Parliament. None the less, it contained propositions that Unionists were bound to find highly objectionable. In particular, it described Northern Ireland as a 'constitutional oddity' and envisaged 'the establishment of joint British-Irish responsibilities in a number of specified fields, politically, legally and otherwise'.[25] While the main thrust of the report was the need for agreement among the political parties in Northern Ireland, its advocacy of the establishment of an Anglo-Irish parliamentary body provided acknowledgment of the relevance of the Irish dimension in any settlement of the conflict. The European Parliament debated the report in March 1984. A resolution embodying the findings and recommendations of the report was passed by 124 votes to three with 63 abstentions. Neil Blaney, John Taylor, and Ian Paisley spoke and voted against the resolution. The British Conservative MEPs, apart from Lord Bethell, abstained, though apparently somewhat reluctantly.[26] The debate was widely interpreted in Northern Ireland as a triumph for John Hume's lobbying of European opinion.[27] The significant political result of the debate was to put added pressure on the British Government to reach agreement with the Republic of Ireland through the Anglo-Irish process.

New elections to the European Parliament took place in June 1984. The main focus of interest in these elections in Northern Ireland was the challenge of Sinn Fein to John Hume. In the event, Sinn Fein suffered its first significant electoral setback since its successes in the Northern Ireland Assembly elections in 1982. Hume was re-elected with 22.1 per cent of first preferences to 13.3 per cent for Danny Morrison of Sinn Fein. Paisley and Taylor were also re-elected. Paisley increased his share of first preference votes to 33.6 per cent.[28] In October 1984 the new Parliament reiterated its predecessor's call for a ban on plastic bullets in a debate that centred on the death of Sean Downes. Following controversy over the arrest of a number of Irish citizens in Britain under the Prevention of Terrorism Act at the close of 1984, the Parliament adopted a resolution in January 1985 calling for an inquiry into the operation of the Act. In October 1985 the Fianna Fáil MEP, Niall Andrews, raised the issue of the strip searching of woman prisoners in Northern Ireland in the European Parliament.[29] However, the Parliament declined to adopt a resolution calling for it to be ended. The case of miscarriages of justice in the British courts in relation to the Provisional IRA's bombing campaign in Britain was also raised in the Parliament. In December 1986 the European Parliament adopted three resolutions 'on public concern over the unsatisfactory nature of the convictions of the Birmingham Six, Guildford Four and the Maguire Seven'.[30] The resolutions called on the British Government to re-open the three cases in the light of new evidence that had become available.

These and similar debates in the previous Parliament revealed the general disposition of MEPs towards the conflict. Although MEPs from the British Isles tended to dominate debates on Northern Ireland, it was clear from their contributions that continental MEPs generally favoured peaceful progress towards the ending of partition, not least because movement in the direction of a united Ireland could be seen as progress towards the fulfilment of the wider Community goal of removing frontiers and ending divisions.[31] As in the United States, hostility towards terrorism provided the main, if weak, countervailing factor to support for the Irish nationalist cause. Criticism of the failure of the Republic of Ireland to sign the European Convention on the Suppression of Terrorism was the one issue on which Unionists were able to elicit support from other MEPs.[32] However, the issue of terrorism also created difficulties for the Unionist position. MEPs were suspicious of the international connections of Republican paramilitaries as well as alarmed by the measure of popular support the paramilitaries were able to generate within Northern Ireland during the 1981 hunger strike campaign. These two considerations taken together enhanced their enthusiasm for political initiatives to shore up the position of constitutional nationalism.

The European Parliament's debate on the Anglo-Irish Agreement in December 1985 resulted in the passage of a resolution that not only welcomed the Agreement but held out the prospect of Community money for a programme of economic development to underpin the new dispensation. It was carried by the large majority of 152 votes to 27 with 11 abstentions.[33] The opposition came from 'a disparate mixture of Fianna Fáil and their Gaullist allies, some British socialists, Flemish nationalists, and Dr Ian Paisley'.[34] The basis on which some MEPs were giving their support to the Agreement was evident in one of the few speeches from an MEP outside the British Isles, that of a Dutch member of the Rainbow Group of left-wing environmentalist parties:

> The only satisfactory solution is a united Ireland free of British occupation. The rights of the Catholics in Northern Ireland will perhaps be more respected as a result of this agreement. This could be the positive result of the signatures of Mrs Thatcher and Mr FitzGerald. However, Ireland cannot be satisfied with this. The

Agreement must now be followed by steps towards full reunification and independence. With this proviso, I shall vote for the
compromise resolution as support by this House for a step
towards unity in independence.[35]

The favourable reaction of the European Parliament to the Anglo-
Irish Agreement eased international pressure on the British
Government over Northern Ireland and was one of the most obvious,
early benefits of the Agreement from a British perspective. At the same
time, the support of the European Parliament, like that of the United
States Congress, had another implication. It locked the two
Governments into the Agreement through the embarrassment they
would suffer internationally if either repudiated what international
opinion had endorsed with their encouragement. While the EEC has
not as yet made any contribution to the International Fund set up by the
British and Irish Governments to handle aid specifically given in the
context of the Agreement, Northern Ireland has in general been a major
beneficiary of funds from the EEC as an economically depressed region of
the Community.[36] Further, in November 1986 the European Parliament
passed a resolution by 155 votes to one, calling 'on the Commission to
draw up an Integrated Development Programme, in conjunction with
the Northern Ireland authorities and the United Kingdom
government'[37] to apply to the whole of the province except Belfast for
which an EEC programme already existed.

None of the other institutions of the Community matched in
importance the role played by the European Parliament in relation to
the conflict. Indeed, the Commission set considerable store by its
capacity to foster co-operation on social and economic questions across
the sectarian divide in Northern Ireland in contexts that were seen as
politically neutral.[38] An indirect influence on the situation was the impact
of European Political Co-operation (EPC) on the development of
Anglo-Irish relations. The aim of EPC was the co-ordination of the
foreign policies of the Community's member states towards countries
outside of the EEC. Formally, therefore, Anglo-Irish relations lay
outside the ambit of EPC. However, the EPC process, involving regular
consultation between officials in the foreign ministries of member states
prior to action at a political level through the Council of Ministers and
at meetings of Heads of Government, greatly enhanced the scope and
status of Irish foreign policy[39] and provided a context in which the
Republic of Ireland enjoyed a measure of equality with the United
Kingdom. EPC itself grew in importance during the 1970s as progress
towards political integration within the Community stalled. At its
lowest EPC provided a justification for closer relations between
London and Dublin and opportunities for informal discussion between

Ministers on the problem of Northern Ireland that did not require public affirmations of their governments' respective positions on the constitutional issue. Significantly, the British Prime Minister, Margaret Thatcher, fended off criticism of the meeting in December 1980 with the Irish Prime Minister, Charles Haughey, which launched the Anglo-Irish process, by justifying the summit as a routine meeting between two Community Heads of Government.[40]

Others went much further in their invocation of the relevance of the European dimension. In May 1981, a leading figure in the British Social Democrat Party, David Owen, suggested that the United Kingdom and the Republic should 'place the whole issue of Northern Ireland into the framework of European Political Co-operation'.[41] A slightly more mundane illustration of the importance of the Republic's input into the affairs of the European Community was the role played by the Irish delegation in securing an increase in Northern Ireland's representation from two to three seats in discussions on direct elections to the European Parliament in 1977. The practical effect of the decision was that the SDLP in the person of John Hume was able to secure representation in the Parliament with far-reaching consequences for the role played by the European Parliament in the conflict. Brigid Laffan in a study of the consequences of membership for Irish foreign policy published in 1983 concluded that 'membership of the Community has not given Ireland significant leverage in its relations with Britain on the Northern question',[42] though she acknowledged that it 'has added a new dimension to the Anglo-Irish relationship'.[43] In the light of the Anglo-Irish Agreement of November 1985, such a judgment seems too cautious. While membership of the Community did not have the dramatic impact on partition that some in the Republic had anticipated prior to 1973,[44] its implications went further than Laffan's conclusion would suggest.

Firstly, membership of the European Community was important in enhancing the status of the Republic of Ireland in the world. This was particularly underlined by the development of European Political Co-operation. Partition became less of a symbol of the Republic's subordination to the United Kingdom. Consequently, for the Republic, it was no longer necessary to view the issue of Northern Ireland in stark all-or-nothing terms. Secondly, the Republic's new status enhanced the value to Britain of closer relations both in regard to Northern Ireland and other matters. Thirdly, because the Republic's stance on the issue appeared accommodatory to European opinion, it became easier for the Republic to enlist support in Europe for a change in British policy. The increased international pressure on Britain over the conflict in Northern Ireland through the directly elected European Parliament and other bodies added to London's interest in an agreement with Dublin. These factors facilitated a convergence of views between the two capitals and form an important part of the background to the Anglo-Irish process, culminating in the signing of the Hillsborough Agreement in November 1985.

The implications of the United Kingdom's and the Republic's membership of the EEC for the problem of Northern Ireland have proved to be very different from many of the expectations that existed prior to entry. Most striking of all has been the negligible impact of functional co-operation between North and South on the conflict. Cross-border schemes promoted by the EEC, while occasionally giving rise to political controversy, have had little discernible impact on attitudes in Northern Ireland. The hopes of liberal Unionists and nationalists that common membership of the Community would make the Border less of a political issue in Northern Ireland and that sectarian divisions might wither as a result have proved false. The Community dimension has failed to transcend sectarianism. The Unionist and nationalist blocs have remained intact, though internally divided. The EEC, far from dissolving the conflict, has internationalised it. This has worked politically to the benefit of constitutional nationalism, though not from the bottom up, but from the top down.

In May 1949 ten European states at the initiative of the European Movement, itself a product of a multitude of organisations established to promote European co-operation in the aftermath of the Second World War, formed the Council of Europe. Both the United Kingdom and the Republic of Ireland were founder members of the new organisation. The aim of the Council of Europe was to achieve greater unity among the democratic countries of Europe through common action in 'economic, social, cultural, scientific, legal, and administrative matters and in the maintenance and further realisation of human rights and fundamental freedoms'.[45] Military matters lay outside the ambit of the Council. The organisation consisted of a Committee of Ministers, made up of the foreign ministers of member states, and a Consultative Assembly, which provided a parliamentary forum for the member states. In the context of Britain's extensive international commitments, the Council of Europe constituted a very minor element in British foreign policy. The same was not the case for the Republic of Ireland. The Republic was not a member of the British Commonwealth. Irish neutrality further limited the scope of the Republic's foreign relations and was responsible for Ireland's exclusion from the United Nations until 1955. So for much of the 1950s, the Consultative Assembly provided a practically unique forum for the articulation of Irish views in an international context. It was used in the main by the Irish representatives as a platform for speeches denouncing partition. F. S. L. Lyons characterised the reaction of other delegates to these speeches as 'one of boredom mingled with bewilderment'.[46]Conor Cruise O'Brien was equally scathing: 'Our Parliamentary delegates to the Council of Europe seemed to devote their time to making speeches about partition; speeches which were designed to be read at home, but which unfortunately had to be listened to abroad'.[47] The failure of Irish efforts to internationalise the question of Northern Ireland through the Council of Europe forms an instructive contrast to what was later to be achieved through the European Parliament.

The establishment of machinery for the protection of human rights in member states was one of the first items to be considered by the Consultative Assembly. The result was the adoption of the Convention for the Protection of Human Rights and Fundamental Freedoms by foreign ministers of the Council of Europe at a meeting in Rome on 4 November 1950. However, the Convention (commonly referred to as the European Convention on Human Rights) did not come into force until September 1953 following its ratification by ten member states. It was a further two years before an Article came into force which granted the right of petition to individuals within member states that chose to allow this procedure. Interest in the Republic in the creation of this machinery reflected not merely general concern about the issue of human rights, but also, according to Hederman, 'a tactical feeling that such a Convention could be used to press for changes in the conditions of the Catholic minority in Northern Ireland'.[48] Ironically, the first case to be considered by the European Court of Human Rights, created for the purpose of enforcing the Convention, involved the Republic.[49] Both the Republic and the United Kingdom chose to allow petitioning by individuals and to accept the compulsory jurisdiction of the Court, but made use of Article 15 to limit their obligations under the Convention as circumstances required.

The first case directly related to the conflict in Northern Ireland was brought by the Irish Government in applications to the European Commission of Human Rights in December 1971 and March 1972. The Irish applications made several submissions concerning the situation in Northern Ireland. In particular, they alleged that persons detained under the Special Powers Act after the introduction of internment in August 1971 had been subjected to torture and inhuman and degrading treatment contrary to Article 3 of the Convention, and they claimed that internment as employed in Northern Ireland constituted a violation of Article 5 (the right to liberty and security of person) and Article 6 (the right to a fair trail) and was exercised in a discriminatory manner contrary to Article 14. The case centred on the question of the interrogation methods used by the security forces in the months following the introduction of internment. These included the hooding of detainees, subjecting them to an ear-splitting noise intended to produce disorientation, forcing them to remain standing against a wall for long periods, deprivation of sleep, and restricted diet. These methods had already been the subject of political controversy in Britain and of two separate inquiries into their use in Northern Ireland, as a result of which the British Prime Minister, Edward Heath, had announced in March 1972 that their use was being stopped.

Partly because the British Government had taken steps relatively promptly to ensure that use of these techniques was discontinued, there was considerable resentment in Britain over the Irish Government's decision to continue to pursue the case under the Convention. It proved to be a lengthy process once the Commission decided that the Irish applications warranted investigation. There were hearings of witnesses put forward by the Irish Government in December 1973 and February 1974 and of witnesses put forward by the British Government in 1974 and as late as February 1975. Altogether 118 witnesses were heard. The Commission's report on the case was sent to the Committee of Ministers in February 1976 and published in September the same year. The Commission accepted that the British Government's derogation from the Convention under Article 15 in respect of detention without trial was justified in terms of the situation in Northern Ireland and that this power had not been exercised in a discriminatory way. However, the Commission held that the interrogation methods employed by the security forces constituted a violation of Article 3. To the dismay and anger of the British Government,[50] the Irish Government referred the case, as it was entitled to do, to the European Court of Human Rights for a definitive judgment. It was the first inter-state case under the Convention to be referred to the Court. Judgment was delivered on 18 January 1978. The Court drew a distinction between torture and inhuman and degrading treatment and found the United Kingdom guilty of the slightly lesser charge.

In any context, such a judgment would have been a grave embarrassment to the British Government. The fact that the interrogation methods in question had been officially authorised in the first place and then accepted retrospectively by a majority on the Committee of Privy Counsellors examining their use added to the indictment. Given international questioning of the legitimacy of Northern Ireland as a political entity, the judgment was bound to have much more far-reaching political implications than would have been the case if the setting had been less politically contentious. The case through its various stages contributed significantly to souring relations between Britain and the Republic. The strong feelings it aroused in the British Government are reflected in the comments of Merlyn Rees on the case in his book on his period as Secretary of State for Northern Ireland:

During all this time, successive British governments faced bloody violence in Northern Ireland, where the Irish government's persistence with their complaint reinforced loyalist feelings about the perfidy of the South and gave respectability to the actions of republican paramilitaries.[51]

From the Republic's perspective, the case demonstrated both its interest in human rights in Northern Ireland and its capacity to secure redress through its membership of international organisations. That was seen as important in the context of the contest for the allegiance of the Catholic minority in Northern Ireland. More widely, the case and its outcome exposed Britain's vulnerability over the issue of Northern Ireland internationally. It was frequently cited abroad by opponents of British rule in Northern Ireland. The case was brought up whenever fresh allegations of misbehaviour by the security forces were made, because it made such claims seem more credible in the light of Britain's past record in Northern Ireland.

The next important case involving the conflict in Northern Ireland was brought by four Republican prisoners in the Maze. Their petition to the European Commission of Human Rights claimed that the conditions of their imprisonment and the denial to them of special category status constituted inhuman and degrading treatment under the Convention. The Commission's ruling was published in June 1980. It rejected their claim and held that they were not entitled to be regarded as political prisoners under British, European, or international law.[52] The outcome of the case was of considerable assistance to the British Government in buttressing its position during the subsequent hunger strikes over the issue of special category status. For example, the ruling was repeatedly referred to in the debate in the European Parliament in 1981 as a reason why the resolutions critical of Britain's handling of the hunger strike should be rejected.[53] However, the rejection of the prisoners' claim was tempered by the Commission's insistence that the Government was under an obligation on humanitarian grounds to show greater flexibility over the protest on the issue, an aspect of the Commission's ruling that provided ammunition for opponents of the Government's handling of the hunger strikes.

The conflict in Northern Ireland was central to two further cases taken to the Commission. The petitions lodged in 1981 by Edith Elliott in respect of the murder of both her husband and her brother in terrorist incidents complained that the Republic of Ireland through its claim to jurisdiction over Northern Ireland and the British Government in failing to implement effective security measures had violated their obligation under the Convention to protect the right to life of the deceased. The case was dismissed by the Commission at a preliminary stage on a technicality. The presentation of the widow's case was made by the Ulster Unionist Party and indicated the readiness of Unionists to

avail themselves of the machinery under the Convention, notwithstanding their general opposition to intervention in the conflict by
international bodies. The other case was brought by the family of Brian
Stewart, a twelve-year-old killed by a plastic bullet in Belfast in 1976.
Their petition complained that the use of plastic bullets constituted a
violation of the Convention. The Commission's ruling, published in
October 1984, held that since the incidence of casualties was relatively
low in relation to the number of baton rounds fired in the course of riots
since 1969, the use of the weapon could not be construed as a breach of
the Convention.

Two other cases were indirectly linked to the conflict in Northern
Ireland. The most important concerned the operation of the Prevention
of Terrorism Act. The three applicants had been arrested and detained
under the Act for 45 hours in February 1977 after disembarking from
the Dublin to Liverpool ferry on their return from a holiday in Ireland.
Two were British citizens, the third an Irish citizen. They complained
that there were no grounds of reasonable suspicion for their arrest. The
Commission took up the case but ultimately ruled against the
applicants in the light of the terrorist threat that lay behind their arrest,
notwithstanding the absence of any evidence that there had been
grounds for suspicion that they as individuals had any connection with
terrorism. Potentially embarrassing to both the British and Irish
Governments was the case brought by the Littlejohn brothers
concerning their extradition to the Republic in connection with a bank
robbery carried out with members of the IRA in October 1972. Their
application highlighted differences in the British and Irish law in
relation to the definition of a political offence for the purposes of extradition and their contention that they had carried out the robbery while
working for British intelligence. The Commission declared their
application inadmissible.

Although it might appear from the generality of cases discussed above
that the Convention has had little impact on the conduct of British
policy towards the Northern Ireland conflict, that would be to
underestimate its influence as a constraining factor not just on security
policy but also on the political options that can be pursued by the
Government. In particular, Britain's adherence to the Convention
effectively rules out the adoption of many of the security measures
pressed for by Unionists and the associated political strategy of seeking
to crush Republican paramilitaries by military means. In the early phase
of the Troubles, the British Government took up the option of dero-
gating from obligations under the Convention on the grounds of the
existence of a state of emergency. However, with the adoption of the
policy of criminalisation in the second half of the 1970s, that option
became less attractive and Britain no longer relies on derogation from

the Convention. The British Government is acutely conscious of the tendency of international opinion to focus on the violation of human rights in territories where political authority is seen as deficient in international legitimacy and of the fact that the use of emergency measures to suppress internal unrest tends to reinforce external perceptions of the conflict in Northern Ireland as a quasi-colonial situation. By keeping within the bounds of the European Convention on Human Rights, the British Government hopes to project an image of Northern Ireland as governed according to the standards of a West European democracy.

This is important in the context of external perceptions of the nature of continuing violence in Northern Ireland. The phenomenon of terrorism within other liberal-democracies in Western Europe has partially enabled the British Government to present political violence in Northern Ireland within this framework. The advantage to the British Government of placing the conflict in this wider context has been that it has been able to avail itself of the machinery that has been developed within Europe to cope specifically with the problem of terrorism. The European Convention on the Suppression of Terrorism, drawn up at the initiative of the Council of Europe, came into force in 1977. It provides for the extradition, or alternatively, the trial in the jurisdiction of the state apprehending the suspect, of anyone accused of a terrorist offence—that is to say, any serious offence involving an act of violence. It thus limits the circumstances in which a suspect is able to prevent extradition on the grounds that the offence for which extradition is being sought is political and therefore outside the scope of co-operation between states to apprehend criminals. The spirit of the Convention ran counter to the wide interpretation that Irish courts initially placed on what constituted a political offence outside the reach of extradition. Successive Irish Governments took the view that the definition of a political offence in use in the Irish courts, which was rooted indirectly in the Constitution itself, was an obstacle to Ireland's adherence to the Convention. This stance caused considerable friction between Britain and the Republic and was seen by Unionists as underlining their contention that the Republic provided a safe haven for terrorists. In this instance, it was the Republic's position that ran counter to European opinion.

However, two important judgments of the Irish Supreme Court in 1982 and 1984 considerably narrowed the definition of a political offence accepted by the Irish courts. In the first of these cases, involving a leading figure in the INLA, Dominic McGlinchey, the Irish Chief Justice laid down as a test of a political offence whether it was within the bounds of 'what reasonable, civilised people would regard as political activity'.[54] The judgment opened the way for extradition to Northern Ireland from the Republic of Ireland for at least some terrorist offences. The way was also cleared for the Republic's adherence to the European Convention on the Suppression of Terrorism. For political reasons the Irish Government linked this step to the Anglo-Irish Agreement of November 1985. By that time, all but two of the twenty-one members of the Council of Europe had signed the Convention, although some states entered reservations when they accepted the Convention. The Republic signed the Convention in February 1986. However, ratification required the consent of the Dáil. It ran into considerable opposition because of the failure of the Government to enter any reservations when it signed the Convention. Concern that there had been a miscarriage of justice in a number of cases connected with the Provisional IRA's bombing campaign in the UK mainland added to the clamour against ratification. In the end, the Government refused to yield on the issue of reservations but secured the support of the Dáil by delaying implementation till December 1987 to allow the British Government time to fulfil the commitments it had entered into to reform the administration of justice in Northern Ireland, which was seen as a *quid pro quo* for the Republic's acceptance of the Convention. However, in view of the post-1982 attitude of the Irish courts to what constitutes a political offence, it seems unlikely that implementation will make very much practical difference to the ease of extradition when it occurs.

The third level of European intervention in the conflict in Northern Ireland arises out of the bilateral relations of the United Kingdom and the Republic of Ireland with other European states. It is also the most difficult to get to grips with, as evidence that other European governments have taken an active interest in the conflict to the point of discussing the issue in bilateral exchanges with either London or Dublin is fragmentary at best. Significantly, the most explicit governmental criticisms of British policy in Northern Ireland coincided with the hunger strike crisis of 1981. No event in Northern Ireland since the onset of the Troubles in 1968 and 1969, including even Bloody Sunday, evoked a greater response in Europe than the death of Bobby Sands in May 1981. It provoked large demonstrations in a number of European cities including Paris, Milan, Brussels, and Athens. The Portuguese Parliament went so far as to observe a minute's silence in honour of Sands.[55] Press comment was also generally hostile to the British stance on the issue, although some papers were concerned that the pressure on the British Government should not lead to a victory for terrorism. The *Frankfurter Allegemeine Zeitung* called Northern Ireland 'this weak point of British democracy'[56], while *Le Monde* described Margaret Thatcher as faithful to her legend as the Iron Lady to the point of caricature, arguing that the British Government had made a martyr of Sands.[57] The Portuguese *Popular Daily* declared that Britain had 'the inglorious distinction of being the only country in free Europe to hold a part of the continent as a colony'.[58] Official comment on the hunger-strike crisis was much more restrained. The most significant response, though couched in general terms, came from the West German Chancellor, Helmut Schmidt, just over a month before Sands's death. Reporting to the Bundestag on a meeting with the Irish Prime Minister, Charles Haughey, Schmidt voiced support for the Anglo-Irish initiative launched at the Dublin summit in December 1980, expressed the view that Northern Ireland was an international problem, and described the situation in Northern Ireland as a source of deep irritation to the West German Government.[59] The victory of the French Left in Presidential and National Assembly elections during 1981 brought a new government to power in France, members of whom had been fiercely critical of British rule in Northern Ireland while in Opposition. In a speech to the National Assembly the new French Foreign Minister, Claude Cheysson said that France supported the stance of the Irish Government on the hunger strike and called for collective action by the international community over the situation in Northern Ireland.[60]

However, despite occasionally tough rhetoric about British policy in Northern Ireland, no European Government was prepared, in practice, to press the British Government on the issue to the point at which it became an irritant in bilateral relations with the United Kingdom. While there was a certain amount of speculation in the press that the issue was raised in bilateral meetings between British and French ministers, it appears to have been accorded a very low priority and no briefing of the press on the content of discussions on Northern Ireland took place. More information has been made public about discussion of Northern Ireland in the context of bilateral relations between the Republic of Ireland and individual European states. Such discussion seems generally to have taken place at the initiative of the Irish Government and much of the Irish effort appears to have been directed at France. In March 1980 the Irish Prime Minister, Charles Haughey raised the issue in discussions with the French President, Giscard d'Estaing, hoping to enlist French support for a new initiative on Northern Ireland. Although the French were sympathetic to the Irish viewpoint, they made it clear that they were unwilling to take up the issue bilaterally with Britain on Ireland's behalf.[61] President Mitterand went considerably further in expressing support for the Irish Government's stance on Northern Ireland, though he also indicated that French help would have to stop short of any interference on the issue.[62] Following the Anglo-Irish Agreement of November 1985, the Irish Prime Minister, Garret FitzGerald, specifically thanked the French Government for helping the Irish Government's efforts to secure the Agreement and for the interest it had shown in the issue.[63] However, clearly, at a national level, European diplomatic intervention over the issue of Northern Ireland, in so far as it has existed at all, has not amounted to much.

The contrast between the reluctance of national governments to take up the issue of Northern Ireland bilaterally with Britain and the willingness of the European Parliament to involve itself in the issue is therefore very striking. There is some irony in the fact that the European Parliament, conceived as a step towards erosion of national differences among West European democracies, has played such a significant role in strengthening international support for constitutional nationalism in Northern Ireland. While John Hume's commitment to political accommodation between the communities in Northern Ireland has aided his efforts to enlist support in the Parliament, it is clear that sympathy for the goal of a united Ireland plays a central role in the Parliament's response to the issue. By contrast, national governments, the very embodiment of the divisions that European idealists wish to see transcended, have declined to get involved in a conflict bound up with the legitimacy of the boundaries of the nation-state. There is a simple explanation for this apparent paradox. Interests dictate the approach of national governments. It is easy to calculate that there is no benefit to involvement and much to lose. By contrast, the Parliament has naturally been the vehicle for a more normative approach. This does not simply apply to the case of Northern Ireland but is reflected in its deliberations on a whole range of issues, including such topics as the invasion of Afghanistan and unrest in South Africa. Expressing a collective view on matters that raise fundamental questions of political principle is necessarily a part of the development of the Parliament's political identity. Its own legitimacy is at stake. Considerable damage would be done to the reputation of the Parliament if it appeared indifferent to public concern about such issues.

Similarly, a Parliament aspiring to be more than simply a meeting place for representatives from different countries could hardly have ignored a conflict within the borders of Western Europe as serious as that in Northern Ireland. Indeed, the more successful the Parliament is in establishing legitimacy for itself as a body politically representative of the people within the boundaries of the member states of the EEC, the larger the issue is likely to loom as a European responsibility and the more the conflict in Northern Ireland will tend to be seen as a blot on European democracy. The European Convention on Human Rights embodies the commitment of the states belonging to the Council of Europe to a common set of principles, but it is subject to the rather different process of legal adjudication. While it places constraints on British security policy, acceptance of the Convention also provides the British Government with a valuable political defence of the manner in which it rules Northern Ireland. However, the overall effect of the three levels of European intervention is to increase international pressures on the British Government over the issue of Northern Ireland. Thus, it is unlikely that Britain would find the issue any less troublesome if its foreign policy tilted towards Europe and away from the United States.

9.

COMPARATIVE PERSPECTIVES

INTERNAL perceptions of the Northern Ireland conflict tend to influence opinions about its comparability with conflicts taking place in other parts of the world. On the one hand, Unionists assert the province's uniqueness, and insist that external agencies have no role to play in the resolution of the conflict; on the other hand, nationalists assert that the province should be made to fall in line with universally accepted political norms by the international community. As the last two chapters illustrated, external parties have tended to favour the nationalist case in Northern Ireland so the attitudes of both Unionists and nationalists on this score are perfectly comprehensible. While it needs to be recognised that polemics often influence the comparisons that are made between Northern Ireland and other societies, the comparative perspective none the less has analytical value. It provides the necessary intellectual incentive to separate out the structural features of each case from the less essential flux of personalities and events. It also provides a context in which to examine whether the trends in a particular conflict are specific to that situation or are representative of the direction of change in a number of societies. Finally, in the particular context of this book, it provides an opportunity to test propositions that have been made about the influence of international norms on the Northern Ireland conflict by examining the relevance of these norms in comparable situations elsewhere.

There are a very large number of situations in the world with which the Northern Ireland problem can be compared. Indeed, the list of possible comparisions appears to be growing longer every year with the contemporary relevance of the conflicts in Fiji, New Caledonia, and Sri Lanka.[1] In this chapter, the comparison will be limited to five cases: Lebanon, Cyprus, Israel, Puerto Rico, and Corsica. Two main considerations determined the choice. In the first place, it was decided to restrict the choice of cases to societies caught up presently or in the recent past in violent conflict, though there is a very wide variation in the scale of violence which the five societies named have experienced.

The level of violence in Lebanon since the outbreak of the civil war in the mid-1970s has been far higher than anything Northern Ireland has experienced during the Troubles whereas in Puerto Rico and in Corsica it has not approached that in Northern Ireland. In the second place, they were chosen either because they have a considerable number of general features in common with Northern Ireland or because of a very particular resemblance to Northern Ireland in one area that is especially illuminating. Like Northern Ireland itself, four of the five are examples of deeply divided societies, though their degree of division varies. The exception is Puerto Rico. Like Northern Ireland, the five are small both in size and population. Three are independent states, though in the case of Cyprus and Lebanon, their existence as single entities is more a question of international law than of political reality. However, independence, real or nominal, remains a significant point of difference between these countries and Northern Ireland. This gives added importance to the two sub-state entities that have been included among the cases for comparision.

Of the five, Lebanon is the society Northern Ireland is probably most often compared with, from outside the province. On television news programmes round the world, Beirut and Belfast project an image of being twinned cities of Hell. Inside Northern Ireland, the case of Lebanon is seen slightly differently as an object lesson of the devastating potential of civil war and of what could befall Northern Ireland, should the worst happen. However, there are more reasons for comparing the two situations than their common experience of the car bomb or their capacity for bloodletting. The boundaries of Lebanon as a political entity were established in the same year as those of Northern Ireland, 1920. Like those of Northern Ireland, they cut across previous boundaries and were without historical precedent. Mount Lebanon had enjoyed a measure of autonomy under the Ottoman Empire from 1861. However, when the French acquired the mandate for Syria and Mount Lebanon under the Treaty of San Remo in 1920, they created the new political entity of Lebanon by attaching to it Syrian districts. They claimed that the enlargement was necessary to ensure the economic viability of the new entity, notwithstanding the hostility to the transfer of territory of the largely Muslim population in these districts. Much the same argument was used by Britain to justify the inclusion of the counties of Fermanagh and Tyrone in Northern Ireland against the wishes of the local population. Like Northern Ireland, Lebanon was widely seen at the outset as 'an artificial country with arbitrary borders'.[2] Consequently, the commitment of the dominant community, the Maronites, to the legitimacy of the entity France had created was rarely fully shared by other communities.

However, in the 1940s the various communities of Lebanon did come together politically, when the Free French tried to maintain the mandate after France itself had been defeated by Germany. This united the Lebanese communities behind a demand for independence. The Muslims swallowed their objections to the boundaries of Lebanon as the *quid pro quo* for the ending of the special relationship between France and the Maronites. The political accommodation of Lebanon's different communities at the time of the country's independence in 1943 was enshrined in an agreement known as the National Pact. Under the Pact, acceptance of the country's boundaries and a double negative, neither Westernisation nor Arabicisation, underpinned a complex formula for the representation of Lebanon's confessional communities in the political system. Under this formula, the communities were represented in the country's Chamber of Deputies and in government on a ratio of six Christians to five Muslims, a ratio which was derived from Lebanon's last official census in 1932. The principle of proportionality was extended to the allocation of particular posts within the system. By far the most important position, the Presidency, was reserved to a Maronite; the Premiership to a Sunni Muslim; and the Presidency of the Chamber of Deputies to a Shi'a Muslim. The result was the entrench-ment of the dominant position of the Maronite minority within an outwardly democratic system, though Maronite dominance was tempered by powers of patronage afforded to the leaders of the other communities. Patronage underpinned the role of wealthy, regionally based notables or traditional leaders in the context of *laisser-faire* economic policies. Indeed, within this system government itself was extremely weak and carried out few of the functions expected of the modern state. Public services, where they existed at all, were at best rudimentary.

The negative nature of the compact among the communities, coupled with their reluctance to cede power to the centre, made the whole arrangement vulnerable from the beginning to any changes that upset the complex balance of power among the communities. The National Pact was, in fact, little more than 'a form of mutual deterrence'.[3] The first breakdown of the system occurred in 1958 when President Chamoun's attempt to align Lebanon more closely with the West provoked a revolt by Muslims inspired by the Arab nationalism of Gamal Abdel Nasser. Equilibrium was restored by the Commander of the Armed Forces, General Chehab, who refused to allow the army to be used on the side of the Maronites. As a result of his judicious restraint he was elected President. Chehab sought to strengthen the institutions of the state as a force standing above the power struggle among the communities. In 1970 the system Chehab had created suffered a serious political reverse with the election by a single vote of a regional clan leader dedicated to restoring patronage as the basis of government and with no interest in sustaining the power of the state as a neutral force at the centre of society. Chehab's system—and Lebanon—never recovered.

Lebanon's slide into civil war began in 1975. Of a number of episodes that marked the country's descent into chaos, the massacre in April of that year of 27 Palestinians on a bus ambushed by Maronite gunmen is perhaps most often mentioned as the turning point. The highlighting of this particular episode provides an indication of the importance of the Palestinian presence and Maronite reaction to it as a cause of the breakdown. The Palestinian presence in Lebanon dated back to the establishment of the neighbouring state of Israel and the first Arab-Israeli war, in the aftermath of which over 100,000 Palestinian refugees settled in Lebanon. The numbers of Palestinians in Lebanon grew still further after the 1967 Arab-Israeli war and the 1970 expulsion of the Palestine Liberation Organisation (PLO) from Jordan. By 1975 there were some 350,000 Palestinians in Lebanon, approximately 10 per cent of the country's population. The Maronites increasingly came to see their presence as a destabilising force within Lebanon, tipping the country politically towards Arab nationalism and disturbing the balance among the communities. The use of Lebanese territory by the PLO as a launching pad for raids into Galilee was turning the country into a target for Israeli retaliation. The terms of the 1969 Cairo Agreement, which committed Lebanon to support the Palestinian cause, and the inherent weakness of state institutions reduced the Lebanese Government to a state of impotence. In some areas, the PLO became virtually a state within a state.

Division within Lebanon over the Palestinian issue was by no means the only factor fuelling conflict between the communities. The rigidity of the formula for the political representation of the communities was an important source of contention as Muslims now constituted a clear majority of the population. Not surprisingly, representatives of the Muslim communities demanded more power within the system. The enormous gulf between the rich and the poor in Lebanon was also becoming a source of conflict, with the process of modernisation itself generating demands for greater economic equity within the country. These issues were reflected in the make-up of the two main contestants that emerged in the first phase of the civil war. They were a right-wing Maronite grouping, the Lebanese Front, and a left-wing, largely Muslim and Druze grouping, the National Movement. However, with 50,000 people killed in 1975 and 1976, the war between communities tended to override the ideological aspects of the conflict. The result was that the army disintegrated under the pressures of communal loyalties.

At the request of the Lebanese President, Syria sent in its troops in April 1976 to restore order. While Syrian intervention prevented the defeat of the Maronites, it failed to bring peace to Lebanon. Indeed, following Syrian intervention fissures appeared within both the Lebanese Front and the National Movement, leading to violent conflicts within each of the blocs. Despite the evident failure of their mission, the Syrian troops stayed in Lebanon, the legitimacy of Syria's action underwritten by a mandate from the Arab League. Concern over Syrian influence in Lebanon and the continuing provocation of Palestinian raids from its territory in turn prompted Israeli intervention in the south of the country in 1978 and a full-scale invasion in 1982. The former led to the establishment of the United Nations Interim Force in Lebanon to stop incursions into Israel from Lebanese territory, the latter to the establishment of the Multinational Force, composed principally of American and French troops, to supervise the withdrawal of the PLO from Beirut. To this catalogue of external interventions must be added the less direct but in most respects much more successful intervention in the conflict by revolutionary Iran. Through the dispatch of revolutionary guards to the country, the influence it wields over the largest of the country's confessional communities, the Shi'a Muslims, and the money it has invested in building schools and clinics in the areas its sympathisers control, Iran has created practically 'a state within a state in Lebanon'.[4] The scale of external intervention in Lebanon is partly a reflection of the strategic location of the country on the frontline of the Arab-Israeli conflict, and partly of the opportunities presented by a state in which government is unable to exercise the most basic of its functions in the realm of law and order. It has immensely complicated the problem of re-establishing a political and institutional consensus among the now far more territorially separated communities, and by dispersing control of different parts of the territory into the hands of particular factions, it has put obstacles in the way of the implementation of any agreement reached by representatives of the different communities. Thus, approximately 180 ceasefires broke down in the period from 1975 to the end of 1983.[5]

The much larger number of deaths in the Lebanese conflict coupled with the qualitatively more lethal nature of the weaponry at the disposal of the paramilitaries constitutes one of the most obvious differences between the situation in the Lebanon and that in Northern Ireland. This is related to a more fundamental difference, the relative absence of external intervention in the Northern Ireland conflict. Northern Ireland's lack of international legitimacy has not prompted the involvement of outside powers that Lebanon has experienced as a consequence of the weakness of the Lebanese state and of the country's strategic location. That puts into perspective the influence of international norms; Lebanon's problems cannot plausibly be attributed to their role. Paradoxically, despite the similarity of Lebanon's origin as a political entity to that of Northern Ireland, the international community has treated Lebanon as a fully legitimate political entity, secure in its status as a sovereign independent state, notwithstanding the *de facto* fragmentation of its territory. Even those states that have intervened most directly in the country's affairs pay lip service to the idea of Lebanon as an independent state. Proposals for the partition of the country as a way of ending the endemic intercommunal conflict have consistently failed to attract international support. What Lebanon's experience suggests is that if Northern Ireland ever were to achieve international recognition as an independent state, the origin of its boundaries from partition might largely cease to matter internationally.

From the perspective of Northern Ireland, perhaps the most significant conclusion that can be drawn from a comparision of the two societies is that the potential for a catastrophe on the Lebanese scale does not exist in Northern Ireland, because there is no foreseeable prospect of paramilitaries in Northern Ireland acquiring the resources of destruction available to the parties to the conflict in Lebanon. Nor is there any likelihood of an escalation of the violence through the direct military intervention of external powers. Further, while Britain's commitment to the existence of Northern Ireland remains conditional and while the security forces remain constrained by British concern over international reaction to violations of human rights in the province, the British state is not weak in Northern Ireland in the sense of lacking the capacity to demonstrate its sovereign control over the territory. Indeed, paradoxically, the role of the state is larger in Northern Ireland, especially in the economic realm, than in any other part of the United Kingdom. In this respect, the contrast with the Lebanese state could hardly be greater. It is therefore with good reason that the scenario of civil war in Northern Ireland is most often discussed in the context of a British withdrawal. Even in such circumstances Northern Ireland's membership of the Western community makes it unlikely that its collapse into chaos would be permitted to proceed very far.

While Lebanon's communal divisions are far more complex than those of Northern Ireland, there are some obvious similarities between the two societies apart from conflict. Residential segregation, separate education, and endogamy are features of both. But politically, there is an ironic contrast between the triumphalist attitudes of Northern Ireland's politicians and the commitment to political accommodation in Lebanon, which appears to have survived the breakdown of the country's consociational system of government. The dominant community in Lebanon, the Maronites, are far more disposed towards power-sharing than are Protestants in Northern Ireland. The Maronites embraced power-sharing in 1943 as a means of safeguarding their position in an independent Lebanon. By contrast Unionists have hitherto argued that guaranteeing a place to nationalists in the govern-

ment of Northern Ireland under power-sharing arrangements constitutes a threat to the status of the province as part of the United
Kingdom. Part of the reason for the difference of attitude is that
Maronites are a minority in Lebanon who could not realistically hope to
govern the country without the involvement of the other communities,
whereas Protestants as Unionists constitute a majority that was able
to govern Northern Ireland for more than four decades in relative tranquillity without even seeking the consent of Catholics as a community.
For that reason they have found it very difficult to face the implications
of the internationalisation of the conflict after 1969.

The implications for Northern Ireland of Lebanon's experience of
power-sharing prior to the breakdown of the system are, firstly, that
power-sharing does not automatically equalise the position of the
communities represented in the system and, secondly, that it is not a
guarantee of stability even when it has apparently been operating
successfully for a number of years. Lebanese experience is therefore a
caution against seeing what remains the main aim of British policy, the
achievement of power-sharing devolution in Northern Ireland, as a
panacea for the province's ills or as a permanent resolution of conflict
between the communities in Northern Ireland. Indeed, on the basis of
the experience of the power-sharing Executive in Northern Ireland in
1974 it is questionable whether the establishment of a power-sharing
government would halt violence between the communities even
temporarily.

Cyprus represents another example of the breakdown of a consociational form of government and of the failure of power-sharing.
However, the breakdown in Cyprus, which was eventually to prompt
Turkish intervention, had very different consequences. Whereas
Lebanon remains racked by political violence, the partition of Cyprus as
a result of Turkey's invasion of the island in 1974 has largely ended the
bloodshed between the communities, though the processs of partition
itself was both violent and destructive. Despite the ending of fighting
between the communities, partition has been overwhelmingly rejected
by the international community as well as by the Greek Cypriot
majority. The present situation is perhaps most accurately described
therefore as one of bloodless conflict. Only Turkey recognised the
Turkish Republic of Northern Cyprus when it was declared an
independent state in November 1983, while the United Nations
General Assembly has passed numerous resolutions reaffirming the
territorial integrity of the island of Cyprus. Northern Cyprus has
suffered economically as a result of its isolation and that has been an
important factor in persuading its representatives to enter into
negotiations under UN auspices to explore the possibility of a federal
solution to the conflict.

Cyprus is about two-thirds the size of Northern Ireland with a population of approximately 700,000. Greek Cypriots outnumber Turkish Cypriots by roughly four to one, but that is balanced by the fact that the island is less than fifty miles from Turkey but 500 miles from the Greek mainland. The island became part of the Ottoman Empire in the sixteenth century. In 1878 Turkey transferred the administration of the island to the British with the purpose of providing them with a strategic base in the area so that they could help the Turks in the event of conflict between the Russian and Ottoman Empires. Ironically, it was never used for this purpose and Britain annexed the island when Turkey entered the First World War on the side of Germany. Because of its status as a British colony Cyprus fell outside the scope of the Treaty of Lausanne in 1923 under which Greece and Turkey arranged large and compulsory exchanges of population between their territories. In Cyprus itself the Greek Cypriot majority aspired to *enosis* or union with Greece.

In the 1950s the campaign for *enosis* became increasingly violent in the face of British reluctance to withdraw from Cyprus because of the island's strategic importance. The reaction of Turkish Cypriots to the Greek campaign was reflected in the demand they put forward for *taksim* or partition. The communal division inevitably generated support for rival paramilitaries, EOKA (National Organisation of Freedom Fighters) among Greeks and TMT (Turkish Defence Organisation) among Turks. Hostility between the communities was exacerbated because one of the principal targets of EOKA's campaign were Turkish policemen who played an important role in the execution of British security policy. However, what Greeks justified as part of their attack on colonial rule was naturally seen very differently by the Turkish Cypriot community. In the first half of 1958 there was an escalation of intercommunal violence, weakening in the process institutions such as the trade unions that had succeeded in bridging the divide between the two communities. The violence also prompted movements of population, increasing the already high level of residential segregation on the island. In August, however, there was a ceasefire, which held. Negotiations among the parties became possible when the leader of the Greek Cypriot community Archbishop Makarios, accepted independence for Cyprus as an alternative to union with Greece; an acceptance prompted by fear that Britain would otherwise implement its threat to partition the island.

However, in the first instance, agreement on the future of Cyprus was reached by the external parties with the most intimate interest in the conflict, namely Greece and Turkey. The Zurich Agreement, the outcome of direct talks between the two countries, was followed in the same month, February 1959, by a tripartite settlement between them and Britain. The settlement was accepted by the internal parties as well, though in essence 'this was a solution imposed from outside Cyprus by the three interested powers'.[6] Under it Cyprus became an independent state on 16 August 1960. An elaborate constitution was bequeathed to the new state to safeguard the position of the two communities. It laid down that the President of the Republic would be a Greek Cypriot with the right to choose seven of the ten ministers in the government, while the Vice President would be a Turkish Cypriot entitled to choose three ministers. Both were given a veto over decisions of the Council of Ministers in respect of foreign policy, defence, and internal security, and a delaying power in respect of other matters. A legislature was established, made up of 35 Greek and 15 Turkish members. Any law imposing taxes or duties required a majority of the representatives of both communities. The constitution also laid down that the civil service should allocate positions to the Greek and Turkish communities on a ratio of 70:30, entailing a slight over-representation of Turks in relation to population. There were similar provisions covering the composition of the security forces. In addition, strong protection for human rights was written into the constitution, which ran to a total of 199 articles.

Furthermore, the constitution was linked to three international treaties which formed part of the overall settlement of the Cyprus problem and which came into effect on the territory's independence. Under the Treaty of Guarantee with Britain, Greece, and Turkey, Cyprus undertook to remain independent and to adhere to the provisions of her constitution, while the three powers for their part guaranteed not just Cyprus's territorial integrity and status as an independent state but also, controversially, the principal provisions of the constitution. The Treaty of Alliance was designed to promote co-operation among Cyprus, Greece, and Turkey in foreign affairs and in defence matters. In particular, it contained provisions for the stationing of Greek and Turkish troops in Cyprus to assist the training of an army for the independent state. The Treaty of Establishment created two enclaves of British sovereign territory on the island totalling 99 square miles for use as military bases. In short, the boundaries of the new state did not encompass the entire island. Taken together, the constitution and the three treaties placed considerable constraints on the new state's effective independence. Indeed, it was questionable whether some of their provisions were legally compatible with the principle of the sovereign equality of states set out in the Charter of the United Nations.

The elaborate structure the three powers created did not last long. There was a widespread attitude among Greek Cypriots that the provisions of the constitution conferred unjustified privileges on the Turkish Cypriot minority, while Turkish Cypriots were determined to use the constitution to ensure communal equality with the Greek Cypriots despite the disparity in the numbers of the two groups. Relations between the representatives of the two communities rapidly deteriorated as a result of disputes about the constitutional provision for proportionality in the civil service, the use by the Turkish members of the legislature of their power to block taxation as a bargaining lever to demand compliance with the 70:30 ratio, the composition of the army, and other matters. Towards the end of 1963, Archbishop Makarios, who had been elected President of the Republic, proposed a series of amendments to the constitution as a way out of the impasse that had been reached. They included ending the Presidential and Vice Presidential vetoes, basing representation in the public service and in the armed forces on the ratio of population between the two communities, and removing the requirement whereby the passage of taxation needed separate majorities of the Greek and the Turkish members of the legislature. The proposals aroused the worst fears of the Turkish Cypriot community about Greek Cypriot intentions, including their desire for *enosis*, and were rejected by both Turkey and the Vice President. The political crisis deepened and such was the atmosphere of tension between the communities that a minor street disturbance in a Turkish quarter of the capital in December 1963 touched off serious intercommunal violence.

The violence spread rapidly, engulfing much of the country and leading to some 500 deaths in the first half of 1964. In these circumstances, ending the violence assumed a higher priority for the external guarantors than restoring the working of the 1960 constitution, which had irretrievably broken down as a result of the violence. With the threat of Turkish intervention looming in the background the Security Council agreed in March 1964 to the establishment of a United Nations peace-keeping force, UNFICYP and to the initiation of international mediation. The arrival of UNFICYP did not immediately stop the fighting between the communities, but it became increasingly effective with the passage of time and an easing of tensions between the communities. However, UNFICYP achieved its greatest success as a peace-keeping force after the 1974 partition of the island clearly defined a buffer zone between the communities. The efforts to achieve a political settlement of the conflict through international mediation were much less successful and little progress had been made towards an agreement between the representatives of the two communities before the military coup in Athens in April 1967. Hostility from the Greek military régime made Makarios more determined to make independent Cyprus free of Greek oversight and the prospects for an agreement between the representatives of the two communities through the talks being held under UN auspices actually improved. However, the Greek regime's support for proponents of *enosis* in the Greek Cypriot community, including a paramilitary organisation known as EOKA B, became a destabilising factor in the situation.

Another instrument of the military régime's influence in Cyprus was the National Guard, the staff of which included officers from the Greek army. At the beginning of July 1974, President Makarios asked the junta to withdraw 650 non-Cypriot officers from the force. His request triggered a coup by the National Guard, backed by Greece. The coup installed a notorious EOKA figure, Nicos Sampson, as President. The crisis led to inconclusive consultations between Britain and Turkey under the Treaty of Guarantee. Then, following the Greek junta's rejection of a Turkish ultimatum which demanded Sampson's resignation, the withdrawal of non-Cypriots from the National Guard, and a reaffirmation by Athens of Cyprus's status as an independent state, Turkish forces invaded Cyprus on 20 July. They met fierce resistance but succeeded in establishing a corridor between the northern coast of the island where they had landed and the capital, Nicosia. There were allegations that Turkish troops had murdered civilians in the Greek villages they had occupied, while Greek Cypriots wreaked vengeance on the many Turkish Cypriot enclaves in the south of the island. A conference of the three guarantor powers and of representatives of the two communities was held in Geneva in August. By this time, the Greek junta had collapsed and Nicos Sampson had resigned. The negotiations reflected the shift in the balance of power between the communities. Now it was the Greek Cypriot side which sought the full restoration of the 1960 constitution. The Turkish Cypriot side demanded federation. The failure of the negotiations was followed by further military action by the Turkish forces on Cyprus which completed the partition of the island. The area they occupied and what was proclaimed in 1983 an independent state covers 36 per cent of the island.

The Turkish action was extremely costly in human terms. It turned more than a third of the population into refugees and was accompanied by widespread bloodshed. However, the ultimate result was the total territorial segregation of the two communities, effectively removing the threat of intercommunal violence. The number of Greeks still living in Northern Cyprus is insignificant (less than 1 per cent of the population) as is the number of Turkish Cypriots in the south. Each of the partitioned entities currently functions as a multi-party democracy, though internationally only the Greek Cypriot government of Cyprus is recognised. It has successfully campaigned to ensure that the Turkish Cypriot entity remains isolated, not just diplomatically, but economically and in terms of communications. While Turkish Cypriots have been disadvantaged by their international isolation, it is difficult to imagine any circumstances in which Turkish Cypriots would agree to arrangements for the future government of the island that did not underwrite their physical security. Partition therefore seems likely to endure in some form, even if it is under a federal system agreed by the parties.

The role played by the external parties to the conflict provides the most interesting point of comparison with Northern Ireland. With the benefit of hindsight, it is apparent that the solution which Britain, Greece, and Turkey imposed on Cyprus in 1960 contained a fatal contradiction. This was the attempt by the three powers to guarantee both Cyprus's independence *and* the workings of its constitution. The first implied that they had forsworn involvement in the internal politics of Cyprus; the second that they were ready and able to intervene. It placed the external powers in an ambiguous position and maximised the likelihood of miscalculation by the internal parties. In particular, in 1974 the Greek junta's supporters in Cyprus clearly believed that opposition by the United States to the invasion of an independent state would prevent Turkish intervention after the coup overthrowing Makarios. By contrast, the political stance of Turkish Cypriots has been strongly influenced by a belief that the proximity of Cyprus to Turkey ensures that the external balance of forces is in their favour and this has reinforced their demand for equality as a community and their resistance to minority status. In the case of Northern Ireland both Britain and the Republic are committed to the establishment of power-sharing, devolved government in the province within the context of the Anglo-Irish Agreement. This objective reflects a desire in both countries to keep the problem of Northern Ireland at arm's length, coupled with a belief that the province cannot simply be left to its own devices. Although there is scope for similar kinds of internal miscalculation to those that developed in Cyprus, the prospect of internal disturbance in Northern Ireland drawing the external actors into confrontation is very much less, while the Anglo-Irish Agreement exists.

International norms have had a siginficant influence on the situation in Cyprus. The doctrine of the sovereign equality of states cast doubt from the outset on the validity of the Treaty of Guarantee, while the international community has strongly upheld the principle of the territorial integrity of the Republic of Cyprus as an island. While support for this principle did not prevent partition (or, for that matter, the establishment by Britain of two small sovereign bases on the island), it has been important in preventing the normalisation of partition. While the international acceptance of Lebanon's boundaries suggests that if Northern Ireland achieved recognition from the international community as an independent state, the genesis of its borders would cease to matter internationally, the implication to be drawn from the case of Cyprus is that international recognition of Northern Ireland whether under present or reduced boundaries would not be forthcoming without the support of the Republic of Ireland.

Conflict over borders provides an obvious point of comparison between Israel and Northern Ireland, though the two societies have much more in common than that. Both are deeply divided societies with a single principal line of cleavage between dominant and subordinate communities. Although the population of Greater Israel (that is to say, Israel plus the occupied territories of the West Bank and Gaza) is more than three times that of Northern Ireland, the ratio of population between dominant and subordinate communities is roughly similar in the two cases. In both the ratio is narrowing, though more rapidly in Greater Israel. In each case, a major influence on the society's politics is the siege mentality of the dominant community and its fear of absorption as a minority within a larger area. Both are in this sense problems of double minorities. Just as Protestants are a majority in Northern Ireland, but a minority on the island of Ireland so while Jews constitute a majority within Greater Israel, they are a very small minority within the Middle East as a whole. By contrast, while Catholics are a minority within Northern Ireland, they are a majority in Ireland as a whole. Similarly, while Palestinians are a minority within Greater Israel, they are part of the Middle East's Arab majority.

To a degree both Northern Ireland and Greater Israel are pariahs in terms of international opinion and distrust of the outside world is a characteristic attitude of both Protestant Unionists and Israeli Jews. A very high level of residential segregation between the communities is a feature of both societies, although in the case of Israel, even excluding the occupied territories, there is far greater territorial segregation of the communities (as is also true of Lebanon). In both societies the behaviour of the security forces and the operation of emergency laws constitute important sources of contention between the communities. In both, allegations of the violation of human rights have been common and have attracted critical international attention. However, despite these similarities, there is a most significant difference in how the two societies are policed, which underlines a major difference in the outside world's perceptions of the two conflicts. Unlike the RUC, the role of the Israeli police in relation to political violence is subordinate to that of the army, and the Israeli police force as an institution has attracted very little attention from the country's Palestinian critics.

While the limited security role of the Israeli police is, in part, the result of historical circumstance,[7] the fundamental explanation is to be found in the legitimising role of the external threat to Israel's existence as a state. In most societies, use of the military in an internal security role represents an unattractive option for government since it will be interpreted by the outside world as evidence of a serious threat to the state. Any government seeking to convey an impression of normality to the international community will deploy the police rather than the military where it can. Indeed, this was the basic reason why the British Government introduced the policy of police primacy in Northern Ireland in the mid-1970s. These considerations do not apply to Israel. On the contrary, Israel's struggle for existence as a state in a hostile region enjoys much greater support internationally, and especially in the West, than would be forthcoming if the conflict between Jews and Palestinians within the country appeared divorced from any threat of inter-state war. Consequently, treating the control of the Arab minority within its borders as a function of the wider conflict with its neighbours, by deploying the army rather than the police in this role, works to Israel's advantage. By contrast, the characterisation of the divide between Jews and Arabs inside the country, including the occupied territories, as a domestic issue would invite damaging comparisons between Israel and other societies which suppressed minorities. In particular, the multitude of restrictions on the right of Palestinians to give expression to their national aspirations would be difficult to justify in a domestic context.

Considering Israel's involvement in five major wars with neighbouring states since the proclamation of the state in May 1948, it is not surprising that the outside world still regards the conflict between Israel and the Palestinians primarily in international terms. None the less, the similarities between Greater Israel and Northern Ireland have grown with the increasing domestication of conflict in the former as Israel's strategic position has become more secure, and with the trend towards internationalisation in the latter. There still remains a considerable disparity in the political strength of the respective subordinate communities. Palestinians are in relative terms not only very much poorer than Catholics but far more marginal politically. This reflects in part the fact that in Israel proper, Palestinians (with some basic rights of citizenship) are a much smaller minority, one that can relatively easily be controlled by the state.[8] By contrast, the anarchic West Bank, where there are frequent attacks on the security forces by Palestinians as well as clashes between Arab villagers and the residents of Jewish settlements, bears a much closer resemblance to troubled areas of Northern Ireland. Politically, Israeli opinion is divided on the issue of withdrawal from the West Bank and Gaza. Their occupation remains the main reason for Israel's pariah status and one of the principal obstacles to a settlement of the conflict. That points to a very considerable difference between Israel and Northern Ireland in terms of international legitimacy. The international legitimacy of Israel's boundaries prior to the 1967 war provides a fallback position for the dominant community in Israel that is not available to its Northern Ireland counterpart. Repartition is consequently a much more likely solution to the Arab-Israeli conflict than it is in Northern Ireland.

A major difference between Northern Ireland and the three countries discussed above is Northern Ireland's status as a subordinate political entity. By contrast, the principal point of comparison between Puerto Rico and Northern Ireland is the question of status. In particular, the Caribbean island of Puerto Rico is to all intents and purposes an ethnically homogeneous society. None the less, the peculiar status of the island as a territory politically linked to the United States but not fully part of it is reflected in political divisions in Puerto Rico strikingly similar to the divisions within Northern Ireland over the province's conditional membership of the United Kingdom. The anomalous nature of Puerto Rico's status in a world of independent states with fixed boundaries has also led to challenges to its international legitimacy. Puerto Rico was ruled by Spain from the sixteenth century when the first settlement was established on the island. It remained a Spanish colony until 1899 when it was ceded to the United States under the Treaty of Paris following the Spanish-American War. For half a century the United States ruled Puerto Rico as a colony. Under the Foraker Act of 1900 Puerto Rico became an 'unincorporated territory'[9] of the United States. The President appointed the island's Governor. The islanders were given the right to elect the lower chamber of the island's legislature. An appointed Executive Council acted as the upper chamber. In 1917 the American Congress enacted legislation making Puerto Ricans American citizens and replacing the Executive Council's role as an upper chamber by an elected Senate. The Depression of the 1930s had a particularly severe impact on the island's sugar-based economy. Politically, it stimulated the growth of nationalism in Puerto Rico and there were violent clashes between nationalists and the police. In March 1937 20 people died and 100 were wounded when the police opened fire on a nationalist demonstration.

In November 1940 the populist PPD (Popular Democratic Party) won a narrow victory in the island's legislative elections. The PPD had been formed in 1938 by Luis Munoz Marin. Its victory marked the start of Munoz Marin's domination of the island's politics which lasted until his retirement in 1964. After the Second World War, new American legislation reflecting the tide of international opinion against colonial rule provided for the direct election of the Governor of Puerto Rico. Munoz Marin was elected in the first gubernatorial elections in the island's history in 1948, while the PPD also scored an overwhelming victory in the legislative elections. From this position of strength

Munoz proposed the establishment of a new constitutional dispensation for Puerto Rico. It was based on the assumption that Congress would not approve statehood, the full incorporation of Puerto Rico into the United States, and that independence would be economically disastrous for the island. The third way put forward by Munoz was autonomy, a status that he encapsulated in the term, *Estado Libre Asociado* (literally, Free Associated State). It was translated into English as Commonwealth. Almost as important as the terms of the arrangement was the process by which it was enacted.

In 1950 the American Congress passed Public Law 600. It provided for Puerto Rico to draw up its own constitution under Commonwealth status and for the relationship between the United States and Puerto Rico to be embodied in new legislation, the Federal Relations Act. The next step was the ratification of Public Law 600 by the Puerto Ricans themselves in a referendum to pave the way for the election of a Constituent Assembly. The purpose of the referendum was to show that Commonwealth status was the free choice of Puerto Ricans and an authentic act of self-determination. The supporters of independence in the PIP (Puerto Rican Independnece Party) boycotted the poll on Public Law 600. It was passed by a large majority, though the numbers actually voting Yes constituted slightly less than half of all those entitled to vote. The opposition of some nationalists to this process was violent. An uprising in the island's interior in October 1950 resulted in 27 deaths, while in the following month two nationalists attempted to assassinate President Truman in Washington.

After the Constituent Assembly had drawn up a draft constitution under Commonwealth status, it was submitted to Congress, which insisted on a number of amendments. The revised document was then endorsed by a further referendum in Puerto Rico and the new constitution came into effect in July 1952 with all the outward paraphernalia of nationhood, including a flag and a national anthem. The United States sought international endorsement of the Commonwealth at the United Nations during 1953. It advised the UN Committee of Information on Non-Self-Governing Territories that Puerto Rico was now a fully self-governing territory, having freely negotiated its relationship with the United States. In a letter to the General Assembly President Eisenhower, anticipating criticism of Commonwealth status as colonialism in a new guise, pledged that should the Legislative Assembly of Puerto Rico adopt a resolution in favour of independence, he would recommend to Congress that its wish should be granted. These tactics were successful and the American claim that Puerto Rico had become self-governing was endorsed by the General Assembly on the recommendation of the Committee of Information. That freed the United States from the slightly humiliating obligation of submitting annual reports on the territory to the United Nations.

Despite the success of the economic policies that accompanied the establishment of the Commonwealth, the new dispensation failed to settle the status issue, which continued to dominate the island's politics. While there was a drop in the level of popular support for independence, dissatisfaction with the *status quo* remained strong, with growing support for the option of statehood and full integration into the United States. The appeal of Commonwealth status was weakened by an erosion of the island's autonomy with the growth of the scope of government in Washington. In addition, as other Caribbean islands achieved full independence, Puerto Rico's status no longer appeared as advanced as it had in the 1950s. Nevertheless, a referendum in 1967 in which Puerto Ricans were given the option of voting for statehood, independence, or the maintenance of Commonwealth status resulted in a clear victory for the *status quo* with 60 per cent of the votes cast. However, nearly 40 per cent of voters supported statehood and in November 1968, the gubernatorial election in Puerto Rico was won by the candidate of the PNP (New Progressive Party), the pro-statehood party, as a result of a split in the PPD. The PNP victor was defeated four years later by the PPD candidate, Rafael Hernadez Colon, who in turn lost to a new PNP candidate, Carlos Romero Barcelo, in 1976. Romero was narrowly re-elected in 1980 but was defeated by Hernandez in 1984. The swing of the political pendulum reflected uncertainty and division over the constitutional issue. In fact, by the 1970s, both the island's main parties were dissatisfied with the operation of the Commonwealth, with the PPD favouring a radical enlargement of the island's autonomy.

The gloss was wearing off Commonwealth status internationally as well. In 1960 the General Assembly established the Decolonisation Committee with the task of speeding the progress of *all* dependent territories towards independence. In the case of Puerto Rico, this largely negated the effect of the UN's acceptance of Commonwealth status in 1953. While free association with an independent state was recognised by the United Nations as a legitimate form of self-determination, Puerto Rico did not satisfy the criteria the UN laid down for this status because of the requirement of Congressional approval for any modification of the island's status. The supporters of independence lobbied for the inclusion of Puerto Rico on the agenda of the Decolonisation Committee. Aided by Cuba they eventually succeeded in 1972. Paradoxically as support for the PIP was falling in Puerto Rico, international support for the cause of Puerto Rican independence was growing. It was expressed in repeated resolutions of the Decolonisation Committee demanding an end to colonial rule in Puerto Rico.[10] These resolutions could not be dismissed by the United States as harmless rhetoric since they gave encouragement to Puerto Rican nationalists ready to use violence in their quest for an end to American rule by providing them, indirectly, with a measure of international legitimacy for their actions. That at any rate was the logic of General Assembly resolutions that justified resort to armed struggle against colonial domination. On the island itself, a group called *Los Macherteros* (machete wielders) has been responsible for a number of attacks on American installations, including the spectacular destruction of nine National Guard aircraft in 1981, while on the mainland of the United States, a terrorist organisation, FALN (the Armed Forces of the Puerto Rican National Liberation), which was particularly active in the 1970s, has been responsible for at least five deaths and more than 100 bombings. Out of five million Puerto Ricans, two million resided on the mainland of the United States at the time of the 1980 census.

Despite the international embarrassment caused by Puerto Rico's anomalous status, there has been only muted support in the United States for statehood as a permanent resolution to the uncertainty over the island's constitutional position. President Ford endorsed statehood in January 1977 just before he left office, while Ronald Reagan came out strongly in favour of statehood in February 1980 when he was merely a candidate seeking the Republican nomination.[11] However, Reagan's actions as President—in particular, the replacement of the Food Stamp programme in Puerto Rico by a block grant—have served to emphasise the territory's separate status, to the considerable disappointment of the PNP. In general, members of Congress have been reluctant to commit themselves to supporting any change in Puerto Rico's current status in the absence of a clear indication that it will be supported by a solid majority of the Puerto Ricans themselves. Consequently, the division among the islanders on the status question has simply reinforced Congressional inertia. Puerto Rico thus remains trapped in a debilitating limbo.[12]

Political violence and the divisions within Puerto Rico over the territory's place in the world provide the most obvious points of comparison with Northern Ireland. Significantly, the homogeneous nature of the island's population has not prevented the status issue from dominating the territory's politics or from giving rise to political violence that, despite its relatively low level, is recognised as posing a threat to the island's political stability. This suggests that attributing the conflict in Northern Ireland *simply* to the province's sectarian divisions underestimates the importance of the province's constitutional position on its own as an obstacle to political stability. From this perspective, it is not necessary to invoke the prevalence of religious bigotry to explain the depth of political divisions in Northern Ireland, given the existence of a constitutional arrangement capable of generating such division by itself. Furthermore, the issue of Puerto Rico has become internationalised as Commonwealth status has appeared increasingly anomalous in a post-colonial world. There is a clear parallel here with the increasing internationalisation of the Northern Ireland conflict.

Unlike Puerto Rico and Northern Ireland there is no real question mark over the international status of Corsica. The island of Corsica has been an integral part of France since the end of the eighteenth century. None the less, the territory spawned a nationalist movement in the 1960s and 1970s. The movement developed a violent aspect with the formation of the FLNC (National Liberation Front of Corsica) in 1976. While the overwhelming majority of Corsicans have continued to support the maintenance of the link with France, nationalists have attracted a small measure of popular support on the island. The FLNC advocated a boycott of the elections to the Corsican Assembly in August 1982. However, a political party closely associated with the FLNC, the MCA (Corsican Movement for Self-Determination) contested the Assembly elections in 1984 and won 5 per cent of the vote, the same level of support that more moderate constitutional nationalists attracted. The French government banned the MCA in January 1987 after arresting an MCA Member of the Assembly with FLNC documents in his possession. The Corsican Assembly had been set up as part of the general decentralisation of government in France carried through under President Mitterrand in 1982, though its powers were specifically tailored to meet Corsican demands for greater autonomy in the hope of bringing an end to the conflict over the island's future. Since the formation of the FLNC there have been hundreds of explosions each year on the island, as well as in metropolitan France, though the number of deaths in the conflict have been relatively small as the FLNC has by and large confined its attacks to property.

Geographically, Corsica is closer to Italy than to the mainland of France and this is reflected in the fact that the language of the indigenous population of the island is closer to Italian than to French. However, prior to the 1960s there was virtually no nationalist tradition to speak of. The island prided itself on its association with Napoleon and patriotic sentiment was cemented by the employment of Corsicans in France's overseas empire. Nationalism was very clearly a product of the post-colonial era. Economic stagnation, reflected in the long-term decline in the island's population of under a quarter of a million, also contributed to the growth of nationalism, while another factor was resentment at the settlement of *pieds noir* from Algeria on the island and the economic success of their enterprises. The resentment was a reflection of Corsica's principal cleavage which splits the island's population in two, that between the indigenous inhabitants and those whose origins lie outside the island. One of the many manifestations of this division was racial hostility directed towards Arab migrant labour brought in by the *colons* from Algeria to work in their vineyards. While the FLNC has presented itself as an anti-colonial movement fighting to liberate the island from France, international interest in the conflict has consisted largely of economically damaging publicity in those countries for which Corsica is a tourist destination. Even if support for independence were at a qualitatively higher level, the hostility of the international community towards secession makes it nearly inconceivable that an independent Corsica could secure international recognition, as only the geographic fact of island status would operate in its favour.

Comparison of the situation in Northern Ireland with that in Corsica has taken the form in the French press of references to the danger of the *irlandisation* of Corsica. Corsica was indeed one of a number of regional nationalist movements in Europe in the 1970s to attract the attention of the Provisionals and the existence of links between the Provisional IRA and the FLNC was given by the French Government as one of its reasons for banning the FLNC in 1983. For its part, the FLNC has consciously imitated the Provisional IRA in the manner of its public appearances. The comparison has also attracted the interest of a civil servant from Northern Ireland, Robert Ramsay. In the conclusion of his book, *The Corsican time-bomb*,[13] he discusses a number of parallels between the two conflicts. Ramsay particularly emphasises the peripheral character of the two territories and their economic dependence on the states of which they are a part, while drawing attention to the proportionately larger subsidy that Corsica receives from the French state, a circumstance that casts considerable doubt on the economic viability of independence in Corsica's case. But the most valuable of Ramsay's insights is the lesson he draws from the impact of political violence on the two societies. 'Once terrorism has taken hold in a situation in which there exists an ethnic cleavage, it is constantly reinforced by the very tensions which it creates in the community.'[14] This underlines an important difference between the cases of Corsica and Puerto Rico. But by contrast, Corsica's international status as part of France remains unambiguous and all the political parties in metropolitan France are fully committed to the retention of the island as an integral part of the country. Northern Ireland suffers from the equivalent of both the international illegitimacy of Puerto Rico and the ethnic cleavage of Corsica at the same time.

No other situation in the world is identical even in broad structural terms with that in Northern Ireland. Comparisons alone therefore cannot provide the basis for making predictions about the future course of events in Northern Ireland or elsewhere. None the less, some substantive generalisations emerge from the comparisons discussed in this chapter that are worth underlining. Firstly, external factors are a paramount consideration in understanding the nature of the conflicts. The apparent exception of Corsica proves the rule, because the FLNC's capacity to become a serious force would depend upon its securing an international legitimacy which Corsica's unambiguous membership of France makes unlikely. In this case it is clearly the hope of the FLNC to internationalise the conflict by tailoring its message to anti-colonial sentiment as best it can and this is the possibility the French fear. Its basis is that the territorial separation of the island from the rest of France will give separatism a measure of credibility. External factors were one of the dominant influences of the conflicts in Israel, Cyprus, and Lebanon from the very outset. In the case of Puerto Rico, inter-nationalisation of the conflict has occurred largely as a consequence of the interpretation that the United Nations Decolonisation Committee has placed on the norm of self-determination. In Northern Ireland's case, too, external views on its lack of legitimacy as a political entity have had an impact on the conflict as it has developed. Secondly, there is an important distinction between external involvement in the form of rhetoric or even assistance to internal parties and direct foreign military intervention. It is most clearly reflected in the difference of scale between the conflict in Lebanon and that in Northern Ireland. It must be emphasised that the influence of international norms is by no means comparable with the impact of a foreign invasion. Further, the support of the international community on normative grounds provides little protection against a military imbalance of power, as Greek Cypriots discovered in 1974. On the other hand, the support of the international community has prevented the normalisation of the partition of the island. Finally, violent conflict tends both to reinforce, and to be reinforced itself by, any ethnic or communal divisions in society.

10.

CONCLUSION

THE theme of this book has been the interconnection between Northern Ireland's sectarian divisions and the province's anomalous international status. Its basic thesis is that internationalisation has made the conflict more intractable because of the role that external factors have played in the legitimisation of violence. The case of Northern Ireland is not unusual. Internationalisation has also exacerbated other conflicts, none more so than that in Lebanon. In contrast to Lebanon, Northern Ireland has not suffered direct external intervention and is fortunate in being a backwater in strategic terms. In fact, internationalisation has been a practically universal phenomenon as evidenced by the greater prominence of foreign affairs in the domestic politics of most countries. Rosenau's assertion twenty years ago that 'politics everywhere, it would seem, are related to politics everywhere else'[1] appears very nearly true. But while theorists in the field of international relations in the late 1960s and early 1970s were right about the significance of the growth of interdependence on a global scale, they were for the most part mistaken in their predictions of the political effects of internationalisation. The role of the nation-state in international affairs has not diminished. The political power of multinational companies has not begun to match their size in economic terms. While the world's largest companies command more resources in economic terms than the majority of the member states of the United Nations, their political influence remains negligible. Force has not become obsolescent as an instrument of foreign policy. And nationalism, far from declining in strength, has thrived.

Even though the control of the nation-state over its own destiny, especially in the economic field, has declined, it still remains the focus of political loyalty. Indeed, the very sense of insecurity that interdependence has engendered has been a stimulant to nationalism, particularly in the industrialised world, where it had seemed to be on the wane in the 1960s. The tide of nationalism has supported governments as ideologically diverse as those of the United States, Greece, Australia, and New Zealand. It is particularly notable that where left-wing parties have been elected against the general trend in the world towards the Right, they have been identified with nationalism. The strength of support for nationalism among the minority in Northern Ireland therefore fits the pattern of political developments elsewhere in the world. Further, there is nothing unusual in its association with ethnic or communal divisions. Unionism is somewhat more difficult to characterise in these terms. But it too has been affected by the global trends. In particular, the hopes that liberal Unionists once attached to interdependence as a process that might help to erode the province's divisions by making the Border matter less have disappeared.

Nationalism has also been very much in evidence in Britain, though it has taken a rather special form. In the absence of a tradition of territorial nationalism in Britain, there has been a revival of jingoism. Its hallmarks are contempt for foreigners, assumptions of racial superiority, and an essentially English ethnocentrism.[2] It is triumphalist in spirit and has been to some extent imperial in its pretensions, stimulated by, as much as embracing, the cause of British sovereignty over the Falkland Islands. It has been a key element in the rhetoric and popularity of Margaret Thatcher, though her policies (except over the Falkland Islands where the actions of the Argentinian junta forced her hand) have been designed to *limit* Britain's international responsibilities and to complete the process of Britain's adjustment to a post-colonial era. Sympathy for the desire of Ulster Unionists to stay British has not been a characteristic of the new jingoism. There is more to the exclusion of Ulster Protestants than the fact of Britain's expedient perception of them as Irish and therefore not British, though that is an important factor. Another is the fact that the siege mentality of Unionists and the institutions associated with the Protestant ascendancy have seemed politically alien to much of British opinion. It is also recognised that the conflict has detracted from Britain's standing in the world. As a result of the failure of successive British political initiatives, there is little expectation in the UK mainland of an early end to the conflict. Consequently, the overwhelming desire of public opinion is to distance Britain from the problem.

The Republic of Ireland has also been affected by the prevailing mood that society's defences against the outside world need to be strengthened. However, in the case of the Republic, it is perhaps questionable whether nationalism is the right label to attach to sentiment, the main features of which have been a reaction against liberal influences on social questions such as divorce and abortion and the focusing of political loyalty on the twenty-six county state. The two are linked in so far as acceptance of the boundaries of the state has been used to justify the reassertion of the traditionally conservative views of the Catholic Church on these issues. The argument that the Republic needs to take into account the views of Northern Protestants on such issues because of the aspiration to Irish unity has made little impression on public opinion, which has become increasingly alienated from the North. This twenty-six county nationalism, if it can be called such, cuts across party divisions in the South.

The disenchantment in both Britain and the Republic with Northern Ireland has made it possible for the two Governments to enter into the Anglo-Irish Agreement without fearing that they would be repudiated by domestic opinion. In fact, the Agreement further reduces the risk that either society will be magnetised by the conflict, provided both Governments adhere to their responsibilities under it. The Agreement has effectively fenced off the conflict and reduced its capacity to inflict political damage on either Britain or the Republic. At times, both Governments are likely to find the commitment to the Anglo-Irish process burdensome. However, while there are bound to be moments of crisis over whether one or other of the Governments is adhering to its obligations under the Agreement, abandonment of the Agreement is likely to remain a most unattractive option for either side. In any event, neither Britain nor the Republic is in a position to disclaim responsibility for the continuation of the conflict, despite their political distance from the actual antagonists.

In this book it has been argued that Northern Ireland's lack of international legitimacy has made a significant contribution to the intensity of violent conflict in the province. The root of that problem lies in the conditional nature of Northern Ireland's membership of the United Kingdom. The arrangement is not the invention of Ulster Loyalists, as the emphasis sometimes given to the conditional nature of their acceptance of British authority might seem to imply. It is clearly derived from a quintessentially British notion of political legitimacy, embodied in the relationship that Britain has with its remaining colonies. This is the notion that consent, and not territory, defines the boundaries to Britain's authority; of course it fits awkwardly in a world divided into states which are clearly defined in territorial terms.[3] Britain therefore cannot escape political responsibility for Northern Ireland's lack of international legitimacy. Further, there seems little doubt that if Unionists were offered the opportunity to remove the conditional nature of Northern Ireland's status through the total integration of the province into the United Kingdom, they would take the opportunity, even if abandonment of the prospect of devolved government appeared to be one of its consequences. In fact, the offer is never likely to be made, for the simple reason that to permit the full integration of the Northern Ireland conflict into British domestic politics would constitute a threat to Britain's own political stability. Similarly, the claim to jurisdiction over Northern Ireland, enshrined in Articles 2 and 3 of the Republic's constitution, lays the South open to the charge that its own irredentism is a cause of the conflict. As long as such a claim forms part of the constitution, the Republic is placed under an obligation to demonstrate that the aspiration to Irish unity does not entail the legitimisation of violence to achieve it. That cannot be done by ignoring the problem. At the same time, the voluntary removal from the constitution of any desire to achieve a united Ireland is not a viable option for a state that is ultimately grounded in the legitimacy of Irish nationalism.

Viewed from a British Isles perspective, the price of stability in Britain and the Republic is instability in Northern Ireland. In these terms, it is a relatively small price to pay. Its burden principally falls on the population of the province, some one and a half million out of approximately 60 million in the archipelago as a whole. What is more, to resolve the problem of Northern Ireland's place in the world would require fundamental changes in the basis of the legitimacy of both the United Kingdom and the Republic. Of course, the conflict is not seen quite in these terms in Britain, the Republic, or the rest of the world, for that matter. The most common external views of the conflict are that it is a weird anachronism, a seventeenth-century religious conflict in modern dress, or that it represents unfinished business from the colonial era. The former is a popular view in Britain itself, with the British Government cast in the role of a mediator between the warring factions. The latter view tends to be more prevalent elsewhere. In support of the former view, conflict between the two communities in the North of Ireland can indeed be traced back to the seventeenth century. However, such an exercise provides little clue as to why conflict should have burst out with such intensity from the late 1960s, though it does clearly highlight the inter-community nature of the conflict and draws attention to the significance of such institutions as the Orange Order. The main drawback of this perspective is that it tends to ignore the international dimensions of the conflict. The advantage of the latter view is that it focuses on the relationship between the passing of the imperial age and Northern Ireland's Troubles.

In the world of empires, Northern Ireland did indeed have its place. During the Second World War the province was a valued, if none the less politically separate, part of the United Kingdom, itself the heart of a vast global empire. The province's contribution to the war effort was rewarded by parity whereby the Government at Westminster undertook to provide the funds to enable the Northern Ireland Government to match social provision in the rest of the United Kingdom. It was a commitment that naturally grew in significance with the development of the welfare state. By contrast, neutral Éire enjoyed a very low status which persisted even after the war was over. In particular, the country's neutrality during the Second World War led indirectly to its exclusion from membership of the United Nations until 1955. The dissolution of the British Empire, the decline of Britain as a world power, and the enhancement of the Republic's status through its role as a member of the United Nations had transformed the relative standing of the two parts of Ireland by the 1960s. The change moderated the Republic's grievance over partition, but it upset the basis of the uneasy and unequal accommodation between the communities in Northern Ireland. In particular, Catholics became simultaneously more willing to consider according a measure of legitimacy to Northern Ireland's political institutions, but less willing to acquiesce in a subordinate position in the society. The rise in Catholic self-confidence as a community was matched by a growth in Protestants fears, especially among lower status groups. However, middle-class Protestants tended to respond rather differently and were more willing to see the change in Catholic attitudes as the opportunity to overcome sectarian divisions in the province than were their working-class co-religionists. In fact, the political polarisation of the Protestant community proved to be a harbinger of the Troubles.

Since the onset of the Troubles, the Republic's status has been further enhanced by membership of the EEC, while that of Northern Ireland has been further diminished by the imposition of direct rule. The Anglo-Irish Agreement of November 1985 under which the Republic secured the right to exercise an influence on British policies in Northern Ireland, underscored the enormous gulf that has developed in the standing of the two parts of Ireland in the post-colonial era. By placing the Government of the Republic on a near equal footing to that of the British Government, the Agreement represented a devastating humiliation for a Protestant community accustomed to think of Ulster and Éire in competitive terms. The huge size of the rally held outside Belfast City Hall to protest against the Agreement eight days after it was signed, with estimates of the number of participants ranging from 100,000 to 200,000, provided eloquent testimony to Protestant resentment. The subsequent course of the campaign against the Agreement suggests that the status implications of the Agreement were far more important as the driving impulse behind Protestant opposition to the Agreement than concern over its practical implications, at least in the short term. In particular, the fall in the Unionist vote in the 1987 Westminster general election was evidence that some Protestants were more concerned about the damaging effect on the province of the campaign against the Agreement than they were about any of the concrete changes resulting from the Agreement itself.[4]

The political impact of the Agreement on Catholics in Northern Ireland has been far less dramatic than its impact on the Protestant community. While there has been a discernible increase in support for the constitutional nationalism of the SDLP and a relatively modest but significant decline in the electoral fortunes of Sinn Fein, the political wing of the Provisional IRA, overt reaction to the Agreement in the Catholic community has been relatively muted. This is partly because the Agreement enhances the status of the Republic more than it does that of the minority in the North, and partly because of alienation among Northern Catholics from the South that reciprocates Southern attitudes towards the North. There was also justified fear among Catholics that they would bear the brunt of Protestant resentment at the Agreement. Furthermore, in so far as the Agreement is successful in isolating the conflict and in securing external support for British policy towards Northern Ireland, it may reduce the international ramifications of continuing violence in Northern Ireland and the standing of all the protagonists in the conflict. While such partial de-internationalisation might have beneficial results in the long run in improving the prospects for political accommodation between the communities, it remains a distinctly double-edged possibility for a community that tends to see international opinion as an ally in its struggle. Part of the appeal of the Provisional IRA is that it lifts individuals out of Northern ghettoes with high levels of unemployment and other forms of social deprivation, and enlists them in a revolutionary movement waging a campaign much of the outside world is ready to endorse as a legitimate anti-colonial struggle. However, what makes support in the outside world for the nationalist cause so double-edged is that it expects of the Catholic community much more than the community could ever deliver by itself, namely a united Ireland. While the cause of Irish unity enhances the self-image of Northern Catholics, it also places an immense burden on their shoulders.

The strength and solidity of Protestant opposition to a united Ireland and the fact that it is autonomous of the British Government's wishes as well of those of British opinion, are factors in the Northern Ireland equation that tend to be under-appreciated by much of world opinion. One of the main reasons for this is the incapacity of Unionists to articulate their opposition to a united Ireland in terms capable of being understood outside the British Isles. To the outside world, the political stance of the Unionist parties seems to involve a demeaning acceptance of a semi-colonial status. At the same time, the reluctance of Loyalists to rely wholeheartedly upon the pledges of British governments tends to be misrepresented as the existence of confusion over their identity rather than the inevitable by-product of the province's marginal position *vis-a-vis* Britain. Further, those elements in the Unionist case that are most easily conveyed to an external audience, such as the argument of economic self-interest, not merely carry little political legitimacy, but are readily, though inaccurately, perceived as resting on the illegitimate foundations of discrimination against Catholics. It is a short step then to argue that the removal of the illegitimate props of Protestant privilege will dissolve Protestant opposition to a united Ireland. From this perspective, the battle for a united Ireland is not a sectarian objective but the route to equality between Protestant and Catholic and the resolution of the conflict. The flaw in the argument is the assumption that Protestant opposition to a united Ireland is (or has been) a function of discrimination against Catholics. It is the other way round. Discrimination is and has been primarily a function of Protestant opposition to a united Ireland. Consequently, the progress that has been made since the imposition of direct rule to eliminate discrimination has not in any way lessened Protestant opposition to a united Ireland, nor is it relevant to it.

Outside of Northern Ireland the perspective that can most obviously be set against the view of the conflict as an anti-colonial struggle is the terrorist perspective. It is particularly influential in other industrialised countries of the West, although the hunger strike in 1981 represented a considerable blow to its credibility in these countries. It tends to have greater political than analytical significance. In particular, condemning political violence in Northern Ireland as an assault on Western liberal-democracy, the main theme of writing in this mould, does little to explain the conflict. None the less, if its tendency to adopt a self-righteous tone can be disregarded, the terrorist perspective does focus attention on some important features of the conflict that might otherwise not receive the emphasis they deserve. In particular, despite the violence, Northern Ireland is governed according to broadly liberal-democratic norms, even though its actual rulers are not representative of the population of the province. Furthermore, the electorate of Northern Ireland has had regular opportunities to demonstrate its wishes through the ballot box and this has played a role in de-legitimising the activities of the paramilitaries on both sides, despite some measure of ambiguity at different times in the attitude of the constitutional parties towards their activities. At the same time, the case of Northern Ireland shows that the survival of liberal-democracy does not immunise a society against high levels of political violence, nor guarantee the political isolation of those employing unconstitutional methods. If this point perhaps seems rather obvious nowadays, it is partly because of the role it has played in Western societies' growing fear of the phenomemon of terrorism. Another reason for the fear is that politically stable societies have been increasingly affected by violence, the political origins of which lie elsewhere. Thus, the instability in Lebanon has made an impact on the people of France, just as at various stages in the Northern Ireland conflict the residents of London have feared IRA bombs.

The increased portability of political violence resulting in the spill-over of violence from unstable into stable societies is a significant by-product of the growth of interdependence. It also provides an explanation for the internationalisation of conflicts generally, since increasingly every conflict carries with it the potential for wider violence touching many other societies. Inevitably, in these circumstances, emphasis on the vulnerability of society to political violence has tended to be given priority over analysis of the political motivation of those engaged in violence. Similarly, the external associations of violent movements have received increased attention, an emphasis justified by the growth of such contact, another by-product of interdependence. To some extent, this has been at the expense of analysis of the wider political problems of the societies in which the violence originates. However, the advantage that can be claimed for the terrorist perspective is that it does not lose sight of the fact that if there were no violence or at least no serious threat of violence, there would be no conflict, as the term is commonly understood.

Regardless of its limitations as a means of analysing the conflict, the terrorist perspective has clearly been very important to the British Government's defence abroad of its policies in Northern Ireland. It is the principal countervailing factor to the general support to be found for a united Ireland. The prevailing climate of opinion in the West on the issue of terrorism has assisted the Government in combating the influence of Republican perspectives of the conflict in most Western states. However, it is of little help to the Government in countering the influence of constitutional nationalism on issues where the interests of the British Government and those of constitutional nationalism conflict. Indeed, the SDLP has had great success in exercising diplomatic leverage over Britain, precisely because constitutional nationalism is seen by important sections of opinion in Europe and in the United States as offering a peaceful way forward that it is in accord with the goal of a united Ireland. Thus, support for Britain on the issue of terrorism is by no means unconditional. It depends on perceptions of the broader aims of British policy, from a perspective that still tends to question the legitimacy of Northern Ireland as a political entity. Furthermore, the presentation of the conflict as an issue of terrorism is by no means unproblematic for the British Government. Within Northern Ireland Unionists continually complain that the Government pursues a policy of appeasement in relation to Republican terrorism, while the Government stresses the political context of the violence and the need for political accommodation between the communities to end the violence. In practice, the Government recognises the weakness of the terrorist stereotype and the danger that measures taken to suppress political violence will strengthen the bonds between the paramilitaries and the population, on one side or other of the sectarian divide. Thus, the Government has resisted demands that it give priority above all else to the military defeat of the IRA, the policy the Unionists unsurprisingly advocate.

The campaign by Republican prisoners against criminalisation, culminating in hunger strikes in 1980 and 1981, highlighted the Government's difficulties in this area. The Prime Minister was eager to demonstrate her resolve in fighting terrorism by making no concessions to the prisoners, while a very different message was being conveyed by Northern Ireland Ministers, conscious of the political consequences in Northern Ireland of the deaths of hunger-striking prisoners. As it was, the Prime Minister's appearance of inflexibility, understandably popular in the UK mainland, was invaluable to the Republican paramilitaries in generating support for their cause. Despite the disastrous consequences for British policy of the 1981 hunger strike, the pressures on government to adopt absolutist policies towards political violence remain strong because of the continuing influence of the terrorist stereotype. For example, the Government has indicated that consideration is being given to disqualifying Sinn Fein from participation in elections on the grounds of its support for violence. It is easy to predict that if such a course of action were followed it would reduce rather than improve the prospects for political accommodation between the constitutional parties. This is because it would highlight the gulf in their attitudes not just on this issue but in relation to violence in general. Further, such a policy would run counter to the daily accommodation between state institutions and the paramilitaries on both sides of the sectarian divide. The Government's acquiescence in such arrangements amounts to a pragmatic recognition of the influence the paramilitaries wield in some parts of the province. Thus, being furnished with a letter from Gerry Adams, the President of Sinn Fein, is of value to residents of West Belfast when seeking certain public services.

It is tempting to regard such instances of co-operation between the state and its sworn enemies as a form of institutionalisation of the conflict. In fact, after nearly two decades of violence, the society has increasingly become adjusted to the likelihood of the conflict's continuation. At a political level, the compromises necessary to reach a settlement that would restore devolved government to the province present a greater challenge even to the constitutional parties than does the persistence of violence at its present level, while the continuation of the political impasse provides each of the parties with a niche in the system. However, what holds the parties back from an agreement is not just self-interest, but doubt as to whether an agreement among the constitutional parties would in fact end the violence. Furthermore, the argument of self-interest can be disputed. In particular, in the second rank of political leadership in the major parties, an agreement has attractions in terms of an enlargement of individual career prospects through politics. At the same time, the fundamentally different perspectives of the political parties in their attitudes towards violence remain a formidable obstacle to the establishment of a political consensus that could sustain an agreement on devolution. Of the parties involved in the conflict, the British Government and the Loyalist para-military organisation, the UDA, have appeared most impatient in wanting an early settlement. By contrast, the Provisionals have proclaimed their expectation that the conflict will continue into the twenty-first century.[5]

While it would be foolish to make predictions as to the future course of the conflict, not least because the growth of interdependence means that the direction of events in Northern Ireland may be shaped as much by developments outside the province as within it, there are several other reasons, besides the attitudes of the Provisionals, for expecting the conflict to continue beyond the year 2000. From an international perspective, the most important is that *no* political development that is consonant with the balance of forces within the province appears capable of resolving the issue of Northern Ireland's place in the world. Under the type of settlement that is envisaged by the British Government, namely the establishment of devolved government with cross-community support within the framework of the Anglo-Irish Agreement, the province would still occupy something of a political limbo, suspended between two states, even if formally part of one. Even a settlement that reduced the influence of the Irish dimension would not end Northern Ireland's conditional status. In short, the province would continue to lack international legitimacy. Those continuing to use violence in the cause of a united Ireland would still be assured of a measure of international support in the form of external legitimisation of their activities. There would still be uncertainty over Northern Ireland's future.

Whatever peace followed the achievement of a settlement among the constitutional parties would be more in the nature of a truce than an end to the conflict. Even in the most favourable circumstances, it seems unlikely that such an agreement would lead to the dissolution of sectarian divisions and the permanent removal of the threat of inter-community violence. However, for all its limitations, agreement on devolution in the context of Northern Ireland's current status does at least lie within the bounds of the achievable. Solutions with the capacity to end the uncertainty over Northern Ireland's existence as a political entity, such as independence, Irish unity, or integration, face seemingly insuperable obstacles to their realisation. The first two clearly run counter to both the interests and the wishes of a large majority of the people of Northern Ireland. The last would require the consent of the British people. That consent clearly would not be forthcoming at present. Indeed, it would take a revolutionary change in public opinion to bring it about. Of the three, a united Ireland is far and away the most popular solution outside of Northern Ireland, but such is the resistance to this option within Northern Ireland from the majority, that its imposition would require the military subjugation of the Protestant community. There is little basis in Loyalist Ideology or history for the supposition that Protestant resistance would dissolve if Britain withdrew its support for the Union.

If Northern Ireland cannot be made to conform to current international norms, short of even greater bloodshed, what prospects are there that international norms will change or evolve in a manner that makes Northern Ireland appear less anomalous in an international context? Existing trends provide few grounds for expecting changes that will do much to ease Northern Ireland's position. The elaboration of the principle of self-determination to provide for the possibility of forms of autonomy for indigenous minorities, short of independence, has been built on the foundations of the territorial interpretation and is not a challenge to it in any fundamental sense. While interest in the plight of minorities has grown, the change has not been so far-reaching as to affect the perceptions of the two communities in Northern Ireland with regard to the disadvantages of minority status. But the perspective of the late 1980s does not provide a particularly good vantage point for predicting how international norms will develop. It is far easier to recognise that political trends have run counter to much of the theorising about interdependence that took place in the late 1960s and the early 1970s than it is to anticipate, for example, a reaction against nationalism or the strengthening of international institutions. Thus, in the case of Northern Ireland, the influence of theories which predicted that the economic effects of interdependence on both parts of Ireland would reduce the salience of sectarian divisions has faded.[6]

It is evident that far from providing the basis of new political departures in Northern Ireland, internationalisation has made the conflict more intractable, and entrenched rather than eroded sectarian divisions. However, that is not to say that this will always be the case. The intractable nature of the conflict has led other researchers, who have not wished to adopt the bald position that there is no solution to the problem, to take refuge in the possibility that environmental changes will alter the nature of the problem itself.[7] The extent of the internationalisation of the conflict means that the range of developments capable of exercising a significant influence on the nature of the conflict has been greatly enlarged. In ways quite beyond the possibility of prediction, internationalisation may yet benefit Northern

Ireland, though at present the role of internationalisation appears to be largely malign. Indeed, Northern Ireland seems more likely to benefit from a reduction in external interest in the problem. None the less, so interconnected is the conflict in Northern Ireland with the nature of the international order that it is not fanciful to suggest that the actual resolution of the conflict is most likely to occur in the context of far-reaching change in global politics. It is still a commonly held view, especially in the British Isles, that the world has passed Northern Ireland by and that this provides an explanation for the durability of the province's sectarian divisions. Part of the purpose of this book has been to correct that impression. Northern Ireland is very far from being isolated from international influences. In particular, external factors have played a central role in the Troubles that began in 1968. To ignore their role is to neglect an essential element of the current conflict.

APPENDIX

Deaths in Northern Ireland
arising out of the security situation 1969-86

Year	RUC[1]	RUC[2]	Army	UDR[3]	Civilians[4]	Total
1969	1	—	—	—	12	13
1970	2	—	—	—	23	25
1971	11	—	43	5	115	174
1972	14	3	103	26	321	467
1973	10	3	58	8	171	250
1974	12	3	28	7	166	216
1975	7	4	14	6	216	247
1976	13	10	14	15	245	297
1977	8	6	15	14	69	112
1978	4	6	14	7	50	81
1979	9	5	38	10	51	113
1980	3	6	8	9	50	76
1981	13	8	10	13	57	101
1982	8	4	21	7	57	97
1983	9	9	5	10	44	77
1984	7	2	9	10	36	64
1985	14	9	2	4	25	54
1986	10	2	4	8	37	61
Totals	155	80	386	159	1,745	2,525

[1] Royal Ulster Constabulary
[2] Royal Ulster Constabulary Reserve
[3] Ulster Defence Regiment
[4] Including members of paramilitary organisations
Source: Chief Constable's Annual Report 1986, RUC, Belfast 1987, p. 70.

NOTES

Chapter 1: Introduction (pp. 1–20)

1. See John Whyte, 'Interpretations of the Northern Ireland Problem', paper presented at a conference of the British Association for Irish Studies at the University of Keele, 2-4 April 1986.
2. Ibid.
3. See, for example, the British Prime Minister's interview with *Newsweek*, 16 May 1983. 'Northern Ireland is free to determine its own future. It is a fundamental part of the United Kingdom. If the majority of the people in Northern Ireland wish not to be, obviously we would honor their wish, whether it was to be independent or to join up elsewhere. Northern Ireland is part of the United Kingdom because of the wish of the majority of its people.'
4. Arend Lijphart, 'The Northern Ireland problem: Cases, Theories and Solutions', *British Journal of Political Science,* Vol. 5, Jan. 1975, p. 102.
5. *Report drawn up on behalf of the Political Affairs Committee on the situation in Northern Ireland.* Rapporteur: N. J. Haagerup, 19 March 1984 (European Parliament Working Documents 1983-84, Document 1-1526/83), p. 37.
6. Martin Wight, *Systems of States* (edited by Hedley Bull), Leicester University Press, Leicester 1977, p. 153.
7. The issue of Gibraltar was first considered by the UN Special Committee on decolonisation in 1963. The General Assembly passed a resolution calling for negotiations between Britain and Spain in 1965, see *Everyman's United Nations: A Summary of the activities of the United Nations during the five-year period 1966-1970,* United Nations, New York 1971, p. 187. In November 1982 the United Nations General Assembly passed a resolution calling for negotiations between Britain and Argentina on the sovereignty dispute over the Falklands, by 90 votes to 12, see *Keesing's Contemporary Archives,* Vol. XXIV, (1983), 32108.
8. Michla Pomerance, *Self-Determination in Law and Practice,* Martinus Nijhoff, The Hague 1982, p. 9.
9. M. Wight, op. cit., p. 168.
10. General Assembly Resolution 1514 (XV), 14 December 1960.
11. General Assembly Resolution 2625 (XXV), 24 October 1970. 25 UNGAOR, Supp. 26 (A/8026) p. 124.
12. There are some examples of secession by mutual agreement between a

central and a regional government or between two governments forming a loose confederation. The most important example was Singapore's secession from the Malaysian Federation in August 1965. The Federation was under two years old at the time. Bangladesh's membership of the United Nations was not uncontested. The People's Republic of China used its newly acquired veto in the Security Council to hold up Bangladesh's membership until 1974. Throughout the actual crisis the United States Government made constant reference to the UN's position on self-determination in defence of its support for Pakistan. See, for example, Kathleen Knight, 'Bangladesh: The Price of National Unity' in Ray Edward Johnston (ed.), *The Politics of Division, Partition, and Unification*, Praeger, New York 1976, pp. 93-5.

13. See, for example, Claire Palley's comments on this point in David Watt (ed.), *The Constitution of Northern Ireland*, Heinemann, London 1981, pp. 187-8.
14. John O'Connor, 'Agreement gives North new international status', *Irish Times*, (Dublin) 21 Nov. 1985.
15. Quoted in Martin Gilbert, *Finest Hour: Winston S. Churchill 1939-1941*, Heinemann, London 1983, p. 433.
16. See, for example, William A. Carson, *Ulster and the Irish Republic*, Cleland, Belfast 1957. Much of the book is devoted to criticism of 'Eire separatists'.
17. *Irish Times*, 21 Nov. 1985.
18. See, for example, the comments of James Molyneaux in 'Government denies talks on rejoining Commonwealth', *Irish Times*, 18 Oct. 1983, in which he said that the South should recognise that the British Isles were a natural unit.
19. See Martin Wallace, *British Government in Northern Ireland*, David and Charles, Newton Abbot 1982, p. 53.
20. See, for example, James Downey, *Them and Us: Britain, Ireland, and the Northern Question 1969-1982*, Ward River Press, Dublin 1983, pp. 188-90 on Haughey's tentative offer of an Anglo-Irish defence pact. William FitzGerald, *Irish unification and N.A.T.O.*, Dublin University Press, Dublin 1982, puts the case for such a deal between Britain and Ireland.
21. In 1983 Tony Benn suggested that one reason why Britain remained in Northern Ireland was 'an analysis by chiefs of staff that an independent and unified Ireland might constitute a defence threat'. *The Guardian* (London), 18 July 1983.
22. See, for example, the report of a speech by Powell in *Belfast Telegraph* (Belfast), 12 Oct. 1982.
23. Colonel Jonathan Alford, 'North's strategic value is a non-issue', *Irish Times*, 31 Jan. 1986.
24. *Irish Times*, 11 Nov. 1983.
25. See, for example, Helen Shaw, 'Robinson sees independence as a viable option for NI', *Irish Times*, 10 Sept. 1986.
26. *Beyond the Religious Divide*, New Ulster Political Research Group, Belfast 1979.
27. *House of Commons Debates*, col. 1049, 2 July 1981.
28. Professor Cornelius O'Leary, 'Northern Ireland: arguments for negotiated independence', *Irish Times*, 29 Oct. 1981.

29. Dervla Murphy, *Changing the Problem: Post-Forum Reflections*, Lilliput, Mullingar 1984, p. 9.

30. For example, Enoch Powell, a keen proponent of integration, dubbed Paisley and the Democratic Unionist Party (DUP) as Protestant Sinn Fein, see *Belfast Telegraph*, 12 Oct. 1982.

31. See note 3 above.

32. See, for example, Phillip Knightley, 'Is Britain Losing the Propaganda War?' *Sunday Times* (London), 31 May 1981.

33. Lloyd George appreciated the weakness of the British case on partition in 1921. He outlined his strategy on the negotiations with the Sinn Fein leaders to his Cabinet colleagues in the following terms: 'If the Conference started without securing in advance Irish allegiance to the Crown and membership of the Empire, the discussion would become entangled in the Ulster problem; that de Valera would raise the question of Fermanagh and Tyrone, where we had a very weak case, the Conference might break on that point, a very bad one. He would rather break—if there was to be a break—now, on allegiance and Empire', see Thomas Jones, *Whitehall Diary: Ireland 1918-1925* (ed. Keith Middlemass), Oxford University Press, London 1971, p. 111. The Irish negotiators held a similar view. See Frank Pakenham, *Peace by Ordeal*, Cape, London 1935, pp. 184-9. In 1986, a junior Labour Party spokesman, Stuart Bell, gave the existence of nationalist majorities in Fermanagh and Tyrone as a reason why independence should not be granted to Northern Ireland in its present form. *Belfast Telegraph*, 7 July 1986.

34. Hispaniola, Tierra del Fuego, Borneo, New Guinea, and St. Martin are the only current cases of islands under divided sovereignty besides Ireland. To this list may be added the *de facto* partition of Cyprus and the presence of an American naval base on Cuba.

35. See Rupert Emerson, *Self-Determination revisited in the era of decolonisation*, Harvard University Center for International Affairs, Cambridge, Mass. 1964, pp. 55-7.

36. Quoted in Pomerance, op. cit., p. 96.

37. See *Keesing's Contemporary Archives*, Vol. XVIII (1971-72), 25444 on Colonel Gadafy's speech on 11 June 1972.

38. *Sunday Tribune* (Dublin), 6 May 1984.

39. *Irish Times*, 3 May 1984.

40. *Irish Times*, 1 May 1984.

41. *Irish Times*, 18 June 1986.

42. *Irish Times*, 19 June 1986.

43. *The Observer* (London), 1 Mar. 1987 and *Irish Times*, 16 Apr. 1987.

44. Claire Sterling suggests that Gadafy was giving the Provisional IRA five million dollars or so a year in the late 1970s. She bases this claim on allegations made by a former member of the Provisional IRA. (See Claire Sterling, *The Terror Network: The Secret War of International Terrorism*, Holt, Rinehart, and Winston, New York 1981, p. 161.) In fact, five million dollars was more than twice the *total* annual income of the Provisionals in this period, according to the analysis done by Brigadier Glover for the British army in 1978. Brigadier Glover estimated the Provisionals' annual income at £950,000 in a confidential British army intelligence document

entitled 'Northern Ireland: Future Terrorist Trends'. He also concluded that the Provisionals were receiving no aid from Libya by this time. The document is reproduced in Sean Cronin, *Irish Nationalism: A History of its Roots and Ideology*, The Academy Press, Dublin 1980, pp. 339-57.

45. *Newsletter* (Belfast), 21 June 1983. Molyneaux has also made allegations of American governmental involvement in aiding Republican paramilitaries. See, for example, 'NATO plot killings claim by Molyneaux', *Irish Times*, 23 Mar. 1982.

46. See Michael McKinley, 'The International Dimension of Terrorism in Ireland' in Y. Alexander and A. O'Day (eds.), *Terrorism in Ireland*, Croom Helm, London 1984, p. 26.

47. Sterling suggests the anti-Communist outlook of the Provisional IRA provided a cover for Soviet assistance. See C. Sterling, op. cit., p. 156. See also Maurice Tugwell, 'Politics and Propaganda of the Provisional IRA' in Paul Wilkinson (ed.), *British Perspectives on Terrorism*, George Allen and Unwin, London 1981, p. 24.

48. Terrance G. Carroll, 'Northern Ireland' in Astri Suhrke and Lela Garner Noble (eds.), *Ethnic Conflict in International Relations*, Praeger, New York 1977, p. 37.

49. See Liam Clarke, 'Fists fly in fascist row', *Sunday News* (Belfast), 17 July 1983. This is an account of a brawl in a town in Belgium among a number of neo-fascist groups prompted by an argument over whether they should support Loyalists or Republicans in Northern Ireland.

50. See, for example 'The South African Link', *Sunday News*, 24 July 1983.

51. See M. McKinley, 'The International Dimension etc.' in Y. Alexander and A. O'Day (eds.), op. cit., pp. 17-19.

52. J. Bowyer Bell, *The Secret Army: The IRA 1916-1979*, The Academy Press, Dublin 1979, p. 438.

53. See, for example, Patrick Bishop and Eamonn Mallie, *The Provisional IRA*, Heinemann, London 1987, pp. 243-4 on a shipment of arms the Provisional IRA purchased from Al Fatah in 1977.

54. *Irish Times*, 12 Jan. 1980.

55. Bishop and Mallie, op. cit., pp. 244-5.

56. *Irish Times*, 21 Dec. 1981.

57. See Sean Flynn, 'The Marxist gunmen of the INLA threaten a resurrection', *Irish Times*, 18 Sept. 1987.

58. Sterling, op. cit., p. 153.

59. *Irish Times*, 20 Feb. 1986.

60. *Belfast Telegraph*, 25 Mar. 1987.

61. Edward Moxon-Browne, *Nation, Class and Creed in Northern Ireland*, Gower, Aldershot 1983, p. 40.

62. Ibid., p. 42.

63. Ironically, the Republic of Ireland may be the one place in the world where expectations of a united Ireland are actually declining. In particular, a poll in 1987 found that 49 per cent of respondents in the Republic believed that there would never be a united Ireland, see *Irish Times*, 1 Sept. 1987.

64. *Irish Times*, 12 Feb. 1986.

65. The remarks made by Ireland's Ambassador to Britain, Dr Eamon Kennedy to the British Prime Minister, Margaret Thatcher, in December

1979 provide a striking example of nationalist hopes. He said: 'Prime Minister, it's Christmas and you've given us the gift of peace in Zimbabwe. It must have demanded great energy and vision and courage to achieve that. Now could we ask that having achieved that in Africa, you might channel those same qualities towards an island next door, where our tribes need to be brought together too?', interview with the *Irish Times*, 15 July 1983. On Loyalist fears, see as an example the comments in the UDA's journal, *Ulster* (Belfast), February 1984.

66. See Leo Kuper, *Genocide*, Penguin, Harmondsworth 1981, pp. 161-5.
67. *House of Commons Debates* (6th Series), Vol. 7, Col. 1048, 2 July 1981.
68. Conor Cruise O'Brien's dire warnings over the years that a British withdrawal would be followed by civil war, repartition, and the emergence of an independent Loyalist state within truncated boundaries have made little impression on nationalist opinion on this issue.
69. See, for example, the remarks of a Sinn Fein local councillor in 'SF, Communists debate socialism', *Irish Times*, 21 Sept. 1987. He argued that 'until the British military presence in Ireland was smashed the Protestants could not be won over to the national struggle'. The Communist speaker said they had to be won over and criticised the Provisional IRA campaign.

Chapter 2: Violence and Legitimacy (pp. 21-39)
 1. Gerald Priestland, *The Future of Violence*, Hamish Hamilton, London 1974, p. 11.
 2. See John Darby, *Intimidation and the Control of Conflict in Northern Ireland*, Gill and Macmillan, Dublin 1986.
 3. J. Darby and G. Morris, *Intimidation in Housing*, Northern Ireland Community Relations Commission, Belfast 1974, p. c.
 4. Kevin Boyle and Tom Hadden, *Ireland: A Positive Proposal*, Penguin, Harmondsworth 1985, p. 16.
 5. *Political Attitudes in Northern Ireland: An Opinion Poll conducted for UTV by NOP Research*, Ulster Television, Belfast 1982.
 6. See, for example, Anthony Arblaster, 'What is violence?' in Ralph Miliband and John Saville, *The Socialist Register 1975*, Merlin, London 1975, pp. 224-9.
 7. See, for example, Paul Wilkinson, 'The Orange and the Green: Extremism in Northern Ireland' in Martha Crenshaw (ed.), *Terrorism, Legitimacy, and Power*, Wesleyan University Press, Middleton, Connecticut 1983, pp. 105-23.
 8. Ibid.
 9. See, for example, Edward Moxon-Browne, *Nation, Class and Creed in Northern Ireland*, Gower, Aldershot 1983, pp. 35-6.
10. Ibid., p. 6.
11. See, for example, the sectarian breakdown on the answers to a poll on eight different constitutional options in *Belfast Telegraph*, 15 Feb. 1986.
12. On the notion of representative violence, see Frank Wright, 'Communal deterrence and the threat of violence in the north of Ireland in the nineteenth century', in J. Darby, N. Dodge, and A. C. Hepburn (eds.), *Political Violence in Comparative Perspective*, Appletree Press, Belfast forthcoming.

13. See, for example, *Newsletter*, 2 July 1987.
14. See the calculations for the period from 1969 to 1984 in D. Roche, 'Patterns of violence in Northern Ireland in 1984', *Fortnight* (Belfast) (no. 218), 29 Apr.–12 May 1985.
15. See, for example, 'Papers censured over IRA toll', *Irish Times*, 16 August 1983. This is a report of the British Press Council's condemnation of the *Daily Star* and the *Daily Express* for referring to the total number of deaths in the troubles as 'victims of the IRA'.
16. See *Common Sense*, Ulster Political Research Group, Belfast 1987.
17. See Merlyn Rees, *Northern Ireland: A Personal Perspective*, Methuen, London 1985, pp. 149-81.
18. Anonymous SAS member quoted in Tony Geraghty, *Who Dares Wins: The Story of the Special Air Services*, Arms and Armour Press, London 1980, p. 161.
19. Quoted in *Fortnight* (no. 177), July-Aug. 1980.
20. *Alliance Assembly Election Manifesto 1982*, Alliance Party, Belfast 1982.
21. Ibid.
22. Quoted in Rob Carmichael, *The Peace People Experience*, Dawn, Dublin 1987, p. 2.
23. Sympathetic onlookers elsewhere in the world were readily able to identify this problem. See, for example, the comments of the President of Zambia in Kenneth David Kaunda, *Kaunda on Violence* (ed. Colin M. Morris), Sphere, London 1982, pp. 23-4.
24. Gerry Adams, *The Politics of Irish Freedom*, Brandon, Dingle 1986, p. 62.
25. Quoted in *Fortnight* (no. 189), Dec. 1982.
26. *Belfast Telegraph*, 24 June 1987.
27. *New Ireland Forum Report*, The Stationery Office, Dublin 1984, p. 27.
28. *Irish News* (Belfast), 23 Feb. 1984.
29. *Fortnight* (no. 190), Jan. 1983.
30. Ibid.
31. *Fortnight* (no. 231), 16 Dec. 1985–26 Jan. 1986.
32. *Irish Times*, 14 July 1987.
33. Quoted in *Fortnight* (no. 183), Oct.–Nov. 1981.
34. *Fortnight* (no. 224), 9-22 Sept. 1985.
35. *UDA* (Belfast), vol. 1, no. 3, n.d.
36. On the urban appeal of the Loyalist paramilitaries, see Keith Maguire, 'A Conspectus on the Loyalist paramilitaries: An outline of the organisation and ideology of Loyalist paramilitary groups in Ulster 1966-1982', M S Sc dissertation for the Department of Political Science, Queen's University of Belfast.
37. John F. Galliher and Jerry L. De Gregory, *Violence in Northern Ireland: Understanding Protestant Perspectives*, Gill and Macmillan, Dublin 1985, p. 184.
38. Ibid., p. 68.
39. John Whyte, 'How is the boundary maintained between the two communities in Northern Ireland?' *Ethnic and Racial Studies*, Vol. 9, No. 2, April 1986, pp. 219-34.
40. John Whyte, 'Interpretations of the Northern Ireland Problem', paper presented at a conference of the British Association for Irish Studies at the

University of Keele, 2-4 April 1986.
41. Richard Rose, *Governing without Consensus*, Faber, London 1971, p. 248.
42. The relatively small difference in the two communities' living standards is the obvious weakness in arguments that suggest that Protestant attitudes are the product of economic privilege. For an example of such a view, see Michael MacDonald, *Children of Wrath: Political Violence in Northern Ireland*, Polity Press, Cambridge 1986.
43. J. Darby, *Intimidation and Control*, op. cit., p. 55.

Chapter 3: Republican Perceptions (pp. 40-61)
 1. See the calculations by Michael McKeown on the agencies responsible for deaths during the Troubles: Michael McKeown, *De Mortuis*, Irish Information Partnership, Gondregnies 1985. This covers the first 2,400 victims.
 2. See 'A Scenario for Peace: A Discussion Paper', *An Phoblacht/Republican News* (Dublin), 7 May 1987.
 3. Ibid.
 4. Ibid.
 5. See, for example, *Republican News* (Belfast), 30 Oct. 1971.
 6. See Conor Cruise O'Brien, *States of Ireland*, Panther, St Albans 1974, p. 193.
 7. See Patrick Bishop and Eamonn Mallie, *The Provisional IRA*, Heinemann, London 1987, p. 94.
 8. The figures are given in J. Bowyer Bell, *The Secret Army: The IRA 1916-1979*, The Academy Press, Dublin 1979, p. 366.
 9. *An Phoblacht* (Dublin), Feb. 1970.
10. Ibid.
11. See Bob Purdie, 'Reconsiderations on Republicanism and Socialism' in Austen Morgan and Bob Purdie (eds.), *Ireland: Divided Nation Divided Class*, Ink Links, London 1980, pp. 74-95.
12. *An Phoblacht*, Feb. 1970.
13. *An Phoblacht*, Mar. 1970.
14. The front page of the August issue of *An Phoblacht* declared 'British troops are invaders' and followed the comment with a list: 'Budapest 1956-Saigon 1966-Prague 1968-Belfast 1970'.
15. See Frank Burton, *The Politics of Legitimacy: Struggles in a Belfast Community*, Routledge and Kegan Paul, London 1978, p. 82.
16. J. Bowyer Bell, op. cit., p. 381.
17. *Republican News*, Mar. 1971.
18. *Republican News*, Apr. 1971.
19. *Fortnight*, 12 Jan. 1972.
20. Quoted in *Fortnight*, 13 Apr. 1972.
21. Tim Pat Coogan, *The I.R.A.*, Fontana, London 1980, p. 469.
22. Ibid.
23. *Republican News*, 2 Jan. 1972.
24. The social and economic programme had first been published under the title, *Éire Nua*, in January 1971. The proposals for a federation were simply tacked on to a reprint of this publication in 1972. See *Éire Nua*, Sinn Fein,

Dublin 1972. However, after 1972, references made to *Éire Nua* often mean simply the constitutional proposals.

25. See the account of the truce given in *An Phoblacht/Republican News*, 6 Aug. 1987.
26. Ibid.
27. Quoted in Jack Holland, *Too Long a Sacrifice: Life and Death in Northern Ireland since 1969*, Dodd, Mead, and Company, New York 1981, p. 133.
28. *An Phoblacht*, 18 Jan. 1974.
29. According to Coogan, op. cit., p. 559, there were talks taking place through intermediaries as late as April 1977.
30. Bishop and Mallie, op. cit., p. 217.
31. Quoted in Coogan, op. cit., p. 579.
32. *Irish Times*, 14 November 1983.
33. See, for example, *Republican News*, Jan./Feb. 1971.
34. *Belfast Telegraph*, 29 October 1979, contains a typical denial in response to a speech by a government minister.
35. Claire Hackett, 'Sinn Fein and Feminism 1979-1984', M S Sc dissertation for the Department of Political Science, Queen's University of Belfast, p. 19.
36. *Irish Times*, 4 Nov. 1985.
37. See *The Politics of Revolution: The main speeches and debates from the 1986 Sinn Fein Ard-Fheis including the presidential address of Gerry Adams*, Sinn Fein, Dublin n.d., pp. 41-3.
38. *Iris* (Dublin), Nov. 1981, p. 94 (a Sinn Fein quarterly).
39. See, for example, Adams's remarks on the necessity of force in his presidential address to the 1984 Sinn Fein *ard fheis*, *Irish Times*, 14 Nov. 1983.
40. See David Beresford, *Ten Men Dead: The story of the 1981 Irish hunger strike*, Grafton Books, London 1987, p. 53.
41. *Irish Times*, 3 Jan. 1981.
42. *Irish Times*, 9 May 1981.
43. *Sunday Tribune*, 8 Nov. 1981.
44. *Iris*, Nov. 1982, p. 3.
45. *An Phoblacht/Republican News*, 16 Sept. 1982.
46. The Irish Government was further alarmed by the outcome of a by-election in Dublin Central in November 1983. The Sinn Fein candidate won 7 per cent of first preferences, outpolling the candidate of the Irish Labour Party. On reaction in the Republic, see *Belfast Telegraph*, 25 Nov. 1983.
47. *The Guardian*, 8 Apr. 1985.
48. Gerry Adams, *The Politics of Irish Freedom*, Brandon, Dingle 1986, p. 105.
49. See, for example, *Troops Out* (London), Dec. 1985/Jan. 1986. The coverage of the Agreement starts with the words: 'The deal signed at the Anglo-Irish summit is a pudding whose proof will be very much in the eating.' See also *Troops Out*, Mar. 1986.
50. *Irish Times*, 4 Nov. 1985.
51. *An Phoblacht/Republican News*, 16 Oct. 1986. Other decisions included modernising the constitution so that its language was non-sexist, the

election of a 12-person Army Executive and a reaffirmation of the order prohibiting offensive action against the administration in the South.

52. See, for example, *The Politics of Revolution*, op. cit., especially pp. 12-13.
53. See, for example, David Morgan, 'Sinn Fein prepare for loyalist strike', *Irish News*, 11 Mar. 1986.
54. See, for example, '"Catholic backlash" anticipated over killing', *Irish Times*, 29 Aug. 1986.
55. See, for example, the remarks of Danny Morrison quoted in the *Irish Times*, 4 Aug. 1986.
56. Adams, op. cit., pp. 126-7.

Chapter 4: Loyalist Perceptions (pp. 62-81)
1. These are the terms used in Jennifer Todd, 'Two Traditions in Unionist Political Culture', *Irish Political Studies*, Vol. 2, 1987, pp. 1-26.
2. The seminal study of conditional loyalty among Ulster Protestants is David W. Miller, *Queen's Rebels: Ulster Loyalism in Historical Perspective*, Gill and Macmillan, Dublin 1978.
3. According to the Irish Information Partnership, in the period from 1969 to the end of 1984, Loyalist paramilitaries were responsible for just over a quarter of the fatalities resulting from the Troubles, see D. Roche, 'Patterns of violence in N. Ireland in 1984', *Fortnight* (no. 218), 29 Apr.-12 May 1985.
4. The name had powerful historical associations for Protestants. The Ulster Volunteer Force was an armed force which Unionists established in 1912 in their successful bid to stop Irish Home Rule through the threat of force. At the outbreak of the First World War, the force was transformed into a division of the British army, suffering heavy casualties at the Battle of the Somme in 1916.
5. See Keith Maguire, 'A Conspectus on the Loyalist Paramilitaries: An outline of the organisation and ideology of loyalist paramilitary groups in Ulster 1966-1982', M S Sc dissertation for the Department of Political Science, Queen's University of Belfast.
6. *UDA*, Vol. 1, No. 1, n.d.
7. Ibid.
8. *UDA*, Vol. 1, No. 2, 19 Oct. 1971.
9. Quoted in Martin Dillon and Denis Lehane, *Political Murder in Northern Ireland*, Penguin, Harmondsworth 1973, p. 282.
10. Ibid., p. 286.
11. *UDA*, op. cit., 19 Oct. 1971.
12. Dillon and Lehane, op. cit., p. 28.
13. See R. Murray, '"Doorstep Murders" in Belfast', paper presented at the Annual Conference of the Institute of Geographers, University of Lancaster, January 1980.
14. See, for example, the piece on the Housing Executive: 'Points system means Prods out', *Ulster*, Aug. 1981.
15. See Sarah Nelson, *Ulster's Uncertain Defenders: Protestant Political, Paramilitary and Community Groups and the Northern Ireland Conflict*, Appletree Press, Belfast 1984, p. 104.
16. Ibid.

17. This was Glen Barr's explanation of the visit. See W. D. Flackes, *Northern Ireland: A Political Directory*, British Broadcasting Company, London 1983, p. 232.
18. See Arthur Aughey and Colin McIlheney, 'Law before Violence?—The Protestant Paramilitaries in Ulster Politics', *Éire-Ireland*, Vol. 17. No. 2, Summer 1984, pp. 65-6 on the nature of the Scottish and Canadian connections.
19. *Ulster*, Sept. 1976.
20. Ibid.
21. *UDA*, Vol. 1, No. 5, n.d.
22. Article headed 'Those "Innocent" Cats', *Ulster*, July 1976.
23. Tim Pat Coogan, *The I.R.A.*, Fontana, London 1980, pp. 558-60.
24. See Chapter 5.
25. See the account of Barr's speech to the conference in *Fortnight* (no. 110), 12 Sept. 1975.
26. *Beyond the Religious Divide*, New Ulster Political Research Group, Belfast 1979.
27. Ibid.
28. Ibid.
29. Ibid.
30. Ian Adamson is an enthusiastic promoter of the notion of a common Ulster identity prior to the seventeenth-century plantations. See, for example, Ian Adamson, *The Identity of Ulster*, W. and G. Baird Ltd., Northern Ireland 1982.
31. *Ulster*, Oct. 1978.
32. Professor Cornelius O'Leary, quoted in *Ulster*, Dec. 1979.
33. *The Guardian*, 27 Aug. 1979.
34. *Fortnight* (no. 174), Dec. 1979/Jan. 1980.
35. Andy Tyrie interview in *Marxism Today* (London), Dec. 1981.
36. See Jim Hunter, 'The Wicked Witch Lives On', *Ulster*, Feb. 1982.
37. *Chief Constable's Annual Report 1986*, Royal Ulster Constabulary, Belfast 1987, p. 64.
38. See, for example, the remarkable letter L. Scott of the NUPRG sent to the *Irish Times*, 28 Apr. 1981, on the result of the Fermanagh and South Tyrone by-election. He pointed out that 'the Catholic population was not asked to support Bobby Sands or indeed the PIRA, but to support certain demands in order to resolve the prison dispute and to save Bobby Sands' life'.
39. *Chief Constable's Annual Report 1986*, op. cit., p. 64.
40. See *Fortnight* (no. 204), May 1984 and *Fortnight* (no. 224), 9-22 Sept. 1984.
41. *Ulster*, July/Aug. 1986.
42. However, it was apparently possible for men to be transferred from the UDF to the UFF. See *Ulster*, Apr. 1985.
43. *Ulster*, July/Aug. 1986.
44. *Irish Times*, 2 July 1983.
45. See McMichael's comments in *Ulster*, Aug. 1983.
46. 'The Battle for Ulster is NOW', *Ulster*, Apr. 1985.
47. *Ulster*, Sept. 1985.
48. *Ulster*, Mar. 1985.

49. *Belfast Telegraph*, 14 Dec. 1983. Duddy contradicted many of the other claims made by the Londonderry spokesman.
50. See, for example, the *Irish Times*, 4 Nov. 1985.
51. See the account in the *Irish Times*, 13 Apr. 1987.
52. *Irish Times*, 27 June 1986.
53. *Common Sense (Northern Ireland—An Agreed Process)*, Ulster Political Research Group, Belfast 1987.
54. Ibid., p. 6.
55. Ibid., p. 7.
56. Ibid., p. 8.
57. Ibid.
58. Quoted in the *Sunday Tribune*, 15 Feb. 1987.
59. Quoted in *Fortnight* (no. 254), Sept. 1987.
60. *Sunday Tribune*, 15 Feb. 1987.
61. See, for example, 'UDA adopts Dunkirk spirit to help move free EEC food', *Belfast Telegraph*, 13 Feb. 1987.

Chapter 5: The British Dimension (pp. 82-107)
 1. See *New Ireland Forum Report*, The Stationery Office, Dublin 1984, p. 14.
 2. *The government of Northern Ireland: a working paper for a conference* (Cmnd. 7763), HMSO, London 1979, p. 2.
 3. See the interview with Austin Currie in *Fortnight* (no. 252), June 1987.
 4. Clause 1 (1)B of the Ireland Act of 1949.
 5. Patrick Buckland, *A History of Northern Ireland*, Gill and Macmillan, Dublin 1981, p. 89.
 6. Ibid., p. 132.
 7. Downing Street Declaration of 19 August 1969, quoted in *The Times* (London), 20 Aug. 1969.
 8. Ibid.
 9. Ibid.
10. Michael Farrell, *Northern Ireland: The Orange State*, Pluto Press, London 1980, p. 287.
11. *Fortnight*, 12 Nov. 1971.
12. Text of Sunningdale Agreement, quoted in *The Times* 10 Dec. 1973.
13. *Sunday Tribune*, 22 Mar. 1987. Rees has demanded an inquiry into the allegations of political misbehaviour by the security services in Northern Ireland on more than one occasion, see the *Irish Times*, 17 Mar. 1987 and 8 Aug. 1987.
14. Rees cites Loyalist talk of independence after the strike as justifying his use of the phrase,Ulster nationalism, to describe Protestant feelings in this period. See Merlyn Rees, *Northern Ireland: A Personal Perspective*, Methuen, London 1985, pp. 90-92.
15. *The Northern Ireland Constitution* (Cmnd. 5675), HMSO, London 1974.
16. The Convention was formally dissolved on 6 March 1976, though its failure was apparent from November the previous year when its majority report was published.
17. See Rees, op. cit., pp. 296-9 and Desmond Hamill, *Pig in the Middle: The Army in Northern Ireland 1969-1985*, Methuen, London 1986, pp. 184-5.
18. *The Conservative Manifesto 1979*, Conservative Party, London 1979, p. 22.

19. See note 2 above.
20. See, for example, M. Rees, op. cit., p. 352: 'Grandiose Anglo/Irish solutions will not work'.
21. See, for example, George Brock, 'Thatcher's U-turn on Ulster', *The Observer*, 14 Dec. 1980.
22. From the text of the communiqué after the summit, quoted in the *Irish Times*, 9 Dec. 1980.
23. *Sunday Times*, 31 May 1981.
24. See Jim Prior, *A Balance of Power*, Hamish Hamilton, London 1986, pp. 189-97.
25. Ibid., p. 199.
26. *Northern Ireland: a framework for devolution* (Cmnd. 8541), HMSO, London 1982.
27. *Irish Times*, 7 Oct. 1982.
28. See David McKittrick, '[Prior] Takes pasting from press', *Irish Times*, 25 Oct. 1982.
29. See David McKittrick, 'SDLP held in low esteem', *Irish Times*, 20 Nov. 1982.
30. See Jim Cusack, 'Policy on RUC tactics changed', *Irish Times*, 22 Dec. 1982 and Patrick Bishop, 'Ulster calm credited to tougher tactics', *The Observer*, 2 Jan. 1983.
31. *Agreement between the Government of the United Kingdom of Great Britain and Northern Ireland and the Government of the Republic of Ireland* (Cmnd. 9657), HMSO, London 1985.
32. FitzGerald quoted in Patrick Keatinge, 'Ireland's Foreign Relations in 1985', *Irish Studies in International Affairs*, Vol. 2, No. 2, 1986, pp. 106-7.
33. See 'The Pestilent Province: Britain's Patience Runs Out', *Sunday Times*, 9 Mar. 1986.
34. George H. Gallup, *The Gallup International Public Opinion Polls: Great Britain 1937-1975*, Vol. 2, Random House, New York n.d., p. 1054.
35. Ibid., p. 1160.
36. Ibid., p. 1333.
37. Two polls cited in Geoffrey Bell, *The British in Ireland: A suitable case for withdrawal*, Pluto Press, London 1984, p. 90.
38. Reported in the *Irish Times*, 11 Feb. 1987.
39. In February 1972 and August 1978 in the case of the *Daily Mirror*; in August 1981 in that of the *Sunday Times*.
40. *Financial Times* (London), 22 Sept. 1983.
41. See the very full report of the Conference decision in the *Irish Times*, 30 Sept. 1981.
42. See, for example, the comments of Labour's deputy spokesman on Northern Ireland, Stuart Bell, quoted in the *Irish Times*, 2 Oct. 1986.
43. See, for example, the responses to other questions on Northern Ireland recorded by Gallup in G. H. Gallup, op. cit., especially p. 1163, pp. 1168-9, p. 1462.
44. Quoted in Paul Bew and Henry Patterson, *The British State and the Ulster Crisis: From Wilson to Thatcher*, Verso, London 1985, p. 9.
45. See *Finance Accounts of Northern Ireland for the Financial Year 1985-86*, HMSO, Belfast 1987.

46. Anthony Kenny, *The Road to Hillsborough: The Shaping of the Anglo-Irish Agreement*, Pergamon Press, Oxford 1986, p. 136.
47. In particular, Tony Benn has proposed a Bill authorising a British withdrawal from Northern Ireland which is based on the Act that was passed to end Britain's responsibility for the government of Palestine.
48. This is notwithstanding the occasional Ministerial speech suggesting otherwise. For example, on 4 December 1985, the Secretary of State for Northern Ireland, Tom King, went so far as to proclaim that it was his 'fervent wish' that a majority in Northern Ireland would want to stay part of the United Kingdom. For the incredulous reaction, see Conor O'Clery, 'Fervent—a new word in Mr King's vocabulary', *Irish Times*, 7 Dec. 1985.
49. *Belfast Telegraph*, 18 May 1984.
50. Kenny, op. cit., p. 130.
51. See note 33 above.
52. See 'The Falklands Constitution', *Financial Times*, 21 Jan. 1985.
53. See 'Hong Kong people "bow to the inevitable" ', *Financial Times*, 30 Nov. 1984.
54. See the *Irish Times*, 28 Dec. 1984.
55. The SDLP gained one seat in the by-elections in 1986 that resulted from Unionist resignations to protest against the Agreement. The party gained a further seat from the Unionists in the Westminster general election of 1987.

Chapter 6: The South and the North (pp. 108-127)

1. See, for example, Peter Smith, *Why Unionists Say No*, Joint Unionist Working Party, n.d., pp. 3-4.
2. For example, in a poll carried out in 1987, only 16 per cent of the sample expected unity within 25 years. Only 7 per cent expected unity within ten years. (In a similar poll in 1983, 26 per cent of respondents had said they expected unity within 25 years.) *Irish Times*, 1 Sept. 1987.
3. The Committee recommended that Article 3 be changed to read: 'The Irish nation hereby proclaims its firm will that its territory be re-united in harmony and brotherly affection between all Irishmen.' Quoted in John Bowman, *De Valera and the Ulster Question1917-1973*, Clarendon Press, Oxford 1982, p. 325.
4. Quoted in Bruce Arnold, *What Kind of Country: Modern Irish Politics, 1968-1983*, Jonathan Cape, London 1984, p. 21.
5. Arnold, op. cit., p. 147.
6. Andrew Boyd, *Fifteen Men on a Powder Keg*, Methuen, London 1971, p. 328.
7. See, for example, Breasal O Caollai, 'Fianna Fáil and the IRA Connection', *New Hibernia* (Dublin), Dec. 1986/Jan. 1987.
8. See John Peck, *Dublin from Downing Street*, Gill and Macmillan, Dublin 1978, pp. 130-34, on the sharp exchanges between Lynch and the British Prime Minister, Edward Heath.
9. Ibid., p. 142.
10. *The future of Northern Ireland: a paper for discussion*, HMSO, London 1972, pp. 33-4.
11. Lynch used the phrase in a speech on 11 July 1970, see Peck, op. cit., p. 53.

12. *Northern Ireland Constitutional Proposals* (Cmnd. 5259), HMSO, London 1973.
13. *The Times*, 10 Dec. 1973.
14. See Dennis Kennedy, 'Shrinking State of Ireland', *Fortnight* (no. 85), 21 June 1974.
15. *Irish Times*, 20 July 1983.
16. Quoted in Arnold, op. cit., p. 147.
17. *Irish Times*, 9 Dec. 1980.
18. Ibid.
19. Arnold, op. cit., pp. 154-5, conveys the scepticism that greeted the communiqué very clearly.
20. See, for example, Brian Girvin, 'The Anglo-Irish Agreement 1985' in Brian Girvin and Roland Sturm (eds.), *Politics and Society in Contemporary Ireland*, Gower, Aldershot 1986.
21. See Patrick Keatinge, *A Singular Stance: Irish Neutrality in the 1980s*, Institute of Public Administration, Dublin 1984, pp. 77-9.
22. The crusade started with an interview on the RTE radio programme, 'This Week', on 27 September 1981 in which FitzGerald said: 'What I want to do is to lead a crusade—a Republican crusade—to make this a genuine Republic on the principles of Tone and Davis . . .', *Irish Times*, 28 Sept. 1981.) The term, Republican, has a different connotation in the South to its association with paramilitaries in the North.)
23. See 'Text of joint communiqué' in the *Irish Times*, 7 Nov. 1981.
24. Quoted in Paul Arthur, 'Anglo-Irish Relations and the Northern Ireland problem', *Irish Studies in International Affairs*, Vol. 2, No. 1, 1985, p. 47.
25. *Northern Ireland: a framework for devolution* (Cmnd. 8541), HMSO, London 1982.
26. Interview on Ulster Television's 'Counterpoint' programme on 20 Jan. 1983, *Irish Times*, 20 Jan. 1983.
27. See the analysis of the New Ireland Forum Report in Clare O'Halloran, *Partition and the Limits of Irish Nationalism*, Gill and Macmillan, Dublin 1987, pp. 195-210.
28. *New Ireland Forum Report*, The Stationery Office, Dublin 1984, p. 20.
29. Ibid., p. 29.
30. Ibid., p. 30.
31. *House of Commons Debates*, Vol. 63, Cols. 23-30, 2 July 1984.
32. *Belfast Telegraph*, 26 Sept. 1984.
33. See 'What Thatcher said at press briefing', *Irish Times*, 23 Nov. 1984.
34. See, for example, the *Sunday Press*, 25 Nov. 1984, the *Irish Times*, 23 Nov. 1984, and the *Sunday Tribune*, 25 Nov. 1984.
35. *Sunday Press*, 25 Nov. 1984.
36. *Irish Times*, 24 Nov. 1984.
37. An early example was a story in a popular British paper, *The Mail on Sunday*, (24 Mar. 1985) predicting peace in Ireland and suggesting the general outlines of an agreement.
38. Patrick Keatinge, 'Ireland's foreign relations in 1985', *Irish Studies in International Affairs*, Vol. 2, No. 2, 1986, p. 94.
39. For example, the Market Research Bureau of Ireland poll conducted in the days after the Agreement was signed showed that 59 per cent of

respondents generally approved of the signing of the agreement and 29 per cent broadly disapproved, see the *Irish Times*, 23 Nov. 1986.

40. See, for example, Gerald Barry, 'Lenihan takes driver's seat', *Sunday Tribune*, 19 July 1987.
41. Their input was reflected in *New Ireland Forum: the macroeconomic consequences of integrated economic policy, planning, and co-ordination*, The Stationery Office, Dublin 1984.
42. *Irish Times*, 5 May 1984.
43. On the growth of differences between the two parts of Ireland, see Richard Rose and Tom Garvin, 'The Public Policy Effects of Independence: Ireland as a Test Case', *European Journal of Political Research*, Vol. 11, No. 4, Dec. 1983.

Chapter 7: The American Connection (pp. 128-152)
1. The main exception until 1987 was Dennis J. Clark, *Irish Blood: Northern Ireland and the American Conscience*, Kennikat Press, Port Washington, New York 1977. In 1987 two relevant books were published: Jack Holland, *The American Connection: US Guns, Money and Influence in Northern Ireland*, Viking, New York 1987 and Sean Cronin, *Washington's Irish Policy: Independence, Partition, Neutrality*, Anvil Books, Dublin 1987.
2. The figures do not include illegal immigrants. On the census generally, see Theodore H. White, *America in Search of Itself*, Jonathan Cape, London 1983, pp. 344-74.
3. Andrew M. Greeley, *The Irish Americans: the rise to money and power*, Harper and Row, New York 1981, p. 6 and William D. Griffin (ed.), *The Irish in America: 550-1972*, Oceana, Dobbs Ferry, New York 1973, p. 144.
4. *The Irishman* (San Francisco), July 1984.
5. Paul Artherton, 'Irish-American lobbies reflect splits at home', *Fortnight* (no. 216), 18-31 March 1985. The Irish-American Partnership, which is supported by the Irish Government, has estimated that some 600,000 Americans could realistically be expected to form the basis of 'an active donor pool' for fundraising for Ireland in the United States, see the *Irish Times*, 7 June 1985.
6. Lawrence J. McCaffrey, 'A Profile of Irish America' in David Noel Doyle and Owen Dudley Edwards (eds.), *America and Ireland: 1776-1976*, Greenwood Press, Westport 1980, p. 86.
7. White, op. cit., p. 363.
8. See Lawrence J. McCaffrey, *The Irish Diaspora in America*, Indiana University Press, Bloomington 1976, pp. 152-78.
9. Williams Adams Brown and Redvers Opie, *American Foreign Assistance*, the Brookings Institution, Washington 1953, p. 164.
10. Edward M. Kennedy, 'Ulster is an international issue', *Foreign Policy*, Vol. 11, Summer 1973, p. 60n.
11. See Clark, op. cit., pp. 18-19.
12. Ibid., p. 22.
13. Quoted in Griffin (ed.), op. cit., p. 134.
14. Ibid., p. 135.
15. See, for example, Richard Howard Brown, *The Passion of Richard Brown*, Gordon and Cremonesi, London 1977, p. 47.

16. See Barry White, 'The American Connection', *Belfast Telegraph*, 15 May 1979.

17. Quoted in Warren Richey, 'The Noraid Connection', *Christian Science Monitor* (international edition), 19-25 Jan. 1985.

18. *The Observer*, 23 Aug. 1981.

19. Ibid. and the *Irish Times*, 12 Sept. 1981. Also see Jack Holland, 'Noraid's Untold Millions', *Magill* (Dublin), April 1987.

20. *Belfast Telegraph*, 15 May 1979.

21. *Irish People* (New York), 1 Aug. 1987.

22. Warren Richey, 'The Noraid Connection' op. cit. 19-25 Jan. 1985.

23. Ibid.

24. Ibid.

25. Brigadier Glover's report is reproduced as an appendix in Sean Cronin, *Irish Nationalism*, The Academy Press, Dublin 1980, pp. 339-57.

26. *Belfast Telegraph*, 15 May 1979.

27. See, for example, the profiles of James Delaney and Joseph Roche in Donal O'Donovan, *Dreamers of Dreams: Portraits of the Irish in America*, Kilbride Books, Bray 1984, pp. 29 and 176.

28. Quoted in S. Cronin, *Irish Nationalism*, p. 345.

29. Warren Richey, 'How the IRA ships its arms from the US to Ulster', *Christian Science Monitor* (international edition), 26 Jan.-1 Feb. 1985.

30. See, for example, 'Provo split', *New Hibernia*, May 1985.

31. See Kevin Kelley, *The Longest War: Northern Ireland and the IRA*, Brandon, Dingle 1982, p. 309 and Warren Richey, 'British, Irish officials advise against donations to Noraid', *Christian Science Monitor* (international edition), 23 Feb.-1 Mar. 1985.

32. S. Cronin, *Irish Nationalism*, p. 224 and Kelley, op. cit., p. 280.

33. Kelley, op. cit., p. 280.

34. Interview with Sean McManus by Barry White, *Belfast Telegraph*, 16 May 1979.

35. *Freedom and Peace for Ireland... An American Issue*, Irish National Caucus, Washington. Undated leaflet c. 1980.

36. See, for example, the following publications of the Irish National Caucus from Washington: *National Newsletter* Sept.-Oct. 1979; *National Newsletter*, July 1980; *National Newsletter*, Oct. 1980; *Irish Lobby*, Sept.-Oct. 1981; *Irish Lobby*, Feb. 1982; *Irish Lobby*, Nov.-Dec. 1982; *Irish Lobby*, Jan.-Feb. 1983; *Irish Lobby*, Mar.-Apr. 1983; and *Irish Lobby*, Spring 1984.

37. See, for example, Bernard Crick, 'The Pale Green Internationalists', *New Statesman* (London), 7 Dec. 1979.

38. *National Newsletter*, Irish National Caucus, Washington, Sept.-Oct. 1979.

39. Barry White, *John Hume: Statesman of the Troubles*, Blackstaff Press, Belfast 1984, p. 191.

40. White, op. cit., p. 186.

41. *Foreign Policy*, Vol. 11, Summer 1973, pp. 58 and 63-4. For use of the Vietnam analogy, see also Ken Ward, 'Ulster Terrorism: the US network news coverage of Northern Ireland 1968-1979' in Yonah Alexander and Allan O'Day (eds.), *Terrorism in Ireland*, Croom Helm, London 1984.

42. *Foreign Policy*, Vol. 11, Summer 1973, p. 71.

43. Ibid., p. 70.

44. Clark, op. cit., pp. 62-3. Clark argues that Federal activity burgeoned after a meeting between President Nixon and the British Prime Minister, Edward Heath, in Bermuda in December 1971.
45. Quoted in Clark, op. cit., p. 64.
46. White, op. cit., p. 194.
47. Quoted in Crick, op. cit. in note 37.
48. Ibid.
49. *The Conservative Manifesto 1979*, London 1979, p. 22.
50. See, for example, Alan J. Ward, *Ireland and Anglo-American relations 1899-1921*, Weidenfeld and Nicolson, London 1969.
51. *Financial Times*, 7 Aug. 1979.
52. *New York Times*, 9 Aug. 1979.
53. See Malcolm Rutherford, 'The military becomes impatient', *Financial Times*, 21 September 1979.
54. *Fortnight* (no. 174), Dec. 1979-Jan. 1980.
55. *New York Times*, 13 Nov. 1979.
56. See, for example, the editorial in the *Financial Times*, 29 Oct. 1979.
57. Quoted in *Fortnight* (no. 178), Oct.-Nov. 1980.
58. Reagan's policy statement on Northern Ireland, dated 1 April 1980, is quoted in full in *National Newsletter*, Irish National Caucus, Washington, May 1980.
59. Quoted in Elizabeth Shannon, *Up in the Park*, Gill and Macmillan, Dublin 1983, p. 280.
60. *Irish Times*, 28 July 1980.
61. Quoted in Shannon, op. cit., pp. 279-80.
62. From the summit communiqué quoted in the *Irish Times* 9 Dec. 1980.
63. Reagan made his attitude clear at the outset. See Conor O'Clery, 'Reagan rules out Northern "interference"', *Irish Times*, 7 Nov. 1980.
64. See, for example, 'Clark's hopes of Irish unity: He offers US aid in trying to solve the Ulster problem', *Belfast Telegraph*, 8 Dec. 1981. Clark was Deputy Secretary of State in the Administration.
65. For example, the *New York Daily News* simultaneously supported the British Prime Minister's refusal to grant political status to the prisoners in the H-Blocks and urged her towards a settlement based on a united Ireland, see the *Irish Times*, 9 May 1981.
66. For example, Mario Biaggi's proposal, which dates back to 1978, for a peace forum that would include Loyalist paramilitaries as well as Republican groups. See Denis Faul and Raymond Murray, *The Sleeping Giant: Irish Americans and Human Rights in N. Ireland*, undated pamphlet c. 1979.
67. O'Donovan, op. cit., p. 28.
68. See, for example, the *Sunday Tribune*, 3 Mar. 1985 and the *Irish Times*, 2 Mar. 1985.
69. *Irish Herald* (San Francisco), May 1984. See also on Haughey's general stance the account of his trip to the United States in 1985 to launch Friends of Fianna Fáil, *Sunday Tribune*, 3 Mar. 1985.
70. See 'Reagan rules out Ulster peace move from US ... but he plans to quiz Thatcher on the Forum', *Belfast Telegraph*, 30 May 1984.
71. 'Reagan praises Forum effort', *Irish Times*, 3 Dec. 1984.
72. *Irish Times*, 24 Dec. 1984.

73. *Financial Times*, 22 Feb. 1985.
74. See the *Irish Times*, 15 and 19 Mar. 1985. On the scepticism he provoked at the time, see Mary Holland, 'Can the Taoiseach share O'Neill's hopes?', *Irish Times*, 20 Mar. 1985.'
75. See *Belfast Telegraph*, 11 Nov. 1983 and 14 Dec. 1984.
76. Quoted in Gregory Teer, 'An Irish Policy in California', *Fortnight* (no. 207), Sept. 1984.
77. See the *Irish Times*, 20 March 1984 and *Irish Lobby*, Irish National Caucus, Washington, Spring 1984.
78. Quoted from the *Irish Lobby*, Irish National Caucus, Washington, Spring 1985.
79. 'Garret FitzGerald, the Irish Prime Minister, has a long history of indifference to the plight of Catholics in Northern Ireland—some would say that he is even hostile to them', *Irish Lobby*, Irish National Caucus, Washington, Spring 1984.
80. See Michael Farrell, 'Why the Taoiseach changed his mind on US investment in the North', *Sunday Tribune*, 26 May 1985.
81. *Irish Times*, 24 Sept. 1987.
82. *Irish People*, 24 May 1986.
83. *Irish Times*, 16 Sept. 1987.
84. *Financial Times*, 25 Sept. 1987.
85. See Sean Cronin, 'Irish-Americans' in 'Annual Review 1981', *Irish Times*, 30 Dec. 1981.

Chapter 8: European Interventions (pp. 153-173)

1. Quoted in Miriam Hederman, *The Road to Europe: Irish Attitudes 1948-61*, Institute of Public Administration, Dublin 1983, p. 48.
2. Hederman, op. cit., p. 16.
3. See *Northern Ireland House of Commons Debates* (NIHCD), Vol. 49, Cols. 57-148 (6 July 1961).
4. NIHCD (O'Neill), Vol. 67, Col. 1838 (14 Nov. 1967).
5. NIHCD (Bailie), Vol. 83, Col. 990 (8 Dec. 1971).
6. Ibid. (Faulkner) Vol. 83, Col. 941 (8 Dec. 1971).
7. Ibid.
8. *The future of Northern Ireland: a paper for discussion*, HMSO, London 1972, p. 34.
9. Garret FitzGerald, *Towards a New Ireland*, Charles Knight and Co., London 1972.
10. Ibid., p. 103.
11. Ibid., p. 104.
12. Ibid., pp. 111-12.
13. *Northern Ireland: Problems and Perspectives*, Institute for the Study of Conflict, London 1982, p. 42.
14. See Edward P. Moxon-Browne, 'Northern Ireland', in Martin Kolinsky (ed.), *Divided loyalties: British regional assertion and European Integration*, Manchester University Press, Manchester 1978, pp. 28-34.
15. Ibid., p. 29.
16. Ibid., p. 31.
17. See, for example, Paul Hainsworth, 'Direct Rule in Northern Ireland: The

European Community Dimension 1972-1979', *Administration* (Dublin), Vol. 31, No. 1, 1983, p. 63.

18. Edward Moxon-Browne, *Nation, Class and Creed in Northern Ireland*, Gower, Aldershot 1983, p. 158.

19. Ibid., p. 161.

20. See, for example, Paul Hainsworth, 'The European election of 1979 in Northern Ireland: Linkage Politics', *Parliamentary Affairs*, Vol. 32, No. 4, Autumn 1979, pp. 470-81.

21. See A. Aughey and P. Hainsworth, 'Northern Ireland and the European Community: the localisation of politics', *Moirae*, Ulster Polytechnic, Jordanstown 1982.

22. *Official Journal of the European Communities: Information and Notices* (OJEC:IN), Vol. 24, C 144/90 (15 June 1971).

23. See John Kennedy, 'Northern Ireland and the European Communities', M S Sc. dissertation for the Department of Political Science, Queen's Univeristy, Belfast, December 1984, p. 21.

24. See *Report drawn up on behalf of the Political Affairs Committee on the situation in Northern Ireland* (Rapporteur: N. J. Haagerup), European Parliament Working Documents 1983-1984, Document 1-1526/83 (19 March 1984).

25. Ibid., p. 37 and p. 73.

26. This was evident from the praise lavished on the report by Lady Elles (pp. 165-7) and Sir Fred Catherwood ('If I were a free agent, I would vote for this report'—p. 174). *Official Journal of the European Communities: Debates of the European Parliament* (DEP), No. 312 (29 Mar. 1984).

27. The BBC correspondent in Northern Ireland, Brian Walker, commented: 'John Hume has pulled off what is known as a "political stroke". He has now added the European Parliament to the list of international forums where pressure can be put on Britain over Northern Ireland'. Quoted in John Kennedy, op. cit., p. 22.

28. See Sydney Elliott, *Northern Ireland: The Second Election to European Parliament*, Queen's University of Belfast, Belfast 1985, p. 28.

29. *Irish Times*, 23 October 1985.

30. From the heading of the resolution introduced by John Hume. OJEC:IN, Vol. 30, C 7/131 (12 Jan. 1987).

31. See, for example, the speech of Bangemann of the European Liberal and Democratic Group ('What does it mean when a nation is divided and people cannot come together because of frontiers, and problems are created by frontiers? It means that this Community has undertaken to do away with such divisions and frontiers. Frontiers and divisions, too, are a sign of outdated national sovereignty.') DEP, No. 312 (29 Mar. 1984), pp. 165-6.

32. See DEP, No. 245 (26 Sept. 1979) pp. 170-88.

33. OJEC:IN, Vol. 28, C 352/67 on the vote and C 352/83-84 on the text of the resolution (31 Dec. 1985).

34. Patrick Keatinge, 'Ireland's foreign relations in 1985', *Irish Studies in International Affairs*, Vol. 2, No. 2, 1986, p. 108.

35. DEP, No. 333 (12 Dec. 1985), (Mr Verbeek) p. 225.

36. In the first ten years of membership, Northern Ireland received £684 million in grants and loans from the European Community, see *Northern*

Ireland in Europe: The impact of membership, European Commission Office in Northern Ireland, Belfast 1983.

37. OJEC:IN. Vol. 29, C 322/460 (15 December 1986).
38. See for example, Geoffrey Martin, 'A European Initiative', *Fortnight* (no. 181), May/June 1981.
39. See, for example, Patrick Keatinge, 'The Europeanisation of Irish foreign policy', P. J. Drudy and Dermot McAleese (eds.), *Ireland and the European Community*, Cambridge University Press, Cambridge 1984, pp. 33-56.
40. Paul Hainsworth, 'Northern Ireland: A European Role?', *Journal of Common Market Studies*, Vol. 20, No. 1, September 1981, p. 10.
41. Quoted in *Northern Ireland: Problems and Perspectives*, op. cit., p. 42.
42. Brigid Laffan, 'The Consequences for Irish Foreign Policy', in David Coombes (ed.), *Ireland and the European Communities: Ten years of membership*, Gill and Macmillan, Dublin 1983, p. 93.
43. Ibid., p. 106.
44. See, for example, S. Kelleher, 'Irish unity through European unity', *Gazette of the Incorporated Law Society of Ireland*, 1972, pp. 110-12.
45. From the Statute of the Council of Europe.
46. F. S. L. Lyons, *Ireland since the Famine*, Fontana, London 1973, p. 591.
47. Conor Cruise O'Brien, *To Katanga and Back: A U.N. Case History*, Hutchinson, London 1962, p. 14.
48. Hederman, op. cit., p. 38.
49. The case concerned the detention without trial in 1957 of a suspected member of the IRA, Gerard Lawless, under the Republic's Offences against the State Act.
50. Merlyn Rees, *Northern Ireland: A Personal Perspective*, Methuen, London 1985, pp. 308-10.
51. Ibid., p. 310.
52. *The Guardian*, 20 June 1980.
53. See the speeches in the debate in the European Parliament on the hunger strike. DEP, No. 271 (7 May 1981, pp. 243-56.
54. Quoted in Michael Farrell, *Sheltering the Fugitive?: the Extradition of Irish Political Offenders*, Mercier Press, Cork and Dublin, p. 98.
55. *Irish Times*, 6 May 1981.
56. As reported in the *Irish Times*, 7 May 1981.
57. As reported in the *Irish Times*, 6 May 1981.
58. Ibid.
59. P. Hainsworth, 'Northern Ireland: A European Role?', op. cit., p. 14.
60. Anne Sington, 'International action on NI urged', *Irish Times*, 16 Aug. 1981.
61. See 'Haughey gets some sympathy: But French won't get involved over Ulster', *Belfast Telegraph*, 14 Mar. 1980.
62. See, for example, 'French offers help on North', *Irish Times*, 16 Dec. 1981.
63. *Sunday Tribune*, 1 Dec. 1985.

Chapter 9: Comparative Perspectives (pp. 174-194)
1. On the two of these, see, for examples, Robin Smyth, 'Rebels control the roads in France's Ulster', *The Observer*, 2 Dec. 1984 and Michael Hamlyn, 'Thatcher finds parallels with Ireland in Sri Lanka', *Irish Times*, 13 Apr.

1985. For a more unusual comparison, see John Elliott's account of his visit to the Indian city of Batala: 'Punjab's Belfast: microcosm of a communal crisis', *Financial Times*, 19 June 1986.

2. David Gilmour, *Lebanon: The Fractured Country*, Sphere, London 1983, p. 27.

3. Quoted in D. Gilmour, op. cit., p. 30.

4. Nora Boustany, 'The benevolent hand of the Ayatollah', *Financial Times*, 25 July 1987.

5. Gilmour, op. cit., p. 182.

6. Keith Kyle, *Cyprus*, Minority Rights Group, London 1984, p. 7.

7. See my chapter on Israel in J. Brewer, A. Guelke, I. Hume, E. Moxon-Browne, and R. Wilford, *The Police, Public Order, and the State*, Macmillan, London 1988.

8. Sammy Smooha, 'Control of Minorities in Israel and Northern Ireland', *Comparative Studies in Society and History*, Vol. 22, No. 2, Apr. 1980, pp. 251-80, in which he contrasts the success of control in Israel with its failure in Northern Ireland.

9. Quoted in Raymond Carr, *Puerto Rico: A Colonial Experiment*, New York University Press, New York and London 1984, p. 36.

10. For example, in August 1986 the Committee voted by 10 votes to 1 with 8 abstentions 'to decolonise' the territory, see the *Irish Times*, 15 August 1986.

11. Oddly, Puerto Rico is represented in the party conventions that nominate the Democratic and Republican candidates for President even though the territory does not vote in the Presidential election itself.

12. See, for example, Victoria Irwin, 'Puerto Rico: Perennial political identity crisis keeps this Caribbean island in limbo', *Christian Science Monitor* (Weekly Edition), 16-22 Feb. 1987.

13. Robert Ramsay, *The Corsican time-bomb*, Manchester University Press, Manchester 1983.

14. Ibid., pp. 220-21.

Chapter 10: Conclusion (pp. 195-206)

1. 'Introduction: Politics in a Shrinking World' in James N. Rosenau (ed.), *Linkage Politics: Essays on the Convergence of National and International Systems*, Free Press, New York 1969, p. 2.

2. Jingoism with these characteristics is to be found at its ugliest in the British popular press, particularly *The Sun*.

3. Furthermore, the British Government has supported the normative basis of a world permanently divided into states defined in territorial terms. See, for example, the British Government's submission in September 1964 to the UN Special Committee on the drafting of the *Declaration on Principles of International Law concerning Friendly Relations and Co-operation among States*. The submission specifically rejects the legitimacy of secession, citing the case of Wales as a hypothetical example. The clear implication is that the British Government would resist secession even if it was supported by a majority of the people of Wales. See UN Doc. A/5725/Add 4 (1964) p. 74. The readiness of successive British Governments to contemplate the secession of Northern Ireland clearly

sets the province apart from any other part of the United Kingdom.
4. See, for example, the analysis of the results of the Westminster general election in Northern Ireland by Sydney Elliott in *Fortnight* (no. 253), July/August 1987.
5. See, for example, Vincent Browne, 'The Provos Settle down for a 20 Year War', *Magill*, August 1982.
6. For an example of a work that argued that external economic influences would create new political possibilities in Northern Ireland, see Belinda Probert, *Beyond the Orange and the Green: The Political Economy of the Northern Ireland Crisis*, Zed Books, London 1978.
7. See, for example, Edward Moxon-Browne, *Nation, Class and Creed*, Gower, Aldershot 1983, p. 178.

SELECT BIBLIOGRAPHY

Arnold, Bruce, *What Kind of Country: Modern Irish Politics 1968-1983*, Jonathan Cape, London 1984.

Arthur, Paul, 'Anglo-Irish Relations and the Northern Ireland problem', *Irish Studies in International Affairs*, Vol. 2, No. 1, 1985.

Aughey, Arthur and McIlheney, Colin, 'Law before Violence?—The Protestant Paramilitaries in Ulster Politics', *Eire-Ireland*, Col. 17, No. 2, Summer 1984.

Baldy, Tom, *Battle for Ulster,* National Defense University Press, Washington, D.C. 1987.

Bell, J. Bowyer, *The Secret Army: The IRA 1916-1979*, The Academy Press, Dublin 1979.

Bishop, Patrick and Mallie, Eamonn, *The Provisional IRA*, Heinemann, London 1987.

Beresford, David, *Ten Men Dead: The story of the 1981 hunger strike,* Grafton Books, London 1987.

Bew, Paul and Patterson, Henry, *The British State and the Ulster Crisis*, Verso, London 1985.

Blumenfeld, Jesmond (ed.), *South Africa in Crisis*, Croom Helm, London 1987.

Bowman, John, *De Valera and the Ulster Question 1917-1973*, Clarendon Press, Oxford 1982.

Boyd, Andrew, *Fifteen Men on a Powder Keg*, Methuen, London 1971.

Buckland, Patrick, *A History of Northern Ireland*, Gill and Macmillan, Dublin 1981.

Burton, Frank, *The Politics of Legitimacy: Struggles in a Belfast Community*, Routledge and Kegan Paul, London 1978.

Carr, Raymond, *Puerto Rico: A Colonial Experiment*, New York University Press, New York and London 1984.

Clark, Dennis J., *Irish Blood: Northern Ireland and the American Conscience*, Kennikat Press, Port Washington, New York 1977.

Clarke, Liam, *Broadening the Battlefield: The H-Blocks and the Rise of Sinn Fein*, Gill and Macmillan, Dublin 1987.

Coogan, Tim Pat, *The I.R.A.*, Fontana, London 1980.

Cronin, Sean, *Irish Nationalism: A History of Its Roots and Ideology*, The Academy Press, Dublin 1980.

Cronin, Sean, *Washington's Irish Policy: Independence, Partition, Neutrality* Anvil Books, Dublin 1987.

Darby, John, *Intimidation and the Control of Conflict in Northern Ireland*, Gill and Macmillan, Dublin 1986.

Dillon, Martin and Lehane, Denis, *Political Murder in Northern Ireland*, Penguin, Harmondsworth 1973.

Downey, James, *Them and Us: Britain, Ireland, and the Northern Question 1969-1982*, Ward River Press, Dublin 1983.

Elliott, Sydney, *Northern Ireland: The Second Election to the European Parliament*, Queen's University of Belfast, Belfast 1985.

Farrell, Michael, *Northern Ireland: The Orange State*, Pluto Press, London 1980.

FitzGerald, Garret, *Towards a New Ireland*, Charles Knight and Co., London 1972.

Flackes, W. D., *Northern Ireland: A Political Directory*, Gill and Macmillan, Dublin 1980.

Galliher, John F. and De Gregory, Jerry L., *Violence in Northern Ireland: Understanding Protestant Perspectives*, Gill and Macmillan, Dublin 1985.

Gilmour, David, *Lebanon: The Fractured Country*, Sphere, London 1983.

Girvin, Brian and Sturm, Roland (eds.), *Politics and Society in Contemporary Ireland*, Gower, Aldershot 1986.

Guelke, Adrian, 'The American Connection to the Northern Ireland Conflict', *Irish Studies in International Affairs*, Vol. 1, No. 4, 1984.

Guelke, Adrian, 'International legitimacy, self-determination, and Northern Ireland', *Review of International Studies*, Vol. 11, No. 1, January 1985.

Hainsworth, Paul, 'Northern Ireland: A European Role?', *Journal of Common Market Studies*, Vol. 20., No. 1, September 1981.

Hamill, Desmond, *Pig in the Middle: The Army in Northern Ireland 1969-1986*, Methuen, London 1986..

Hederman, Miriam, *The Road to Europe: Irish Attitudes 1948-61*, Institute of Public Administration, Dublin 1983.

Holland, Jack, *Too Long a Sacrifice: Life and Death in Northern Ireland since 1969*, Dodd, Mead, and Company, New York 1981.

Hull, Roger H., *The Irish Triangle: Conflict in Northern Ireland*, Princeton University Press, Princeton, N.J. 1976.

Keatinge, Patrick, 'The Europeanisation of Irish foreign policy' in P. J. Drudy and Dermot McAleese (eds.), *Ireland and the European Community*, Cambridge University Press, Cambridge 1984.

Keatinge, Patrick, *A Singular Stance: Irish Neutrality in the 1980s*, Institute of Public Administration, Dublin 1984.

Kelley, Kevin, *The Longest War: Northern Ireland and the IRA*, Brandon, Dingle 1982.

Kenny, Anthony, *The Road to Hillsborough: The Shaping of the Anglo-Irish Agreement*, Pergamon Press, Oxford 1986.

Kyle, Keith, *Cyprus*, Minority Rights Group, London 1984.

Laffan, Brigid, 'The Consequences for Irish Foreign Policy' in David Coombes (ed.), *Ireland and the European Communities: Ten years of membership*, Gill and Macmillan, Dublin 1983.

McKeown, Michael, *De Mortuis*, Irish Information Partnership, Gondregnies 1985.

Merkl, Peter H. (ed.), *Political Violence and Terror: Motifs and Motivations*, University of California Press, Berkeley 1986.

Miller, David W., *Queen's Rebels: Ulster Loyalism in Historical Perspective*, Gill and Macmillan, Dublin 1978.

Morgan, Austen and Purdie, Bob (eds.), *Ireland: Divided Nation Divided Class*, Ink Links, London 1980.

Moxon-Browne, Edward, *Nation, Class and Creed in Northern Ireland*, Gower, Aldershot 1983.

Moxon-Browne, Edward P., 'Northern Ireland' in Martin Kolinsky (ed.), *Divided Loyalties: British regional assertion and European integration*, Manchester University Press, Manchester 1978.

Murphy, Dervla, *Changing the Problem: Post-Forum Reflections*, The Lilliput Press, Mullingar 1984.

Nelson, Sarah, *Ulster's Uncertain Defenders: Protestant Political Paramilitary and Community Groups and the Northern Ireland Conflict*, Appletree Press, Belfast 1984.

O'Donovan, Donal, *Dreamers of Dreams: Portraits of the Irish in America*, Kilbride Books, Bray 1984.

Peck, John, *Dublin from Downing Street*, Gill and Macmillan, Dublin 1978.

Pomerance, Michla, *Self-Determination in Law and Practice*, Martinus Nijhoff, The Hague 1982.

Priestland, Gerald, *The Future of Violence*, Hamish Hamilton, London 1974.

Probert, Belinda, *Beyond Orange and Green: The Political Economy of the Northern Ireland Crisis*, Zed Press, London 1978.

Ramsay, Robert, *The Corsican time-bomb*, Manchester University Press, Manchester 1983.

Rees, Merlyn, *Northern Ireland: A Personal Perspective*, Methuen, London 1985.

Rose, Richard, *Governing without Consensus*, Faber, London 1971.

Rose, Richard and Garvin, Tom, 'The Public Policy Effects of Independence: Ireland as a Test Case', *European Journal of Political Research*, Vol. 11, No. 4, December 1983.

Smooha, Sammy, 'Control of Minorities in Israel and Northern Ireland', *Comparative Studies in Society and History*, Vol. 22, No. 2, April 1980.

Suhrke, Astri and Noble, Lela Garner (eds.), *Ethnic Conflict in International Relations*, Praeger, New York 1977.

White, Barry, *John Hume: Statesman of the Troubles*, Blackstaff Press, Belfast 1984.

Whyte, John, 'How is the boundary maintained between the two communities in Northern Ireland?', *Ethnic and Racial Studies*, Vol. 9, No. 2, April 1986.

Wight, Martin, *Systems of States* (edited by Hedley Bull), Leicester Univeristy Press, Leicester 1977.

Wright, Frank, 'The Ulster Spectrum' in David Carlton and Carlo Schaerf (eds.), *Contemporary Terror*, Macmillan, London 1981.

INDEX